The
Four
Immigrants
Manga

A marvelous historical document and history that offers astute commentaries on both the daily lives of workers and the momentous events that formed their contexts. This is a fascinating work—funny, pointed, moving—of extraordinary significance.

Gary Y. Okihiro, Professor of History and Director
of the Asian American Studies Program, Cornell University,
and co-editor of the *Journal of Asian American Studies*

A story of hope.... Some of the [immigrants'] exploits are tragic, most are humorous, but all share a masterful insight that all readers can relate to. This is an important—and highly enjoyable— book. Henry Kiyama is a wonderful storyteller.

Stan Sakai, graphic novelist and creator
of the award-winning *Usagi Yojimbo* series

Frederik L. Schodt's discovery and translation is a major contribution to Asian American Studies, Japanese American history, California Studies, and popular culture.... The use of humor by Kiyama to capture the struggles faced by the immigrants is a breakthrough, and the use of visuals—be they called comics, cartoons, or manga—is a pioneering way to tell this story. Schodt's preliminary comments as well as his afterword and notes are very informative and valuable.

Professor Isao Fujimoto, founder,
Asian American Studies Program, U.C. Davis

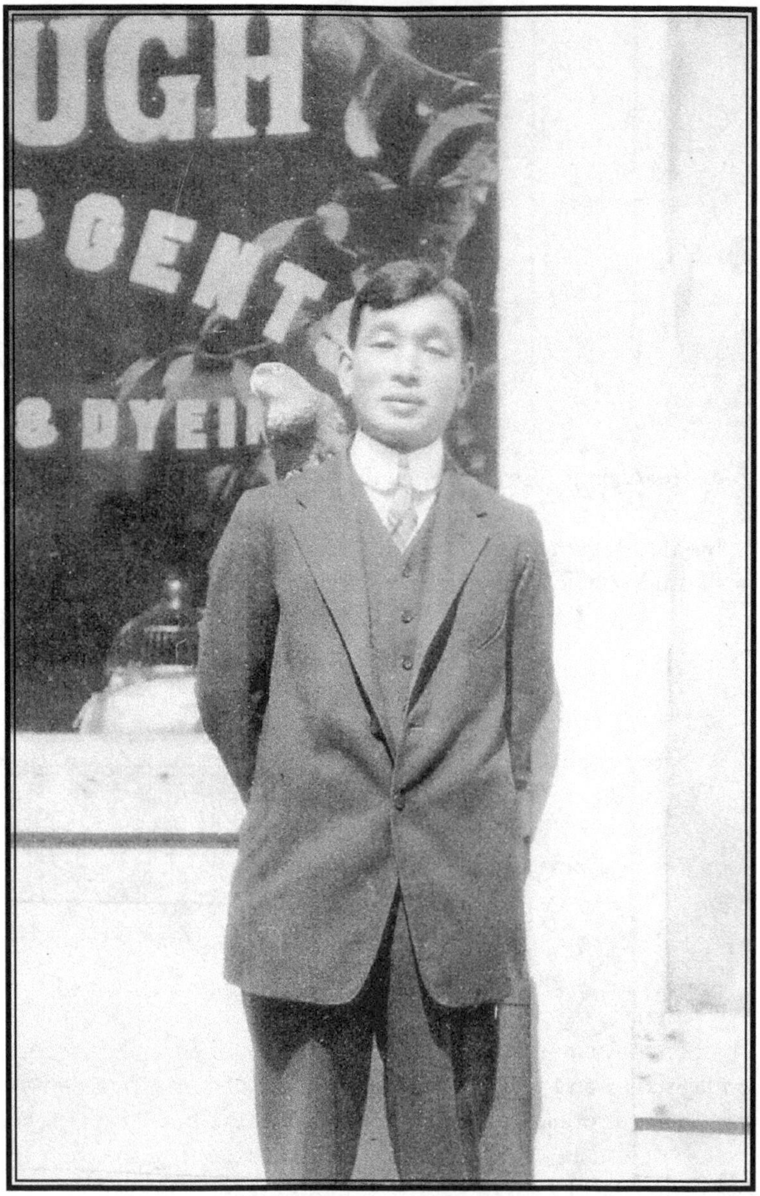
UGH
GENT
& DYEI

The Four Immigrants Manga

A Japanese Experience
in San Francisco, 1904–1924

HENRY (YOSHITAKA) KIYAMA

Translated, with an introduction and notes, by
FREDERIK L. SCHODT

Stone Bridge Press • Berkeley, California

Published by
Stone Bridge Press, P. O. Box 8208, Berkeley, CA 94707
tel 510-524-8732 • sbp@stonebridge.com • www.stonebridge.com

Front cover image: Panel from cover of Henry Kiyama's original Japanese-language edition, 1931.
Photograph on back cover and facing title page: A young Henry Kiyama in front of a San Francisco laundry, probably on Gough Street. Courtesy Kiyama Family.

Originally published as *Manga Yonin Shosei.*

Artwork © Estate of Yoshitaka Kiyama.
All photographs used by permission of their respective owners.
English text and translation © 1999 Frederik L. Schodt.
First on-demand printing 2023.

Cover design by David Bullen.

Printed in the United States of America.

LIBRARY OF CONGRESS CATALOGING-IN-PUBLICATION DATA
Kiyama, Henry (Yoshitaka), b. 1885.
    [Manga yonin shosei. English]
    The four immigrants manga: a Japanese experience in San Francisco, 1904–1924 / Henry (Yoshitaka)
Kiyama; translated with an introduction and notes by Frederik L. Schodt.
      p. cm.
    Includes bibliographical references.
    ISBN 1-880656-33-7
    1. Japanese Americans—California—San Francisco—xComic books, strips, etc.   I. Schodt, Frederik L.
II. Title.
F869.S39K5913   1998
979.4'61004956—dc21   98-41117
                                                    CIP

CONTENTS

Henry Kiyama and The Four Immigrants Manga

It was around 1980, and I was doing research for a book on Japanese comics in the East Asian branch of a University of California library. In the old card catalog, under the Japanese word for "comics," or *manga*, I saw an intriguing listing for something titled *Manga Yonin Shosei* (literally, "The Four Students Comic") by a "Henry Yoshi-taka Kiyama." It turned out to be a hardbound book of 112 pages, with a cover that was dusty and decorated with a faded sketch of four young Japanese men. When I opened it, I was shocked to find that the work was bilingual, written in Japanese and English and requiring a knowl-edge of both to read. Moreover, the place of publication was listed as—not Japan—but San Francisco, 1931. It was not until nearly eighteen years later that I realized I had accidentally come across a rare document of Japanese American immigrant history in San Francisco, and one of the first modern "comic books"—especially of a lengthy autobiographical nature—ever pub-lished in America.

* * * * *

When I first read Henry Kiyama's work, I viewed it mainly in the context of the develop-ment of Japanese, and not American, comics. I saw it as a sort of "bridge work" in the sense that it showed how Japanese artists had early on adopted American formats.

At the dawn of the 21st century, nearly 40 percent of all published books and magazines in Japan are in the form of comics. Nearly everyone reads them, and they are an inseparable part of everyday, even intellectual life. Often they are long and highly personal, with novelistic plots; often they are documentary in nature, and used to impart information on everything from his-tory to the stock market. Increasingly today, they influence trends in pop culture around the world, either directly in translation or indirectly through animation.

Although the modern Japanese love of com-ics may have its roots in a love of entertaining line art that goes back nearly a thousand years, the basic grammar for modern manga comes from the United States, where, at the end of the 19th century, newspaper cartoonists began using a sequence of panels and "word balloons" with dialogue to tell a story. In the 1920s and earlier some popular American newspaper strips were compiled and sold as "books," but what most people today think of as American "comic books" (thin, "comics" magazines, usually with color printing) did not appear until the 1930s; again, they were at first merely compilations of popular newspaper comic strips. What is often regarded as the first true "comic book" with all-new material—*New Fun Comics*—did not appear until February 1935.

Japanese artists began paying attention to American-style newspaper comic strips almost as soon as they appeared. As early as 1902, in *Jiji Manga*, Rakuten Kitazawa began emulating the panel structure of American strips, although he rarely used word balloons. In the '20s and '30s a surprising number of Japanese artists toured the United States and reported on, or even studied, American comic strips. Ippei Okamoto, one of the most famous political and social satire car-toonists of his time, visited the *New York World* in 1922 and wrote back to the *Asahi* newspaper on the popularity of the "Sunday Funnies":

> The American people love to laugh, but not in the stiff manner of the British. Their laugh is an innocent one that instantly dispels fatigue.…American comics have

become an entertainment equal to base-ball, motion pictures, and the presidential elections. Some observers say that comics have replaced alcohol as a solace for work-ers since Prohibition began.

Shortly after Okamoto's visit, American strips such as George McManus's *Bringing Up Father* began appearing, translated, in Japanese news-papers. They were soon followed by Japanese-authored strips, which at first carefully emulated the American style and format and even required Japanese readers to read from left-to-right. It took several years for most Japanese artists to reorder the panels of American-style comics so that readers could read in the native "right-to-left" format. Sakō Shishido, one artist who did this in the '30s, had lived in the United States for many years and studied cartooning through cor-respondence courses.

It was in this connection that I first viewed Henry Kiyama's work and briefly introduced it in my 1983 book, *Manga! Manga! The World of Jap-anese Comics*. I found it fascinating that Kiyama drew in the style of U.S. cartoonists like George McManus and used page layouts and designs that were completely American (even down to the order in which the panels are read)—but created a lengthy and very original story of four Japanese young men who spoke both Japanese and English.

I had it in mind that it would be an interest-ing work to translate some day, but between one thing and another I never seemed to get around to it. Some eighteen years later I finally have, and the result is this reproduction in English, retitled *The Four Immigrants*.

When I started work on this book, howev-er, there was one big problem. I knew nothing about the artist, and when I carefully reread the story I realized that, because of its documentary nature, translating it properly would require considerable knowledge of the time in which Kiyama lived, and of Kiyama himself.

ON THE TRAIL OF HENRY KIYAMA

In 1997, I embarked on a quest to learn as much as I could about Kiyama and his unusual work. Only one or two people I knew in San Francisco had ever heard of him or read his book; in Japan, at least in the world of comics, he also seemed a virtual unknown.

So I did what most people at the end of the 20th century started doing when they wanted to find information: using the Internet, I ran a search of libraries around America. Nothing came up under "Yoshitaka Kiyama," except in the Library of Congress. There, among the Japa-nese books, was a listing for a small booklet on someone of the same name. In rather pithy text, it indicated the booklet had been issued by the Yonago City Art Museum, in Tottori Prefecture, Japan, in conjunction with a 1993 exhibition of art. It also indicated that the artist had lived between 1885 and 1951.

Assuming that the person in the listing and the Kiyama I was interested in might be one and the same, I traveled to the Library of Congress in Washington, D.C., and excitedly asked one of the librarians to show me the booklet. After what seemed an eternity, she reported, to my horror, that it had somehow been "misplaced" and that "no one could find it."

Nonetheless convinced that the missing booklet must be about "my" Kiyama, I had a friend in Japan get the museum's phone num-ber in Yonago. Then I called and spoke to an assistant curator. Why, yes, she said, they had lots of the booklets; they had been created for a spe-cial exhibit of sketches and oil paintings by an artist named Yoshitaka Kiyama who had lived in America for many years. And had he ever done any cartooning? I asked. Why, yes, she replied, he had even published a comic book, the artwork for which was in the museum vault. Moreover, she said, his daughter lived in the rural village of Neu, only forty minutes from the museum.

That June, while in Japan on other business,

I traveled to Yonago, met the curator, and saw the original artwork in the museum vault. This alone was a thrill, but in terms of my quest for information it was the meeting with Kiyama's then seventy-three-year-old daughter, Hideko, and family that was the most productive. I surely appeared to her like an apparition out of the distant past, and when I told her of my dream of translating and reprinting her father's long-forgotten work, and making it better known to the world, she and her family were overjoyed, and eagerly shared with me as much information as they had. Kiyama is not widely known as a cartoonist in Japan, but in the area of his birth he has a certain reputation as a local, early master of Western-style art. Thanks largely to the archival efforts of Hideko's husband, Teruaki, not only Kiyama's artwork but a considerable number of early photographs and newspaper articles about him have been carefully preserved.

By the time I left Yonago City, I had enough leads to begin fitting the missing pieces into the Kiyama puzzle. I had a fairly good idea of who he was and of how he had come to create his most unusual manga over seventy years earlier. And the first thing I realized is that while Kiyama took certain liberties and created some composites of experiences, the story in the manga—about four young men—was far more of a documentary than I had originally suspected.

* * * * *

Henry "Yoshitaka" Kiyama was born on January 9, 1885, in Neu. A little village in Tottori Prefecture, on the Japan Sea side of Honshū island, Neu is far removed from the major metropolitan areas of Tokyo or Osaka that so dominate modern Japan. It is a town of many inns because of its proximity to a major highway in feudal times. Kiyama's family itself ran an inn, and his father, apparently of some local standing, at times served as the village headman.

Japan was isolated from the West for over two centuries until 1853, but by the turn of the century more and more Japanese began working and studying overseas to help modernize their nation, to better themselves, and to escape limited opportunities at home. With a population explosion and food shortages, emigration to foreign lands and especially to the United States became an increasingly attractive option for people in the poorer regions of Japan. An uncle of Kiyama's had early on pulled up stakes and moved to America, so with this connection Kiyama, too, sailed to San Francisco in 1904. He was nineteen years old.

San Francisco was the port of entry for most Japanese immigrants to the West Coast at the turn of the century, and most of them were laborers. But there was also a large percentage of young men who came to study and learn Western ways. The less affluent worked for a living at various jobs during the day and attended school at night, or worked as "houseboys," which allowed them to go to school in the day and perform chores for their employer-families in the morning and evening. The young men in this latter category were thus often referred to as "schoolboys."

In his book *The Issei: The World of First Generation Japanese Immigrants, 1885–1924*, author Yuji Ichioka quotes a wonderful description of this subculture from the March 8, 1890, issue of the *Japan Weekly Mail*:

> The Japanese community in San Francisco …has been growing by leaps and bounds within the past few years, until it numbers over three thousand souls.…The rank and file are of the poor student class, who have rashly left their native shores.…Hundreds of such are landed every year, with miserable scant funds in their pockets.…Their object is to earn, with the labor of their hands, a pittance sufficient to enable them to pursue their studies in language, sociology, and politics.

Kiyama himself belonged to this class of

impoverished student-workers. It must have provided wonderful material for a cartoonist, for among the cast of Japanese characters in San Francisco were not just serious students but loafers, romantics, political refugees, and even an anarchist later executed for plotting to overthrow the emperor. Kiyama's true love was art, however, and as his manga story indicates, his friends regarded him as a bit of a fanatic in his studies. While making his living at a variety of jobs, he attended the San Francisco Art Institute, which today remains the city's premier art school. Surviving records from 1914 show that he paid a tuition of $5.50 per month to take a popular nighttime life-drawing class and that one of his teachers was Pedro J. Lemos.

Kiyama soon distinguished himself at art, and between 1915 and 1920 he won several awards and mentions, especially in life drawing, as well as a scholarship from the New York Art Students League. He also exhibited in San Francisco, not only in the San Francisco Art Institute but at the prestigious Palace of Fine Arts. An April 20, 1920, article in the *San Francisco Bulletin* reports on the exhibit at the Palace of Fine Arts, and sure enough, above an era-revealing ad for pills proclaiming "Plumpness Makes Health; Thin People Heed This," is a restrained description of Kiyama's work:

[His work no. 115], Old Wagon Shed, is a solidly modeled, well balanced and vigorously colored design, and his 114, Old House at North Beach, in room 15, in soft green and gray, is quietly effective.

Kiyama's works are still occasionally exhibited today in the Yonago City Art Museum. Both his paintings and drawings show a remarkable skill, but in today's light they are rather orthodox, for Kiyama's primary goal was clearly mastery of the Western techniques of color, shading, and perspective, and not bold experimentation. What gives his portrait work special poignancy is its historical value, as when he documents the

ordinary people of San Francisco who modeled for him. In his homeland, of course, his art has the added significance of demonstrating how Japanese painters were able so quickly to master Western techniques. All of his fine artwork is marked by considerable seriousness.

At some point Kiyama took the radical step of dabbling in cartoons. Cartoons and comic strips were present in all the local San Francisco newspapers at the time, including the Japanese-language ones, but "high brow" art and cartooning did not necessarily coexist well in those days. For a serious artist with a reputation to maintain, what Kiyama did must have been regarded as rather bold, to say the least. In mid-February 1927, at the age of forty-two—just before temporarily returning to Japan for the second time—he had an exhibit of his work. And it is here that we see the first mention, not only of his cartooning, but of what would later become *The Four Immigrants*.

The February 16 edition of the *Nichi Bei* (*The Japanese American News*), describes it quite succinctly in an article titled "An Interesting Cartoon Exhibit with Numerous Attendees":

Between February 13th to 15th, in two separate areas of the Kinmon Gakuen [Golden Gate Institute] social hall, on the occasion of Mr. Yoshitaka Kiyama's return to Japan, the Primary Color Art Group is sponsoring an exhibit of his drawings and paintings, as well as an exhibit of his cartoons. While there have been several exhibits [of Mr. Kiyama's work] before in this city, this is the first public display of anything in the cartoon vein. The cartoon exhibit consists of 52 pieces dealing historically with the life of Japanese residents here. It is extremely interesting, and has proved to be very popular, with many people attending. The show lasts until 10:00 pm, Tuesday.

Two days later, on the 17th, in the same paper, a columnist who went by the name of

The young Kiyama, probably in San Francisco. Courtesy Kiyama Family.

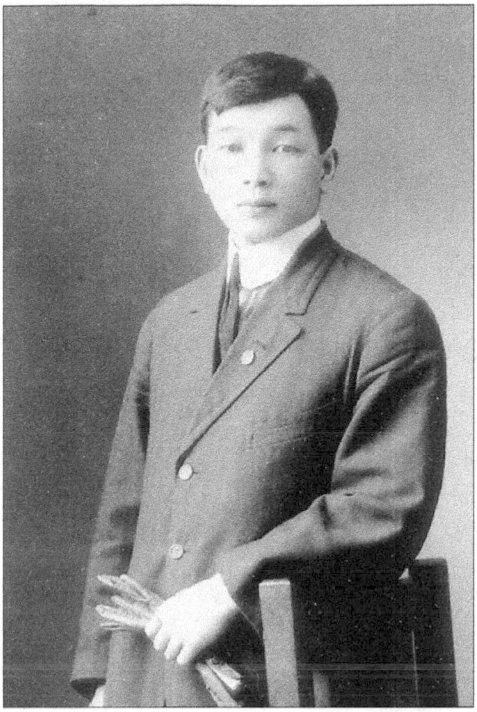

Two Japanese appear to be in this photograph of a ca. 1910 life-drawing class at San Francisco Institute of Art, California School of Design. Kiyama is not identifiable but certainly took this class. Photo by Gabriel Moulin; courtesy San Francisco Art Institute.

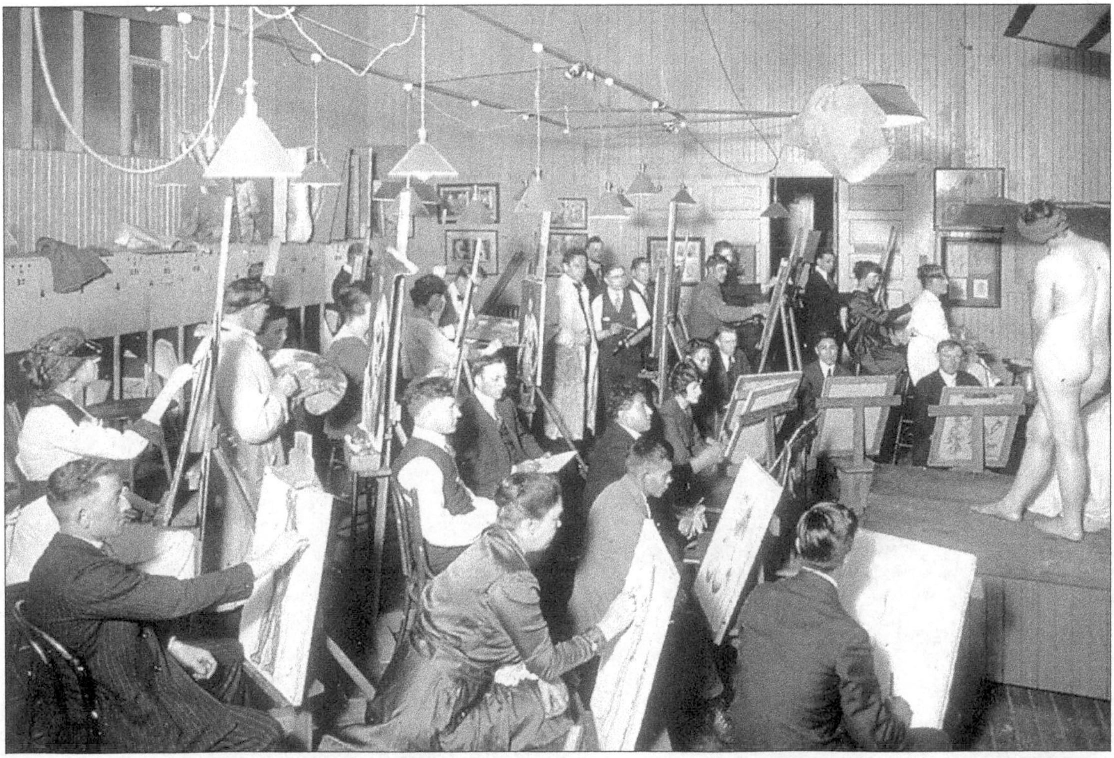

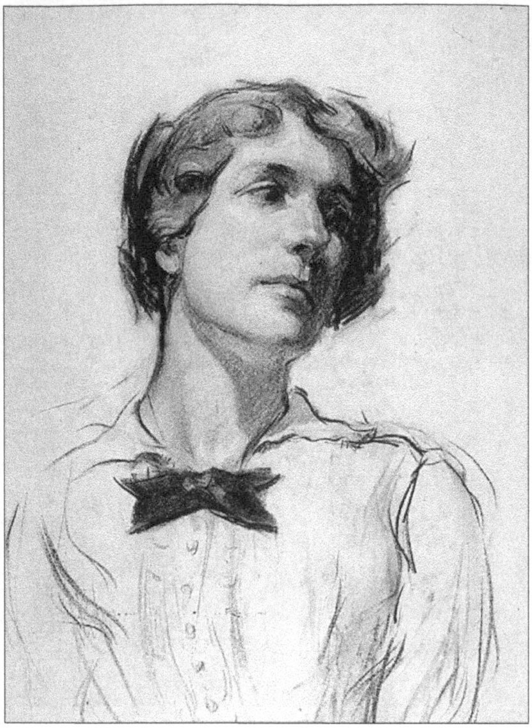

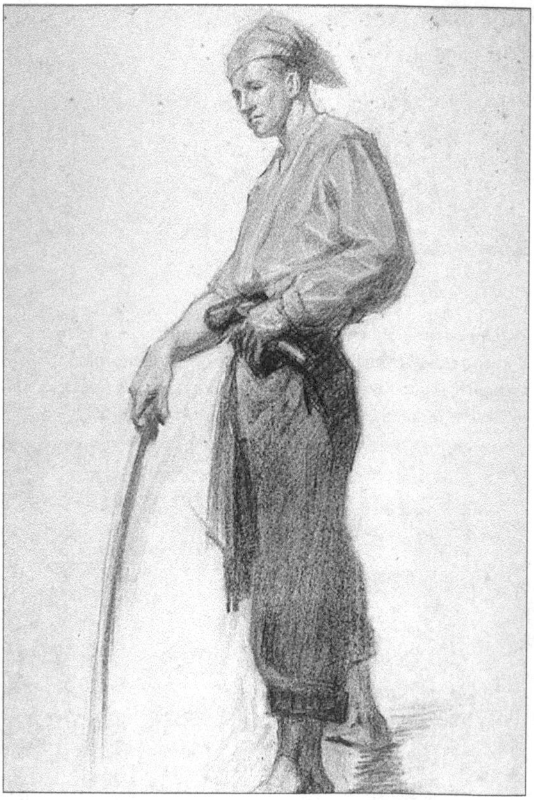

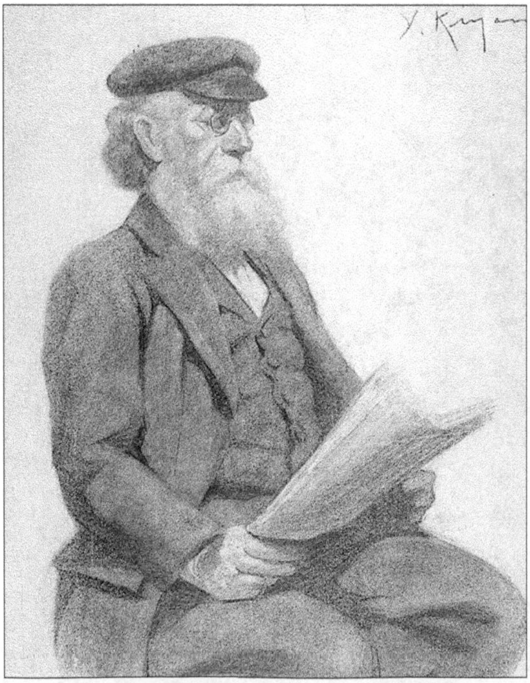

Life drawings of San Franciscans, by Henry (Yoshitaka) Kiyama. Clockwise from top: "Portrait of a Woman," "A Man Dressed in Japanese Clothes," "An Old Man Holding a Newspaper." Courtesy Yonago City Art Museum.

Shunshūrō wrote at greater length on the exhibit. In his column he gives modern historians the answer not only to when and how Kiyama created his eccentric comic, but why he eventually had to resort to self-publishing. Noting that the cartoon art exhibited was titled *Manga Hokubei Iminshi* ("A Manga North American Immigrant History"), Shunshūrō states:

> Much of the work is apparently based on the personal experience of the author, or of his friends. At other times he has used anecdotes or tales of some of the most notorious blunders made in the Japanese community.
>
> Mr. Kiyama originally intended to have his work serialized in the Sunday edition of one of this country's Japanese language newspapers, which is why there are fifty-two episodes, to form a year's worth.
>
> I do not know what sort of negotiations Mr. Kiyama had with the newspapers when he first came up with his plan for this work, but it is extremely unfortunate for him that it was never serialized. Had it had been serialized on a weekly basis in a newspaper, it might well have been a more satisfying work overall.

Shunshūrō then goes on to gently chide Kiyama for having created a complete work of such length, for concentrating on such a "journalistic" theme, and for making the four heroes of the story too "realistic." Of the first point, which he develops at the greatest length, he asserts that comic strips need to have a sense of "immediacy" and currency that can only be provided by daily or weekly serialization and by having feedback from readers. It is this aspect that is lost, he notes, when an entire story such as Kiyama's is presented as an integral piece.

There was a certain irony in Shunshūrō's comments, since he worked for the *Nichi Bei* and was in a position to help Kiyama get his work serialized had he wanted to. Furthermore, the criticisms he makes of Kiyama's approach are most certainly due to the fact that at the time it was very difficult to conceive of using the "comics" format in the way Kiyama did.

Kiyama was working within the context of his era. Newspaper comic strips for the family were enormously popular in America, and many had a strong immigrant theme. Yet Kiyama was far ahead of his time in discovering that the same short, newspaper comic strip format could also be employed to create a 104-page, integrated story of a documentary and adult nature, using sophisticated characters. In short, he was creating what might be called a "graphic novel" today. In America, at least, it would be another seven years before flimsy, magazine-style "comic books" with original material appeared—and they were for children.

Four years later, in 1931, Kiyama returned to San Francisco from Japan with bound and printed copies of his book-length work. The back page lists the printer as Kumaya in Tokyo (still in business today) and the publisher as Yoshitaka Kiyama Studios, 1901 Sutter Street, San Francisco. It is an impressive package, selling for what must have then been an expensive three dollars, and it has forewords and words of praise from the Japanese Consul General in San Francisco, prominent local artists and intellectuals, and none other than columnist Shunshūrō himself.

KIYAMA AND IMMIGRANT HISTORY

In essence, *The Four Immigrants* is the story of Henry Kiyama and three friends who arrive by boat in San Francisco in 1904 to seek their fame and fortune. They immediately have to find work in San Francisco and cope with living in a foreign country with a very foreign language. Each takes a typical American name—Yoshitaka becomes "Henry," and his friends become "Charlie," "Frank," and "Fred"—and each has a different dream. Henry wants to become a skilled artist; Frank a successful businessman; Fred, a farmer;

and aphorism-spouting Charlie, the real character in the bunch, wants to study the workings of American society. According to Henry Kiyama's daughter, Hideko, the characters are loosely based on real people that he knew. Frank is based on Sakuji Hida, Charlie is modeled after Chūji Nakada, and Fred is probably based on a man named Kiichirō Katō.

As was typical in those days, some of the characters begin life in the city by boarding at the local Buddhist church, where they also get help finding local jobs as domestic servants or houseboys. For most of the tale, Henry keeps to the background and focuses on his three friends. With an always amusing, sometimes bittersweet touch he shows how they manage to survive in a new land until what is presumably 1922, when he and Frank return to Japan for the first time in seventeen years. In the meantime, they have experienced the great earthquake of 1906, a World's Fair, World War I, the influenza epidemic, and the beginning of Prohibition in 1918. In the process, they also mature from youths into men.

To connoisseurs of local San Francisco history, The Four Immigrants has a lot to offer. A close look at the backgrounds Kiyama drew reveals that much of his San Francisco survives today, despite the passage of two major earthquakes and nearly a hundred years. The Ferry Building at the end of Market Street, the California Palace of the Legion of Honor, Seal Rock, Golden Gate Park, and the individual street names—all are easily recognizable here, as are the "homeless" in Union Square and the city's reputation for colorful characters. Pedestrians, of course, are still occasionally being robbed.

But as the original title of Kiyama's work suggests, this is the story of immigrants, especially Japanese immigrants, and it is this aspect of the book that gives it its most permanent value.

Kiyama and his friends did not arrive in San Francisco at a particularly auspicious time. There has always been a cyclical component to American relations with Japan, and 1904 was the beginning of the downside of one such cycle. European and Asian civilizations were for very different reasons both expanding, and in California they met head on and clashed.

The American public's awareness of Japan, it is safe to say, did not really start until after 1853, when U.S. warships led by Commodore Perry forced Japan to end its long isolation and begin trading with the outside world. For several decades thereafter, Americans seemed to be in love with all things Japanese, the "quainter" the better. But in California, in particular, several factors would cause this love affair to turn sour.

Large-scale immigration from Japan to America really began after 1882, when Congress adopted the Chinese Exclusion Act, banning the importation of skilled and unskilled Chinese labor. In order to develop California and newly acquired Western lands, European Americans had relied heavily on Chinese for cheap labor; the "coolie" and other contracting systems, at their worst, had parallels with the slave trade in Africans that had been banned earlier in the century. Chinese laborers therefore helped build much of the West in the latter half of the 19th century, but also bore the brunt of much white resentment and racism. The Chinese, it was felt, were too foreign, could never assimilate, were too subservient, and undercut white workers with low wages. Chinese populations in California were regularly harassed and attacked, and occasionally murdered and massacred. They were, in fact, treated considerably worse than the Japanese ever would be.

When European American landowners and capitalists were deprived of fresh Chinese labor, they discovered the Japanese and increasingly began using laborers imported directly from Japan, or indirectly through Hawaii, often through a highly developed contracting system. These laborers were a different class of people from the student immigrants; they often came from rural farms in Japan, hoping to escape grinding poverty exacerbated by the population explosion that occurred as Japan rapidly modernized. Like many immigrants from Europe, their initial goal was often not to live in America forever, but to make some money and then return home. Unfortunately, by stepping into the shoes of the Chinese workforce, they also incurred the same resentments from the white population; indeed, as Kiyama's story shows, many whites couldn't tell the difference between Japanese and Chinese anyway.

International developments further complicated matters. Right around the time Kiyama and his friends arrived in San Francisco, Americans began to perceive Japan in a different, more threatening light. In 1853, Japan had been a quaint, hermit feudal nation, with an army of samurai warriors in topknots carrying swords, bows and arrows, and a few antique matchlock guns. But within the space of fifty years, Japan had rapidly modernized in an attempt to catch up with the colonialist West, and by 1904, when it went to war with Imperial Russia, it was able to roundly trounce Russia's army and navy in Asia with fully modern weaponry and military organizations. In contrast to so many of its neighbors, therefore, Japan had not only successfully avoided becoming a colony of the Western powers—it had become the first non-white, non-Christian nation to industrialize and challenge the hegemony of the Western colonial, imperialist powers. Since Japan, in emulation of the West, was becoming a colonialist, imperialist power of its own in Asia, and since the United States at this time was also in an expansionist mode with its own colony in the Philippines, the two nations were on a collision course in the Pacific that would eventually culminate in full-scale war in 1941.

Although today San Francisco is famed for its racial diversity and tolerance of different ideas, from the time Henry Kiyama and friends arrived it was not the best place to be if one were Japanese. Local newspapers such as the *San Francisco Chronicle* conducted inflammatory campaigns against the local Japanese population and against Asian immigration in general. Prominent citizens such as James D. Phelan (San Francisco mayor and later U.S. senator) lobbied vigorously against the Japanese, calling for their expulsion. Eventually a "Japanese Exclusion League" was formed. The result of all this anti-Japanese sentiment was not just physical and verbal attacks on Japanese, but—starting right around the time Kiyama arrived—what one writer later referred to as an "orgy of anti-Japanese legislation." Much of this legislation forms the backdrop for Kiyama's story.

As can be seen in *The Four Immigrants*, Henry Kiyama and friends were also in a psychologically difficult position. They were from a proud and independent nation, and they belonged to a class of people not inclined to be or to act subservient, even if they had to work in menial jobs to earn a living in America. Unlike the Chinese, many of whom still wore traditional garb and "queues," Kiyama and his friends dressed in modern, Western-style clothing (as did all their countrymen), and they were very modern in their thoughts. It is probably safe to say that they were better educated than many of the whites they worked for and fully considered themselves as equals, but they were constantly being made aware of their "outsider" status, and they could hardly have been ignorant of the rigid racial hierarchy that existed in the city, which was firmly controlled by European Americans.

Some readers may find the depictions of other races in *The Four Immigrants* offensive. Certainly, in modern parlance, the drawings of Chinese and African Americans are by no means "politically correct." In fact, the images of Chinese men with slanted eyes and pigtails and the big-lipped African Americans who appear once or twice in the story are rendered in styles pioneered by white cartoonists in the early part of the 20th century. Kiyama was merely imitating the cartoon styles that he would have found in any American newspaper at the time. There is a subtle racial democracy implemented in the story, however, for there is something to offend nearly everyone—even the whites are often referred to in highly derogatory terms.

One convention of American cartooning of the time Kiyama does not adhere to is that of drawing obsequious Japanese with slanted eyes and buckteeth (later with glasses and eventually cameras added). On the contrary, he draws his Japanese characters with round eyes and a far more "Western" look than the Chinese—a convention that survives to this day in modern Japanese comics. Perhaps unconsciously following the admonishments of the famous Japanese philosopher Yūkichi Fukuzawa (1835–1901)—who promoted the highly influential datsu-a-ron, or philosophy of Japan distancing itself from Asia in order to modernize—in the story Henry and his pals (especially Charlie) want little to do with the old Asia of feudalism and stagnation. Moreover, they are not proud of some of the more "backward" aspects of their own culture, as we see in at least one episode where Charlie is deeply ashamed of the behavior of his working-class countrymen.

It is important to remember that no matter how dissatisfied Kiyama and his friends might have become with life in America, they were far more limited in what they could do about it than other immigrants from Europe, or even Americans of African descent, for they were denied citizenship. Indeed, as Yuji Ichioka eloquently reminds his readers in the beginning of his book on the issei, or first generation of Japanese Americans, starting in 1790 Congress had granted the right of naturalization to immigrants who were "free white people"; in 1870 it had revised it to include former slaves and people of African descent. With few exceptions, issei were not allowed to become U.S. citizens until 1952, when the law was finally changed.

Ultimately, reading the story of Henry Kiyama and his friends is like listening in on a nearly private conversation. Unlike history books written by second- or third-generation descendants of immigrants, or by historians in universities, or even unlike accounts by Japanese who went back to Japan and wrote about their experiences for the Japanese market, The Four Immigrants is written by a first-generation Japanese immigrant for other Japanese first-generation immigrants living in California. Because of its bilingual nature, it would have been unreadable by Japanese in Japan, unless they knew English. Similarly, most Americans could never read the book because it required knowing Japanese. And even people who were bilingual would have had a hard time reading the book unless they were familiar with the local Japanese community and its history. A cynic would comment that Henry Kiyama was a terrible entrepreneur, for he was unconsciously limiting the market for his books to his immediate friends. But it is this very "limitation" that has given modern readers a rare look at the inner thoughts of early Japanese immigrants.

ON TRANSLATING KIYAMA'S BOOK

All translation requires a compromise of sorts, between the need for accuracy and the need for "readability," but with The Four Immigrants I have tried to achieve both. At times this has felt like being simultaneously pulled by two different horses in two different directions, but if you, the reader, can enjoy and derive meaning from the result, then I will have been successful.

Kiyama created an exceedingly unorthodox book with some very challenging translation problems, so a few comments are warranted on some of the solutions employed.

Mixing Japanese and English. The text in the original edition of The Four Immigrants was handwritten in a very old style of Japanese, difficult even for native speakers to read today. But it was originally bilingual, which means that when

American characters spoke English, their words were written in English; when Japanese characters spoke English to Americans (or mixed English with Japanese in their speech in a type of "pidgin"), their English words were also written in English. Everything else, such as the conversations in Japanese between Japanese characters, was in Japanese. The only exception was a few lines of Chinese, which was written in either Chinese characters or phoneticized Cantonese.

In order to preserve this unusual bilingual aspect of the original comic book, I have reproduced Kiyama's often fractured and somewhat rudely lettered English as is; the Japanese text, however, I have translated into natural English and rendered in word balloons using a lowercase type style reminiscent of the era. In modern American comic books, dialogue is usually handwritten in uppercase, but in *The Four Immigrants* I wanted to achieve a visual contrast with Kiyama's original English lettering. Also, Kiyama's Japanese handwriting is so cramped that it would have been impossible to fit the dialogue into the balloons and make it readable without using a small-point, lowercase type.

In the English version, the small typeset text therefore represents "Japanese," while the rough hand-lettered text represents "English." It may seem odd to have the Americans speaking in broken English and the Japanese speaking fluently, but there is an intended logic here. In popular American novels and in Hollywood movies, foreigners often speak in a crude pidgin English while the Americans speak perfectly. Yet in the world of immigrants, the immigrants obviously speak their own native language fluently, and it is only when they try to speak unfamiliar English that their speech sounds odd (to native English speakers). Similarly, the English used by Americans around them never sounds perfect, for their ears are not attuned to it enough to pick it up completely. I hope the textual device I have employed will allow readers to imagine what it might be like to live in a sea of foreign language and to appreciate the charming bilingual format in which Kiyama's book was originally written.

Panel Sequence. In translating *The Four Immigrants* the order in which the characters speak occasionally presented a major problem. It took many years for the modern Japanese manga, or comic book, to evolve. Japanese comics today, like most other Japanese publications, open and are read from right-to-left, rather than English-style left-to-right. Pages and panels are read from the top right corner across and down to the bottom left corner, the mirror image of American comics. And the writing in the word balloons is always vertical, rather than horizontal. But in the late 1920s, when Kiyama drew his book, he did what most of the first Japanese cartoonists did: he copied American (or English) format and tried to force the reader to read both pages and panels from left-to-right and to read the dialogue horizontally. In other words, he was asking Japanese readers to read the story in the mirror image of the progression that their natural instincts craved. Numbering each panel individually certainly helped, but could not have solved the problem.

Unfortunately, every once in a while Kiyama made a mistake because he was thinking in Japanese. In some panels where there are two characters engaged in a dialogue, rather than having the one on the left say, "How are you?" and the one on the right answer "Fine," he would reverse the order. For Japanese readers who subconsciously were more comfortable with this "wrong" order anyway, this switching was probably not that big a problem, but for English-speaking readers it completely throws off the logic of the story.

Thanks to modern computer technology, a few such problem panels have been flipped, or "mirrored." Where it was impossible to flip panels because of some complicating visual element (such as a background or identifying feature that cannot be changed without creating discontinuity in the story), I have tweaked the dialogue to make it more readable. Even so, in a few places readers may occasionally perceive a slight awkwardness in the sequence of the characters' speech.

Translation Problems. Puns and regional dialects are the bane of all translators of Japanese, and Kiyama uses both. As readers of *The Four Immigrants* will I hope discover, Japanese have a wonderful sense of humor, but a core element of it is the use of puns revolving around words that sound the same yet have different meanings. These are usually impossible to translate, especially when linked with a visual element, and even in the rare times when they can be translated they tend to elicit groans rather than laughter in English. In a few places in the story, I had to rewrite the dialogue slightly to try to come up with a gag that worked in English. For those interested I have explained the original Japanese joke in the notes at the back of this book.

The Importance of Context. Since there are many aspects of this story that cannot be understood out of a historical and cultural context, I have supplied notes at the end, thus keeping them out of the way of the story itself. Kiyama's work can therefore be enjoyed in English in a state as close as possible to the original. The notes offer deeper understanding, and I strongly recommend reading them.

* * * * *

It is my sincere hope that, nearly seventy-five years after it was first created, *The Four Immigrants* can be read both as a comic book for entertainment and as a historical document. Tragically, there are relatively few books in English of any sort on the first-generation Japanese Americans, the issei. Part of this is due to language problems, but it is due also to the human disaster of World War II and the effects of the incarceration of Japanese Americans in concentration camps. Many important documents were destroyed and lost; the issei were demoralized and confused; and the experience of the camps—like the Holocaust for Jewish writers—was so overwhelming that it has dominated subsequent writing on Japanese Americans. Yet the history of Japanese Americans today cannot be fully understood without understanding the issei and the experiences of people like Henry Kiyama.

On March 9, 1931, on the first page of the *Nichi Bei*, Shunshūrō again wrote at some length on the publication of Kiyama's newly printed book. It was four years since he had first written about Kiyama's unpublished work when first exhibited in San Francisco. This time, in typically restrained prose, he is grudgingly admiring:

> It includes most of the major incidents and problems of the time, and has considerable value as a profile of Japanese in America. It's far more interesting than reading some poorly written history book.

漫画
四人書生

ヘンリー木山義喬著

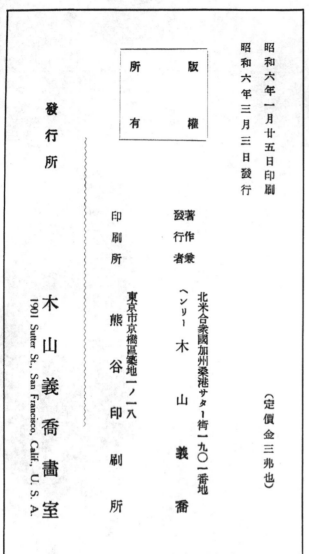

昭和六年一月廿五日印刷
昭和六年三月三日發行

版權所有

（定價金三弗也）

著作者兼發行者　ヘンリー　木山義喬
北米合衆國加州桑港サター街一九〇一番地

印刷所　熊谷印刷所
東京市京橋區築地一ノ一八

發行所　木山義喬畫室
1901 Sutter St., San Francisco, Calif., U.S.A.

Printed January 25, 1931
Published March 3, 1931
Price $3.00

AUTHOR AND PUBLISHER
Henry (Yoshitaka) Kiyama
1901 Sutter Street, San Francisco, California

PRINTER
Kumaya Printers
1-18 Tsukiji, Kyōbashi-ku, Tokyo

PLACE OF PUBLICATION
The Yoshitaka Kiyama Studio
1901 Sutter St., San Francisco, Calif., U.S.A.

漫 畫
四 人 書 生

ヘンリー 木山義喬著

MANGA
Yonin Shosei
(The Four Students Comic)

by Henry (Yoshitaka) Kiyama

Large brush writing
Twenty-five years of wry, bittersweet smiles. This book is a magnificent harvest, given to us as a record of our lives, in the wonderful spirit of Henry Kiyama himself.

Signed
Shunshūrō

Small brush writing on right side
Over twenty years of humor and sweat
For Kiyama-san

Sign and seal
Chiura Obata

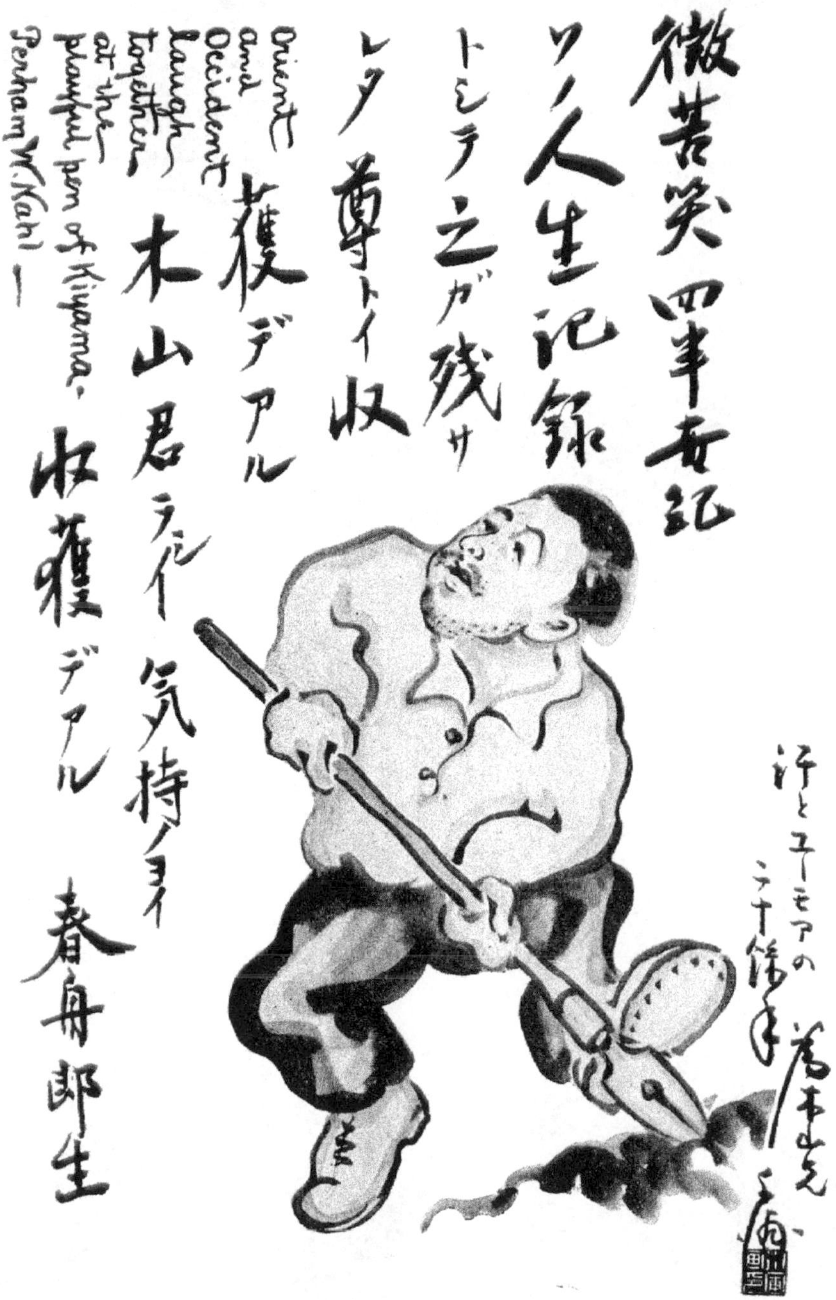

微苦笑四半世紀
ソノ人生記録
トシテ之ガ残サ
レタ尊トイ収
穫デアル
木山君ラシイ 気持ノヨイ
収穫デアル
Orient and Occident Laugh together at the playful pen of Kiyama, — Penham W. Kahl —
汗とユーモアの

Laughter cures almost anything in this world. So does death, for that matter, but laughing's a lot warmer and pleasant and makes you feel better, whereas death's terribly cold and forlorn. For most living creatures, death's the worst thing possible.

I always wish I could laugh more, myself—just laugh my troubles away. But I'm always betrayed by a little bug hiding somewhere in my brain that won't let me. This invisible bug's an awfully stingy fellow, and he only lets me laugh freely when I'm really happy; when I'm not—when I'm upset or angry, or when I run into something sad—he makes it very difficult for me. And if I try to laugh when I don't really feel like it, he makes me seem sarcastic, hypocritical, and mean-spirited.

Henry Kiyama's always laughing. Whenever I see him he's laughing. No matter what happens to him, he seems to be laughing. He's a person who's spent twenty-five years living in America laughing, laughing and observing, laughing and listening. Years ago when he was attending the San Francisco Art Institute, he quietly and earnestly pursued his studies in art, his easel lined up with those of Kazuo Matsubara and Kamesuke Hiraga. But ultimately he started laughing. And the product of his laughter is this book. As a personal history of our countrymen living in America, done by someone whose view of life is interesting, perceptive, and wise, it's truly extraordinary. I'm particularly happy to see what a good artist Henry Kiyama has become, too.

Hibutsu

A cartoonist working for the famous London humor magazine Punch once noted that "cartoons are not jokes; they are observations about life, which isn't serious." Our lives as Japanese in America have a unique historical significance eminently worthy of study. There have been aspects of our lives here that are tragic, and aspects that are comic, things to be proud of, and things that are to be regretted. I do not know exactly what the artist's thoughts were when he created his work, yet I am pleased to report that when I began reading it, I was so captivated by his careful observations and remarkably informed drawings that I read it through in one sitting. I found it immensely fascinating and instructive.

Kaname Wakasugi
San Francisco
March 27, 1931

LIST OF EPISODES

EPISODE 1

Arrival in San Francisco

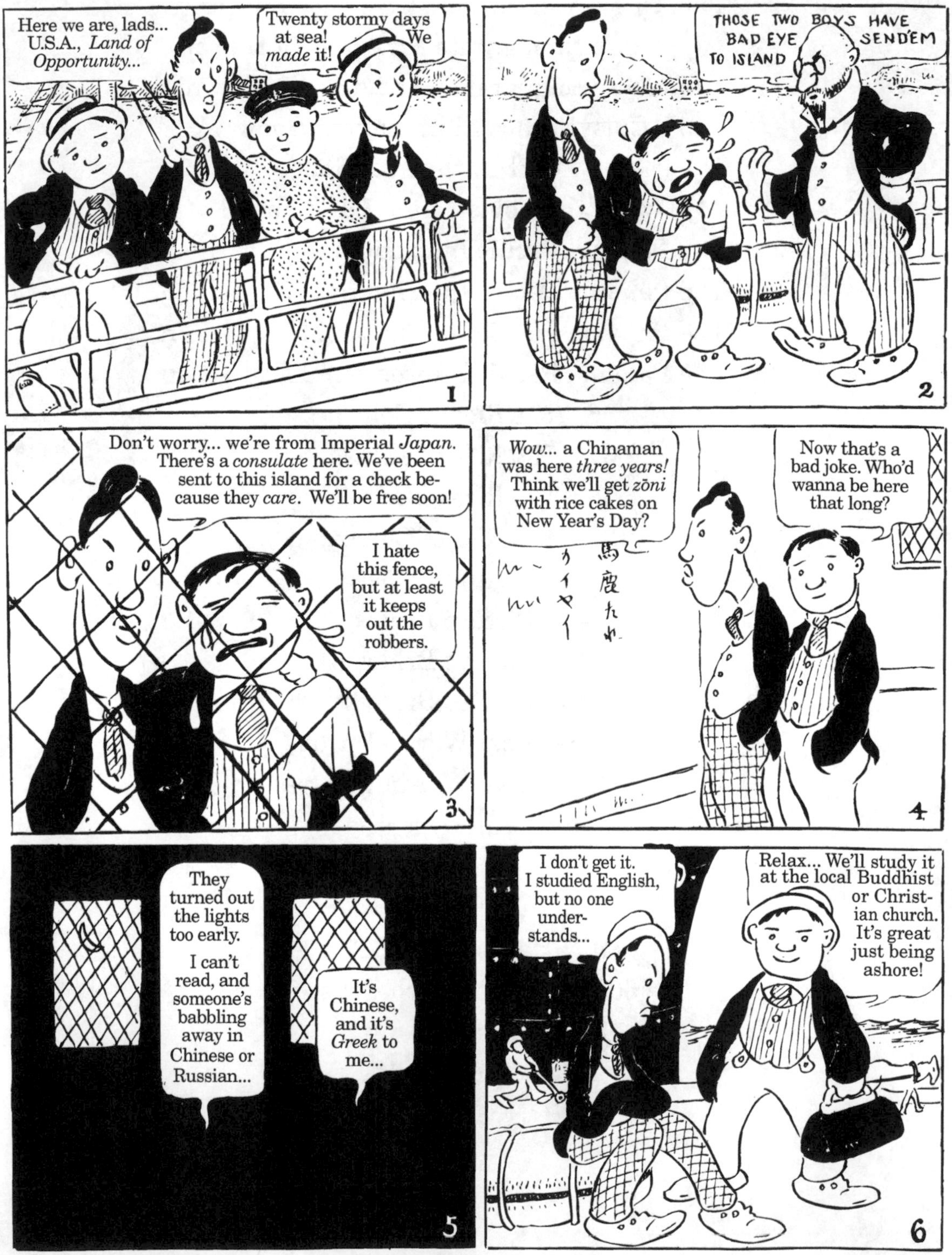
Here we are, lads... U.S.A., *Land of Opportunity*...
Twenty stormy days at sea! We *made* it!
1
THOSE TWO BOYS HAVE BAD EYE SEND'EM TO ISLAND
2
Don't worry... we're from Imperial *Japan*. There's a *consulate* here. We've been sent to this island for a check because they *care*. We'll be free soon!
I hate this fence, but at least it keeps out the robbers.
3
Wow... a Chinaman was here *three years!* Think we'll get *zōni* with rice cakes on New Year's Day?
Now that's a bad joke. Who'd wanna be here that long?
馬鹿たれ
4
They turned out the lights too early. I can't read, and someone's babbling away in Chinese or Russian...
It's Chinese, and it's *Greek* to me...
5
I don't get it. I studied English, but no one understands...
Relax... We'll study it at the local Buddhist or Christian church. It's great just being ashore!
6

Japanese part of graffiti on wall: *Hey, stupid!*

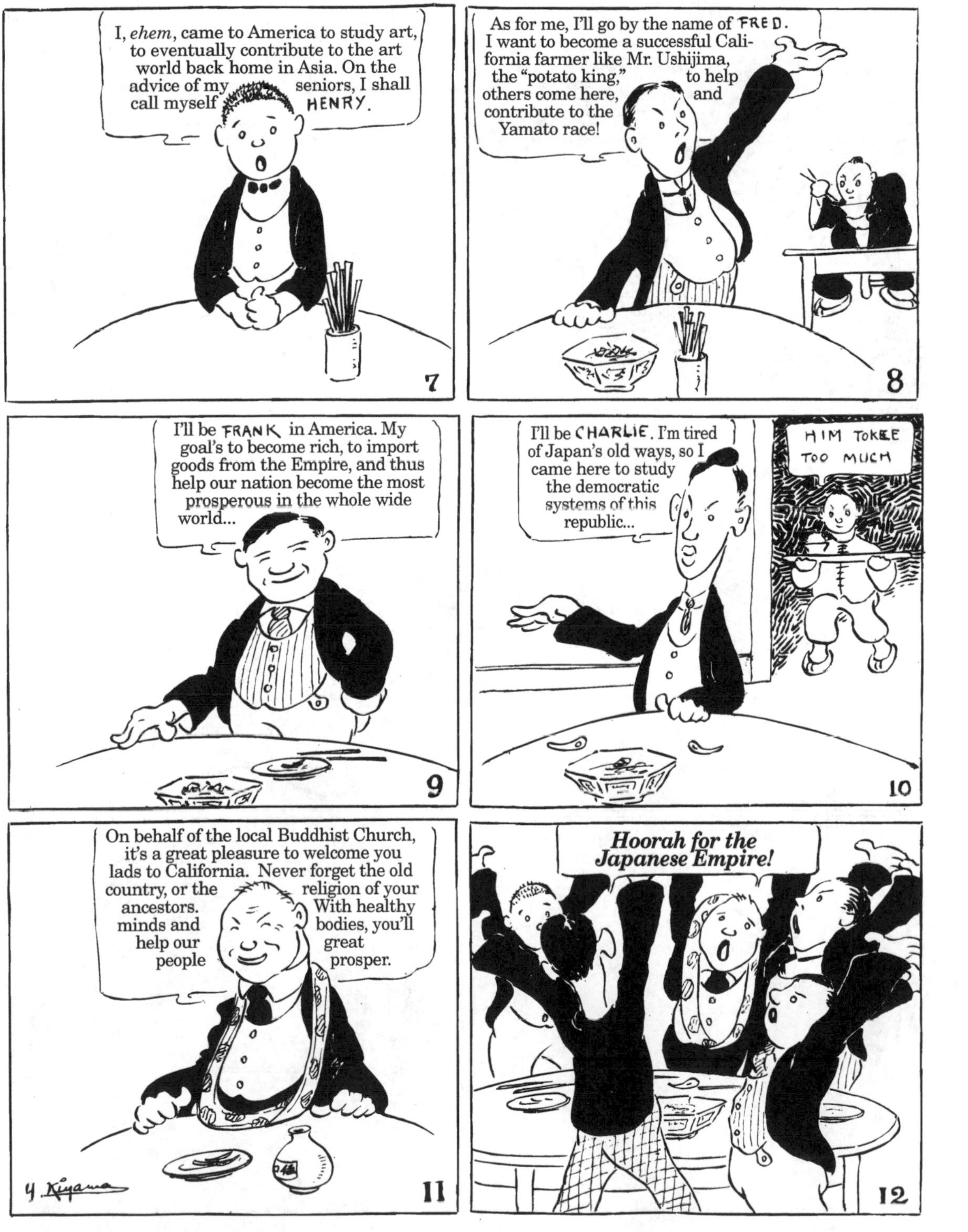
I, *ehem*, came to America to study art, to eventually contribute to the art world back home in Asia. On the advice of my seniors, I shall call myself HENRY.
7
As for me, I'll go by the name of FRED. I want to become a successful California farmer like Mr. Ushijima, the "potato king," to help others come here, and contribute to the Yamato race!
8
I'll be FRANK in America. My goal's to become rich, to import goods from the Empire, and thus help our nation become the most prosperous in the whole wide world...
9
I'll be CHARLIE. I'm tired of Japan's old ways, so I came here to study the democratic systems of this republic...
HIM TOKEE TOO MUCH
10
On behalf of the local Buddhist Church, it's a great pleasure to welcome you lads to California. Never forget the old country, or the religion of your ancestors. With healthy minds and bodies, you'll help our great people prosper.
Y. Kiyama
11
Hoorah for the Japanese Empire!
12

"Schoolboys"

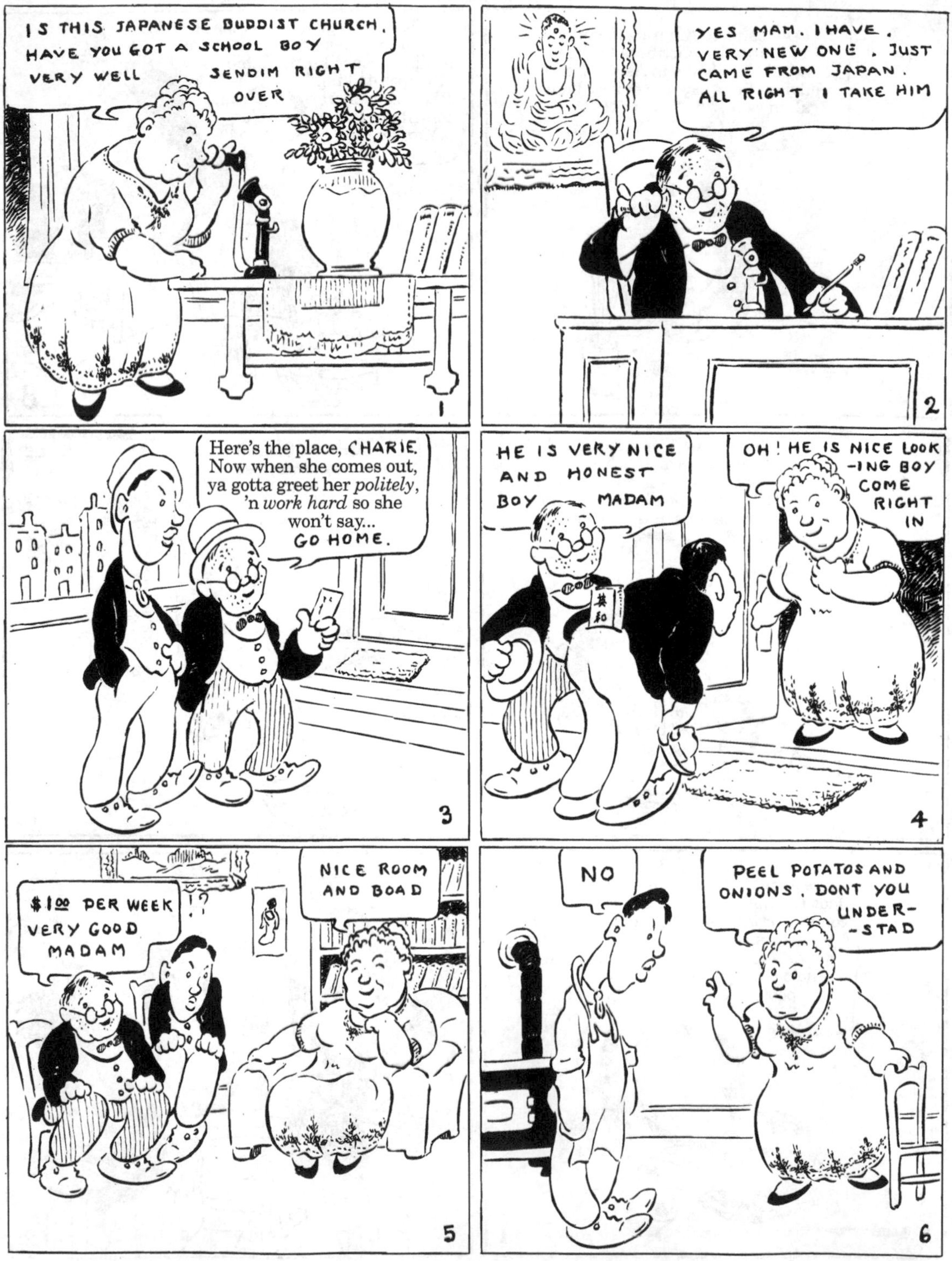
IS THIS JAPANESE BUDDIST CHURCH. HAVE YOU GOT A SCHOOL BOY VERY WELL SENDIM RIGHT OVER
1
YES MAM. I HAVE. VERY NEW ONE. JUST CAME FROM JAPAN. ALL RIGHT I TAKE HIM
2
Here's the place, CHARIE. Now when she comes out, ya gotta greet her *politely*, 'n *work hard* so she won't say... GO HOME.
3
HE IS VERY NICE AND HONEST BOY MADAM
英和
OH! HE IS NICE LOOK-ING BOY COME RIGHT IN
4
$1.00 PER WEEK VERY GOOD MADAM
!?
NICE ROOM AND BOAD
5
NO
PEEL POTATOS AND ONIONS. DONT YOU UNDER-STAD
6

Book in back pocket: *English-Japanese Dictionary*

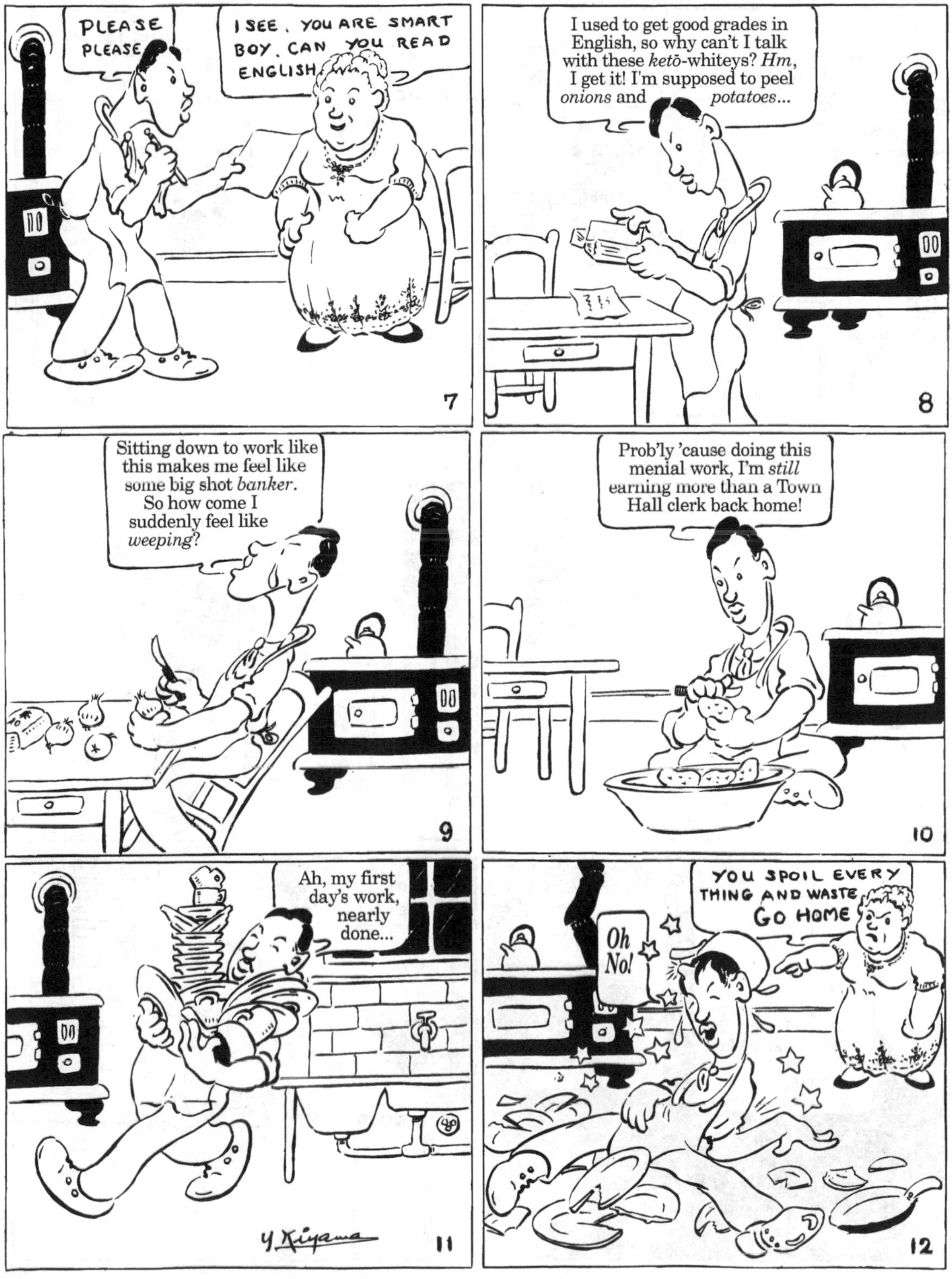
PLEASE PLEASE
I SEE. YOU ARE SMART BOY. CAN YOU READ ENGLISH
7
I used to get good grades in English, so why can't I talk with these *ketō*-whiteys? *Hm*, I get it! I'm supposed to peel *onions* and potatoes...
8
Sitting down to work like this makes me feel like some big shot *banker*. So how come I suddenly feel like *weeping*?
9
Prob'ly 'cause doing this menial work, I'm *still* earning more than a Town Hall clerk back home!
10
Ah, my first day's work, nearly done...
Y. Kiyama
11
Oh No!
YOU SPOIL EVERY THING AND WASTE GO HOME
12

EPISODE 3

"Schoolboys"

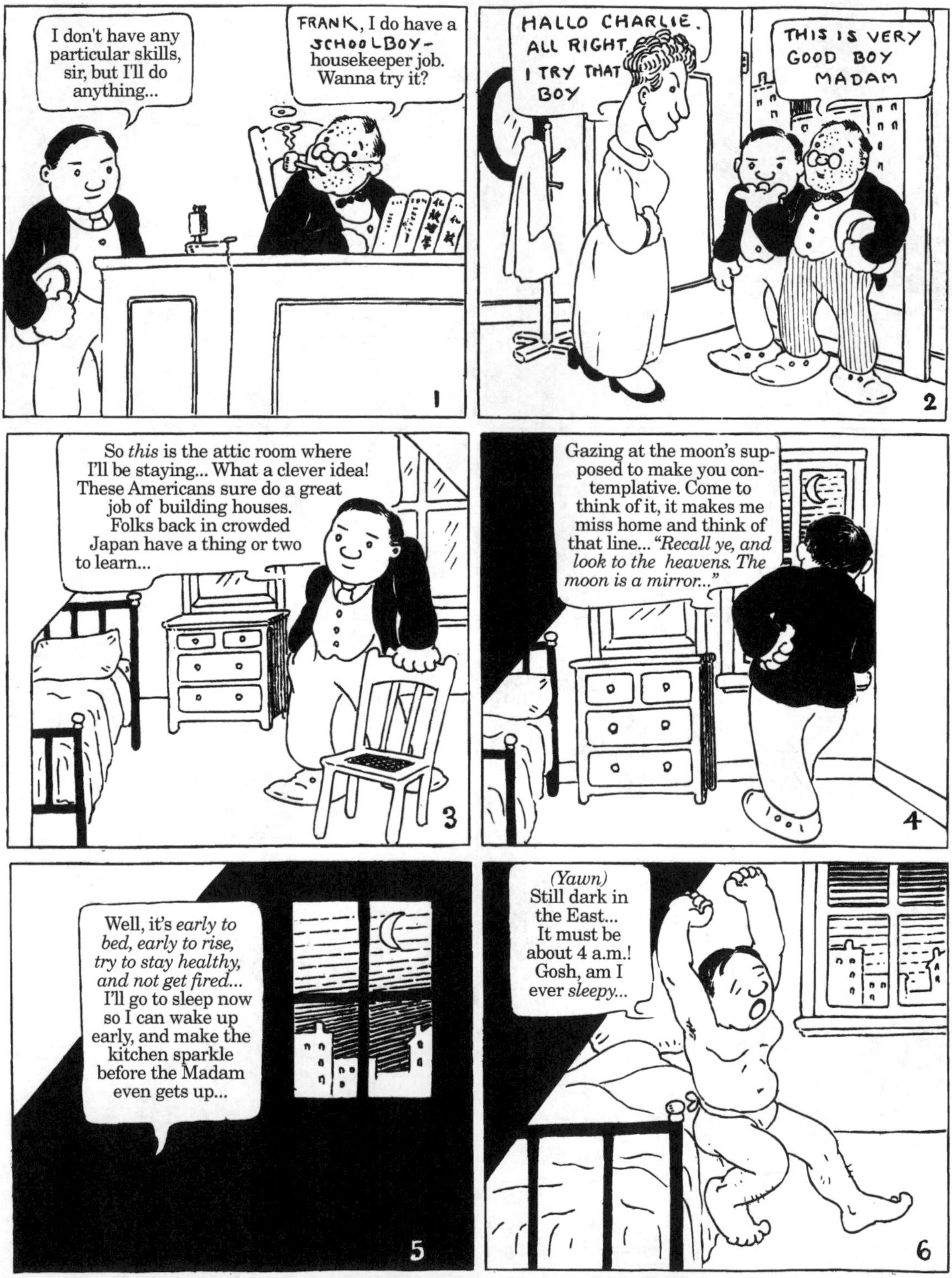
I don't have any particular skills, sir, but I'll do anything...
FRANK, I do have a SCHOOLBOY-housekeeper job. Wanna try it?
HALLO CHARLIE. ALL RIGHT. I TRY THAT BOY
THIS IS VERY GOOD BOY MADAM
So *this* is the attic room where I'll be staying... What a clever idea! These Americans sure do a great job of building houses. Folks back in crowded Japan have a thing or two to learn...
Gazing at the moon's supposed to make you contemplative. Come to think of it, it makes me miss home and think of that line... *"Recall ye, and look to the heavens. The moon is a mirror..."*
Well, it's *early to bed, early to rise, try to stay healthy, and not get fired...* I'll go to sleep now so I can wake up early, and make the kitchen sparkle before the Madam even gets up...
(Yawn) Still dark in the East... It must be about 4 a.m.! Gosh, am I ever *sleepy...*

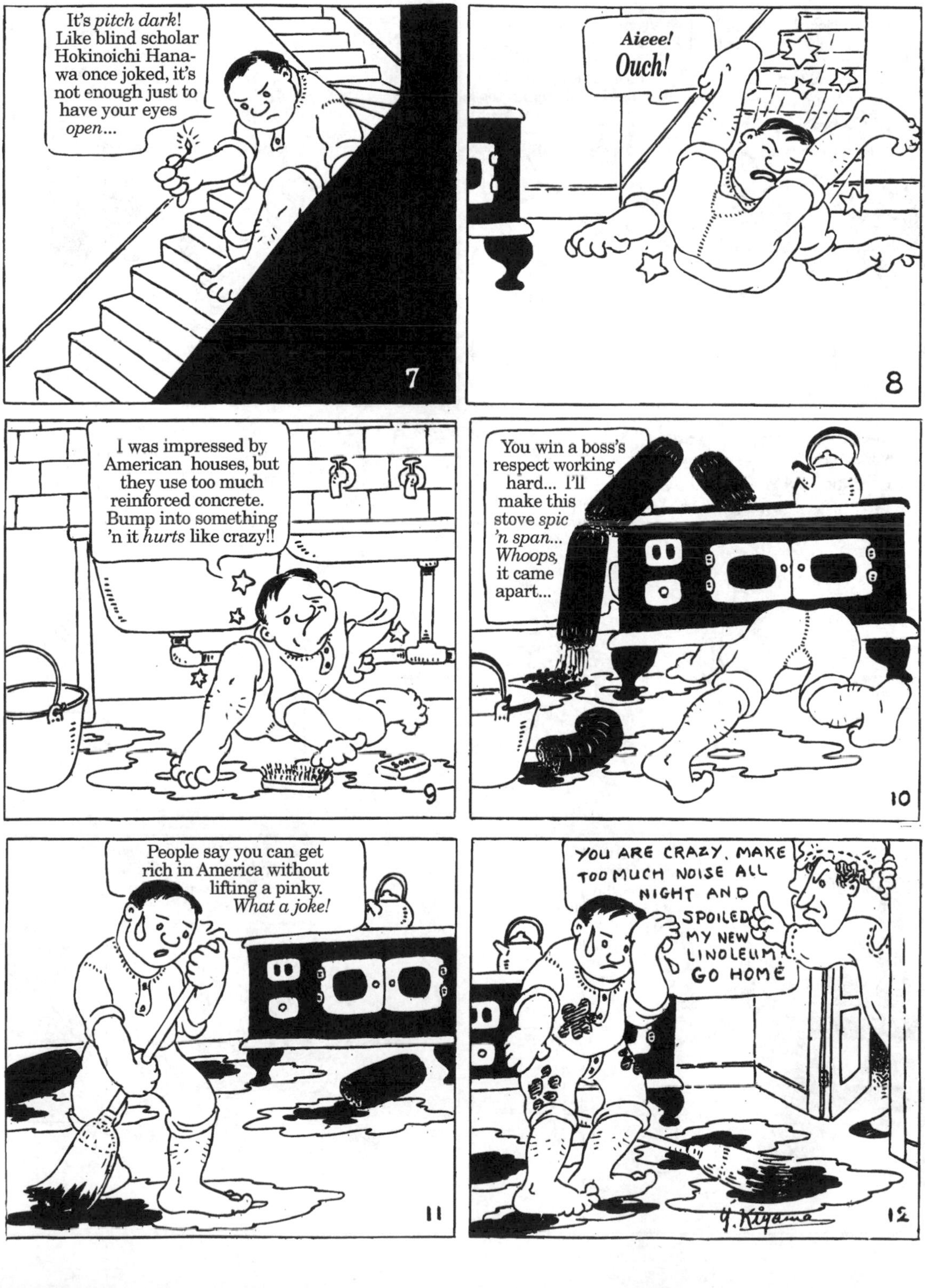
It's *pitch dark*! Like blind scholar Hokinoichi Hana-wa once joked, it's not enough just to have your eyes *open*...
Aieee! Ouch!
I was impressed by American houses, but they use too much reinforced concrete. Bump into something 'n it *hurts* like crazy!!
SOAP
You win a boss's respect working hard... I'll make this stove *spic 'n span*... *Whoops,* it came apart...
People say you can get rich in America without lifting a pinky. *What a joke!*
YOU ARE CRAZY. MAKE TOO MUCH NOISE ALL NIGHT AND SPOILED MY NEW LINOLEUM. GO HOME
Y. Kiyama

"Schoolboys"

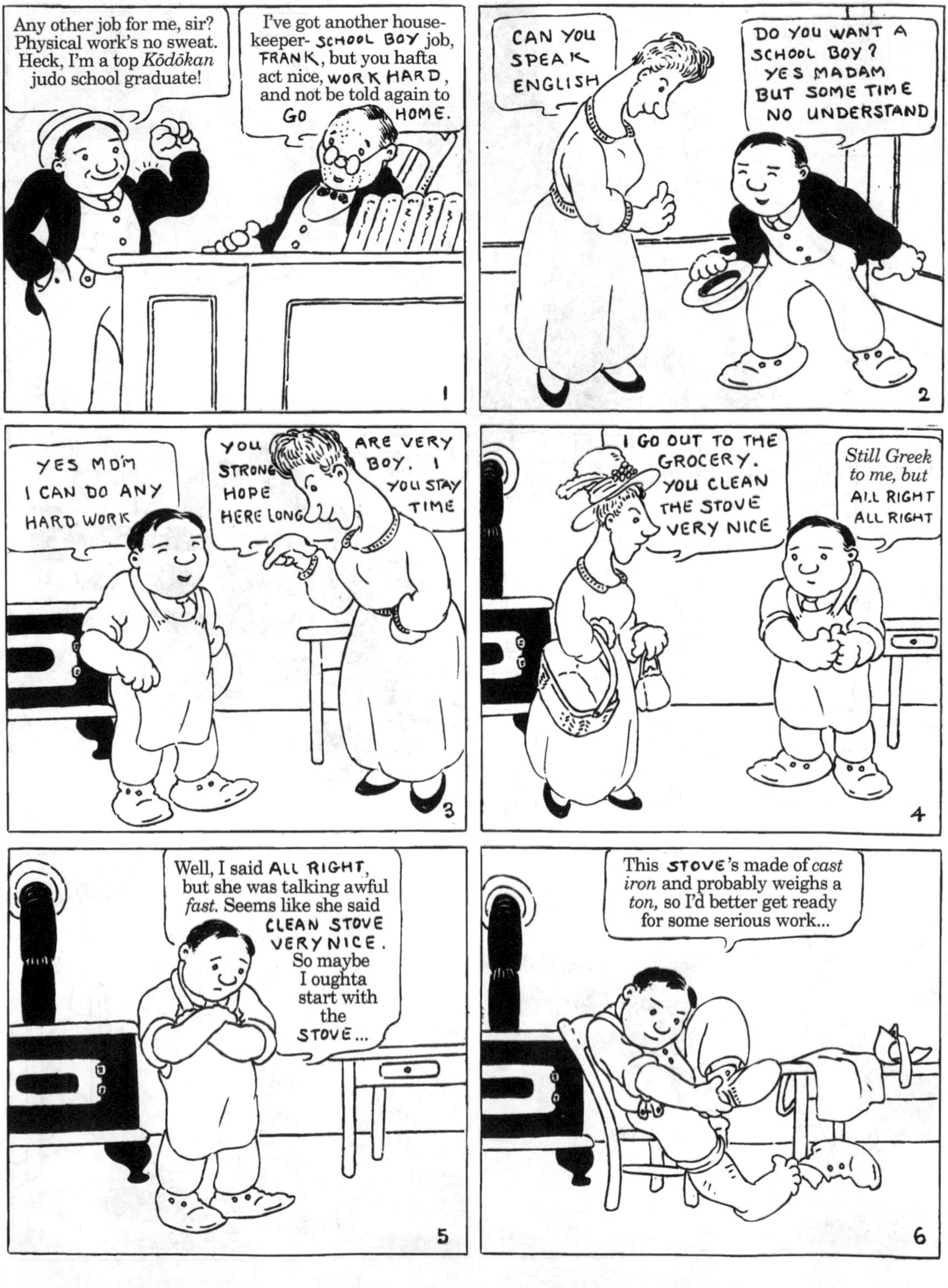
Any other job for me, sir? Physical work's no sweat. Heck, I'm a top *Kōdōkan* judo school graduate!
I've got another house-keeper- SCHOOL BOY job, FRANK, but you hafta act nice, WORK HARD, and not be told again to GO HOME.
1
CAN YOU SPEAK ENGLISH
DO YOU WANT A SCHOOL BOY? YES MADAM BUT SOME TIME NO UNDERSTAND
2
YES MD'M I CAN DO ANY HARD WORK
YOU ARE VERY STRONG BOY. I HOPE YOU STAY HERE LONG TIME
3
I GO OUT TO THE GROCERY. YOU CLEAN THE STOVE VERY NICE
Still Greek to me, but ALL RIGHT ALL RIGHT
4
Well, I said ALL RIGHT, but she was talking awful *fast*. Seems like she said CLEAN STOVE VERY NICE. So maybe I oughta start with the STOVE...
5
This STOVE's made of *cast iron* and probably weighs a *ton,* so I'd better get ready for some serious work...
6

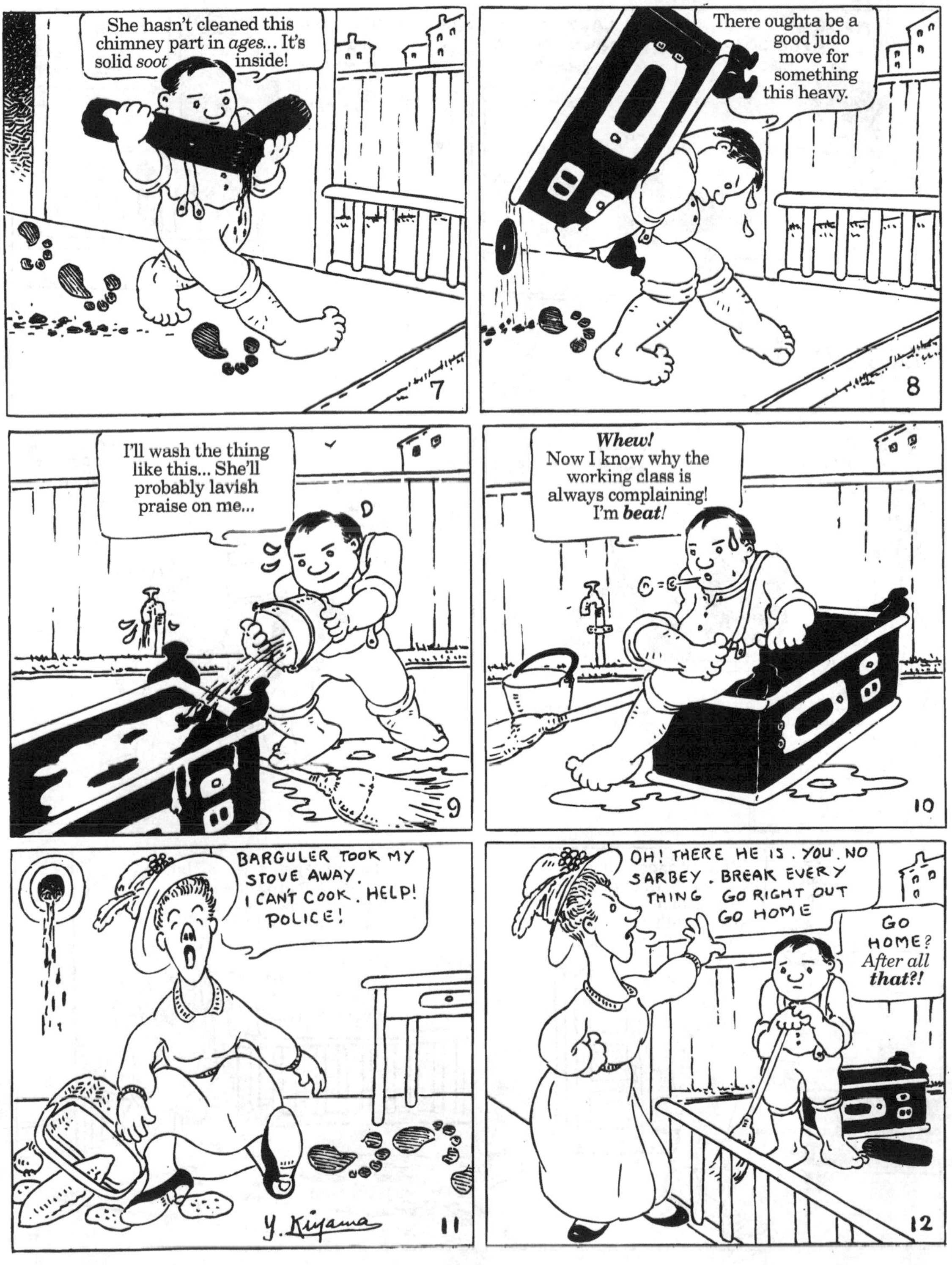
She hasn't cleaned this chimney part in *ages*... It's solid *soot* inside!
7
There oughta be a good judo move for something this heavy.
8
I'll wash the thing like this... She'll probably lavish praise on me...
9
Whew! Now I know why the working class is always complaining! I'm ***beat***!
10
BARGULER TOOK MY STOVE AWAY. I CAN'T COOK. HELP! POLICE!
Y. Kiyama
11
OH! THERE HE IS. YOU NO SARBEY. BREAK EVERY THING GO RIGHT OUT GO HOME
GO HOME? *After all **that?!***
12

EPISODE 5

"Schoolboys"

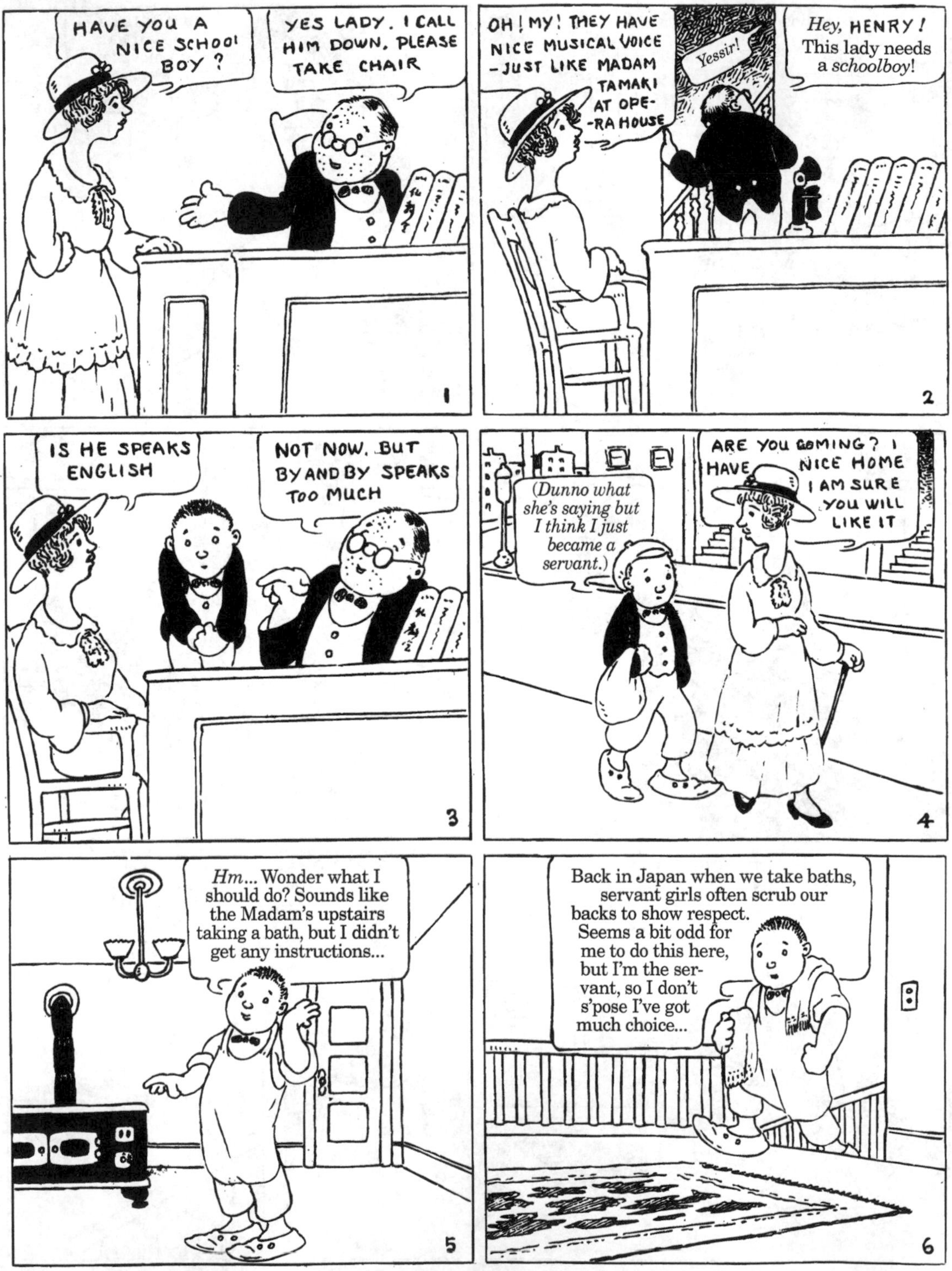

HAVE YOU A NICE SCHOOL BOY ?
YES LADY. I CALL HIM DOWN. PLEASE TAKE CHAIR
1
OH! MY! THEY HAVE NICE MUSICAL VOICE -JUST LIKE MADAM TAMAKI AT OPE--RA HOUSE
Yessir!
Hey, HENRY! This lady needs a *schoolboy*!
2
IS HE SPEAKS ENGLISH
NOT NOW. BUT BY AND BY SPEAKS TOO MUCH
3
(Dunno what she's saying but I think I just became a servant.)
ARE YOU COMING? I HAVE NICE HOME I AM SURE YOU WILL LIKE IT
4
Hm... Wonder what I should do? Sounds like the Madam's upstairs taking a bath, but I didn't get any instructions...
5
Back in Japan when we take baths, servant girls often scrub our backs to show respect. Seems a bit odd for me to do this here, but I'm the ser-vant, so I don't s'pose I've got much choice...
6

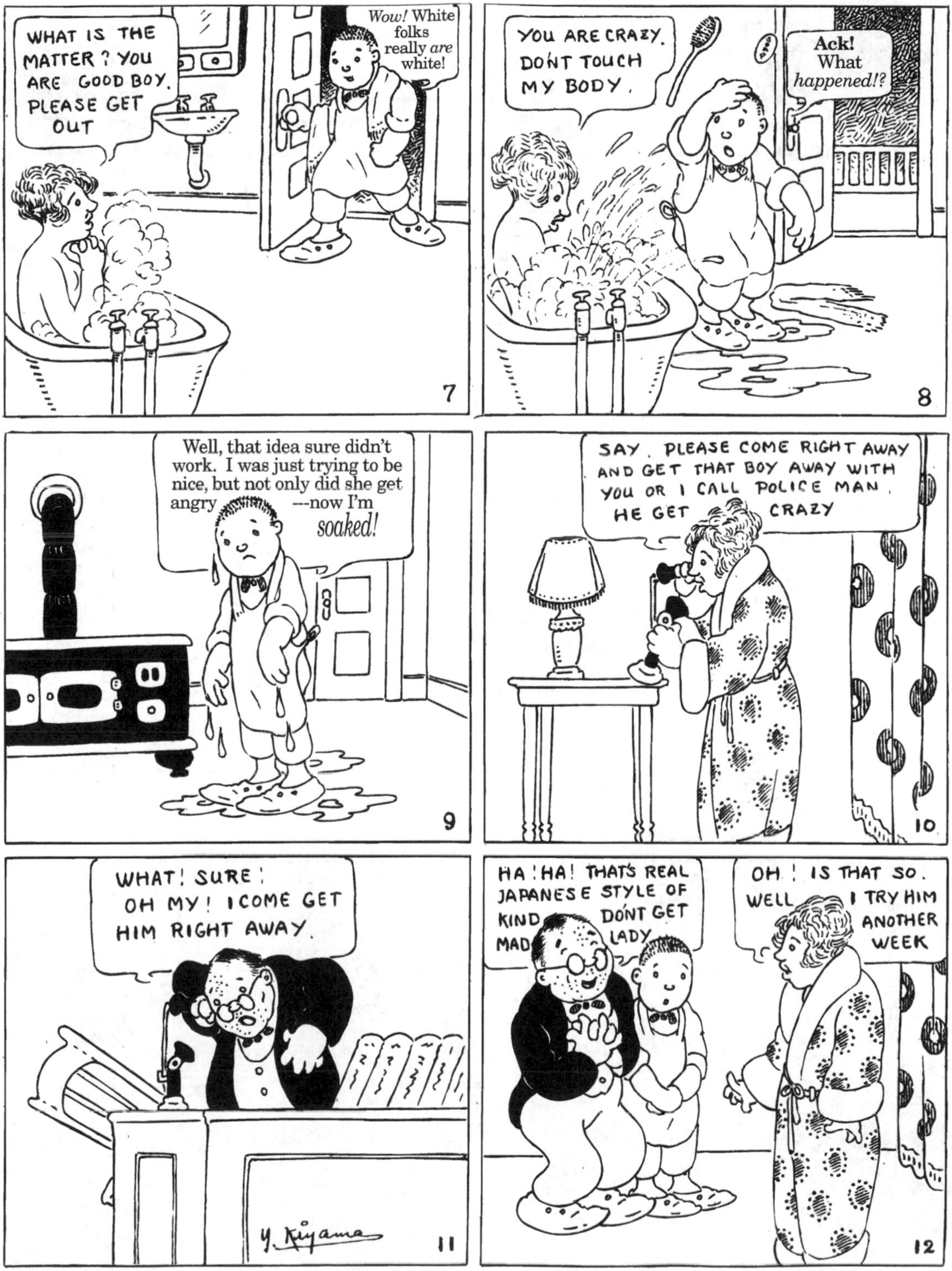
WHAT IS THE MATTER ? YOU ARE GOOD BOY. PLEASE GET OUT
Wow! White folks really *are* white!
7
YOU ARE CRAZY. DON'T TOUCH MY BODY.
Ack! What *happened!?*
8
Well, that idea sure didn't work. I was just trying to be nice, but not only did she get angry --now I'm *soaked!*
9
SAY. PLEASE COME RIGHT AWAY AND GET THAT BOY AWAY WITH YOU OR I CALL POLICE MAN. HE GET CRAZY
10
WHAT! SURE! OH MY! I COME GET HIM RIGHT AWAY.
Y. Kiyama
11
HA! HA! THAT'S REAL JAPANESE STYLE OF KIND DON'T GET MAD LADY.
OH! IS THAT SO. WELL I TRY HIM ANOTHER WEEK
12

EPISODE 6

"Schoolboys"

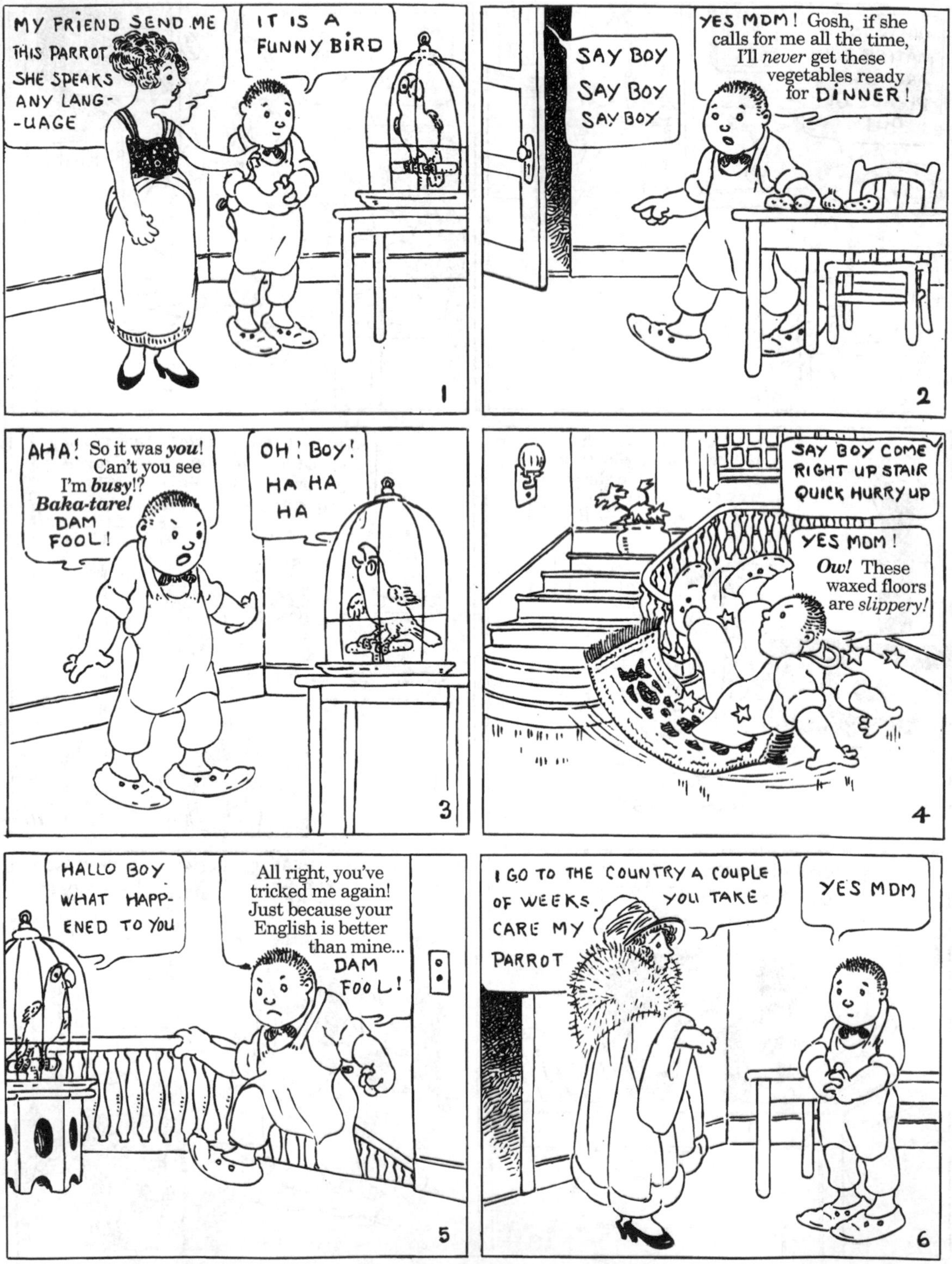

MY FRIEND SEND ME THIS PARROT SHE SPEAKS ANY LANG-UAGE
IT IS A FUNNY BIRD
1
SAY BOY SAY BOY SAY BOY
YES MDM! Gosh, if she calls for me all the time, I'll *never* get these vegetables ready for DINNER!
2
AHA! So it was ***you***! Can't you see I'm ***busy***!? ***Baka-tare!*** DAM FOOL!
OH! Boy! HA HA HA
3
SAY BOY COME RIGHT UP STAIR QUICK HURRY UP
YES MDM! ***Ow!*** These waxed floors are *slippery!*
4
HALLO BOY WHAT HAPP-ENED TO YOU
All right, you've tricked me again! Just because your English is better than mine... DAM FOOL!
5
I GO TO THE COUNTRY A COUPLE OF WEEKS. YOU TAKE CARE MY PARROT
YES MDM
6

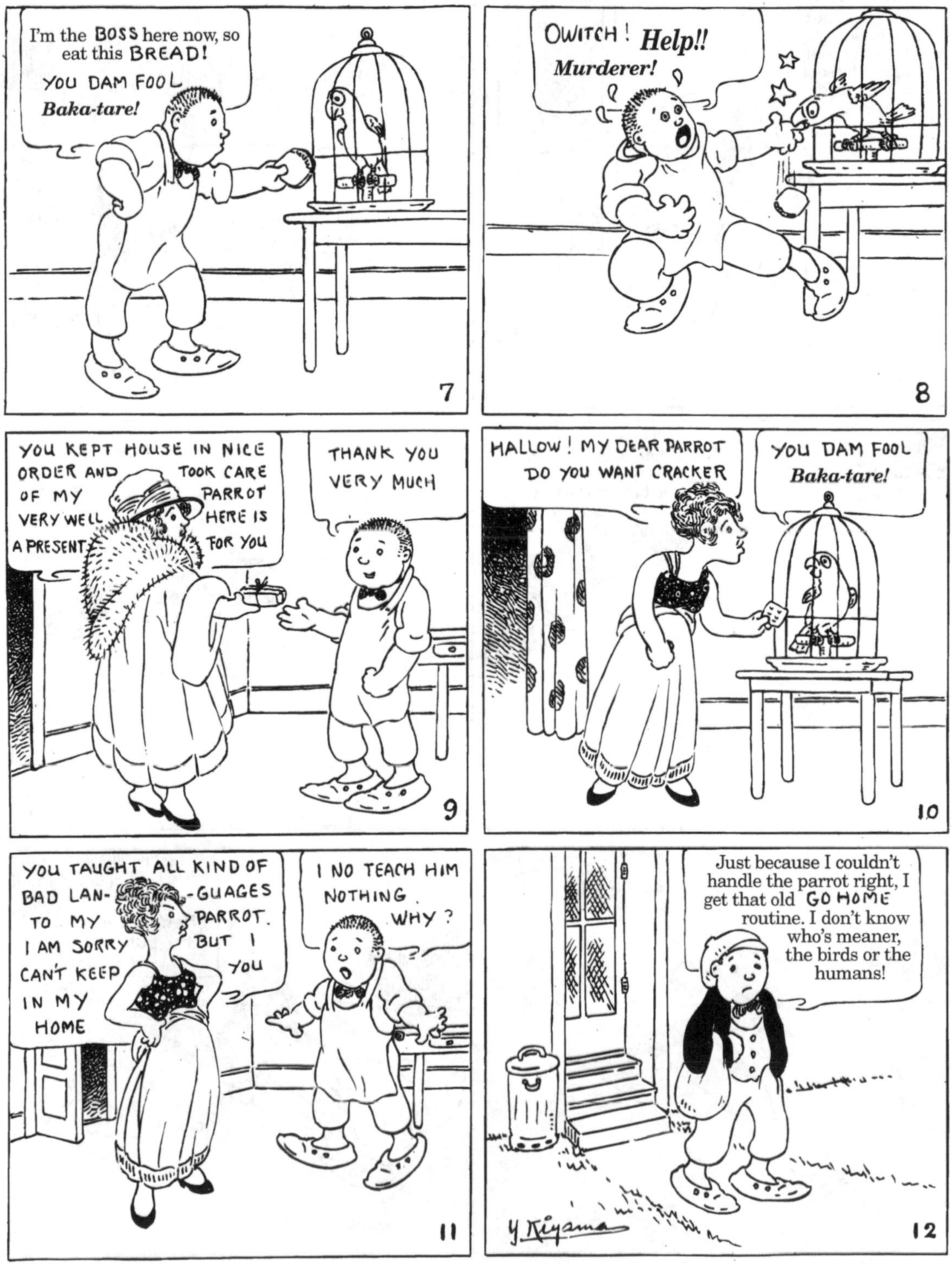
I'm the BOSS here now, so eat this BREAD!
YOU DAM FOOL
Baka-tare!
7
OWITCH! Help!! Murderer!
8
YOU KEPT HOUSE IN NICE ORDER AND TOOK CARE OF MY PARROT VERY WELL HERE IS A PRESENT FOR YOU
THANK YOU VERY MUCH
9
HALLOW! MY DEAR PARROT DO YOU WANT CRACKER
YOU DAM FOOL
Baka-tare!
10
YOU TAUGHT ALL KIND OF BAD LAN- -GUAGES TO MY PARROT. I AM SORRY BUT I CAN'T KEEP YOU IN MY HOME
I NO TEACH HIM NOTHING. WHY?
11
Just because I couldn't handle the parrot right, I get that old GO HOME routine. I don't know who's meaner, the birds or the humans!
Y. Kiyama
12

"Schoolboys"

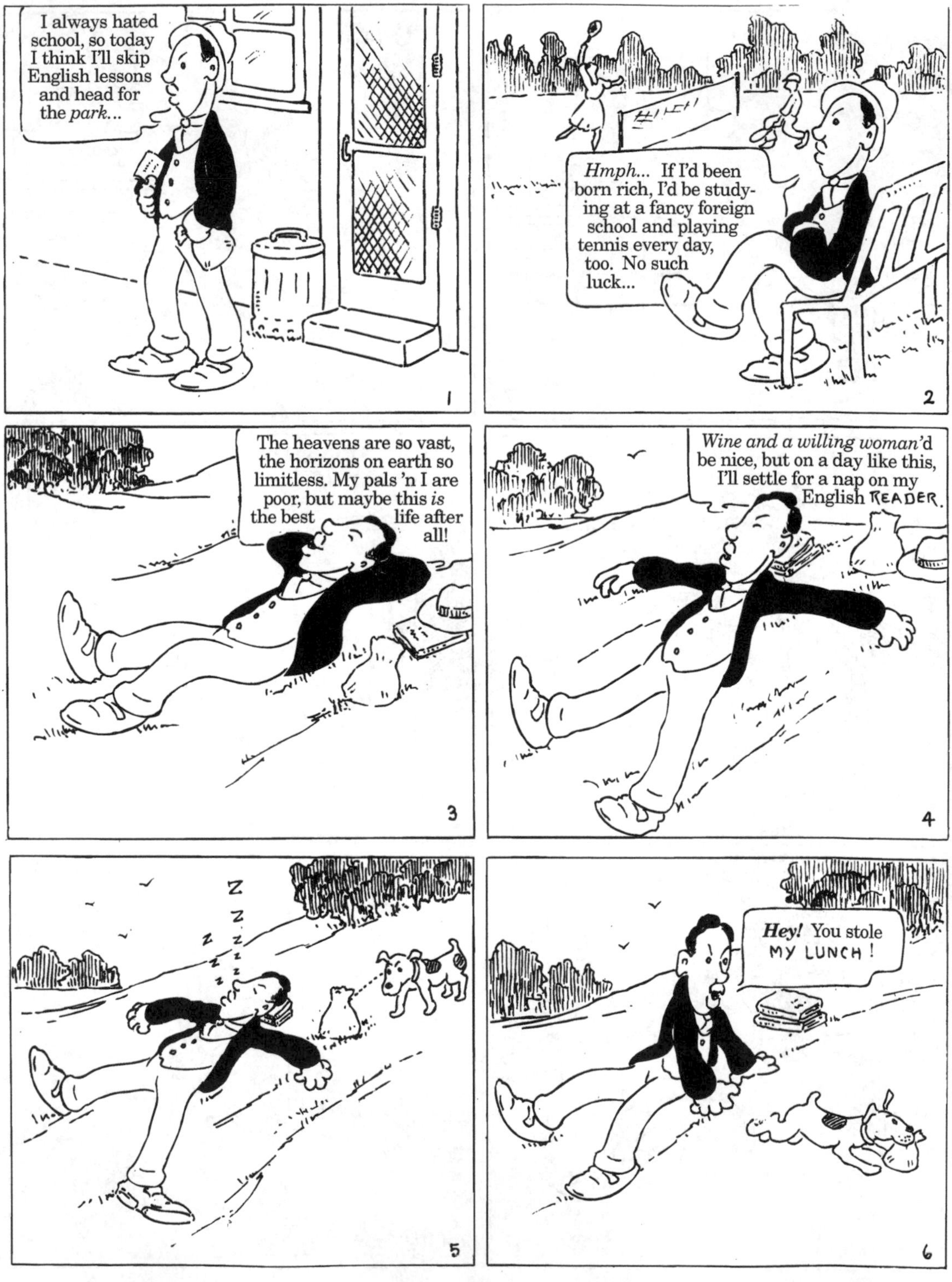
I always hated school, so today I think I'll skip English lessons and head for the *park*...
1
Hmph... If I'd been born rich, I'd be studying at a fancy foreign school and playing tennis every day, too. No such luck...
2
The heavens are so vast, the horizons on earth so limitless. My pals 'n I are poor, but maybe this *is* the best life after all!
3
Wine and a willing woman'd be nice, but on a day like this, I'll settle for a nap on my English READER.
4
Z Z Z Z Z Z Z Z
5
Hey! You stole MY LUNCH!
6

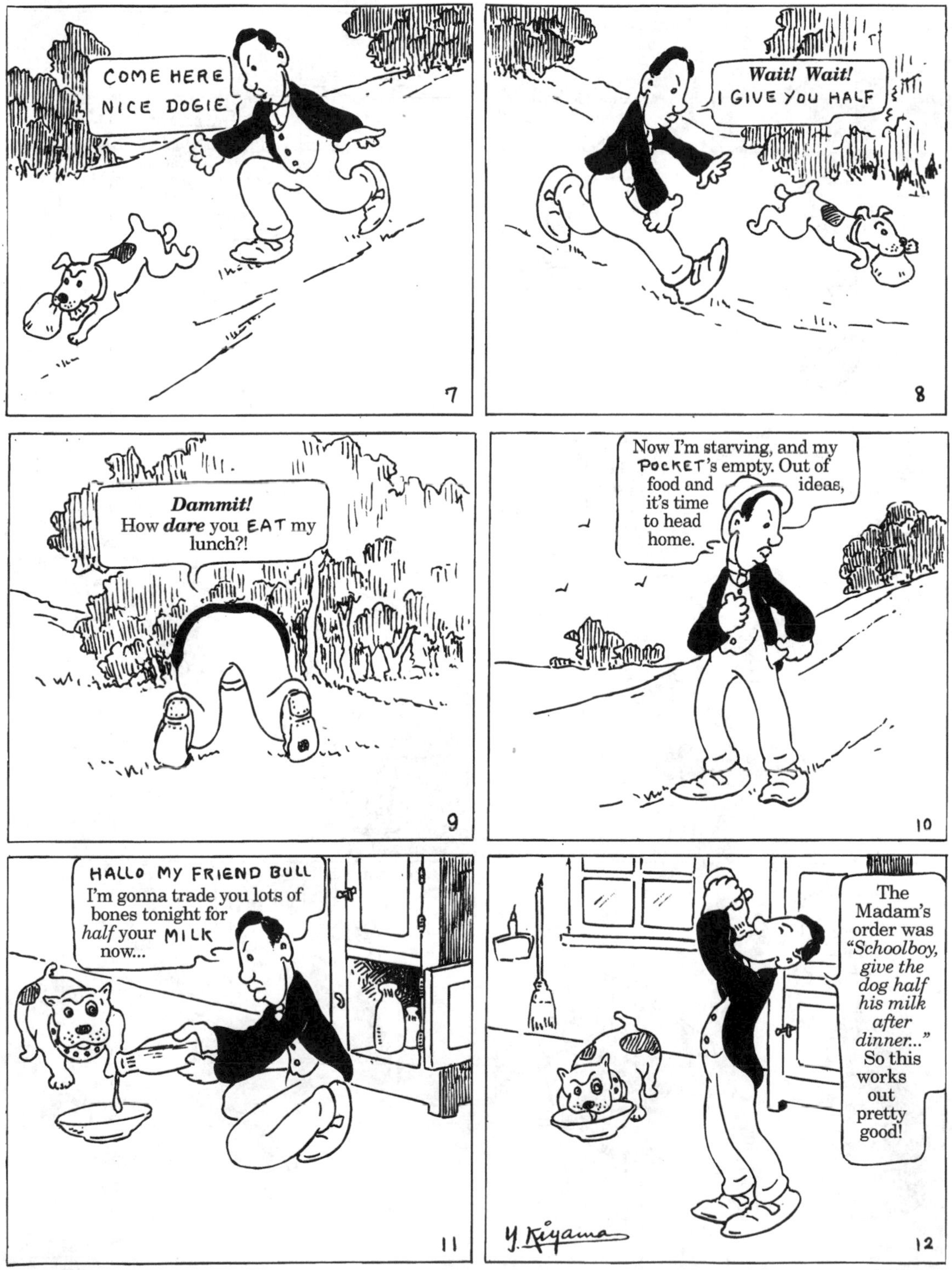
COME HERE NICE DOGIE
7
Wait! Wait! I GIVE YOU HALF
8
Dammit! How dare you EAT my lunch?!
9
Now I'm starving, and my POCKET's empty. Out of food and ideas, it's time to head home.
10
HALLO MY FRIEND BULL I'm gonna trade you lots of bones tonight for half your MILK now...
11
The Madam's order was "Schoolboy, give the dog half his milk after dinner..." So this works out pretty good!
Y. Kiyama
12

EPISODE 8

"Schoolboys"

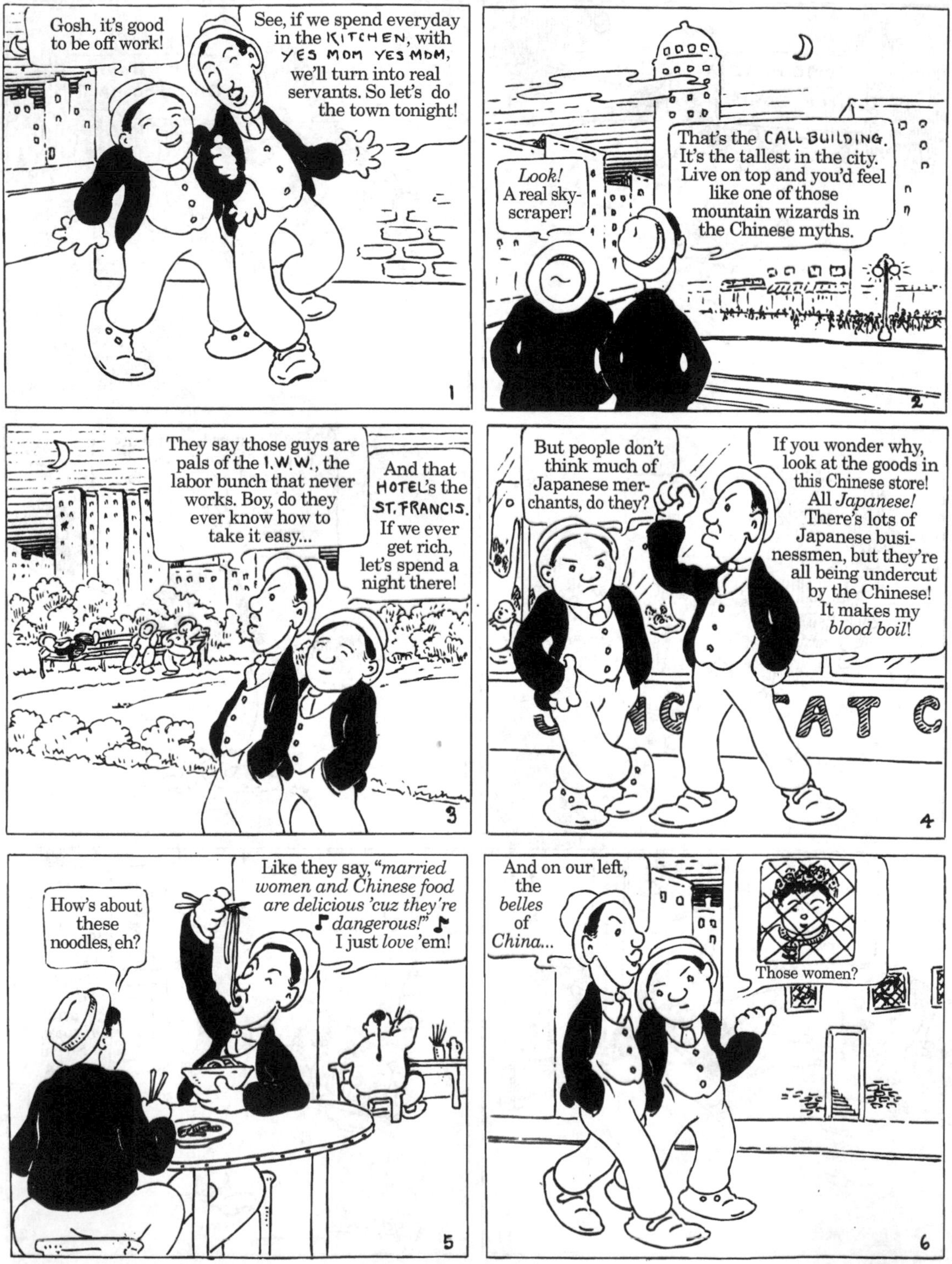

Gosh, it's good to be off work!
See, if we spend everyday in the KITCHEN, with YES MOM YES MOM, we'll turn into real servants. So let's do the town tonight!
Look! A real sky-scraper!
That's the CALL BUILDING. It's the tallest in the city. Live on top and you'd feel like one of those mountain wizards in the Chinese myths.
They say those guys are pals of the I.W.W., the labor bunch that never works. Boy, do they ever know how to take it easy...
And that HOTEL's the ST. FRANCIS. If we ever get rich, let's spend a night there!
But people don't think much of Japanese merchants, do they?
If you wonder why, look at the goods in this Chinese store! All *Japanese!* There's lots of Japanese businessmen, but they're all being undercut by the Chinese! It makes my *blood boil!*
How's about these noodles, eh?
Like they say, "*married women and Chinese food are delicious 'cuz they're* ♪ *dangerous!*" ♪ I just *love* 'em!
And on our left, the *belles* of *China...*
Those women?

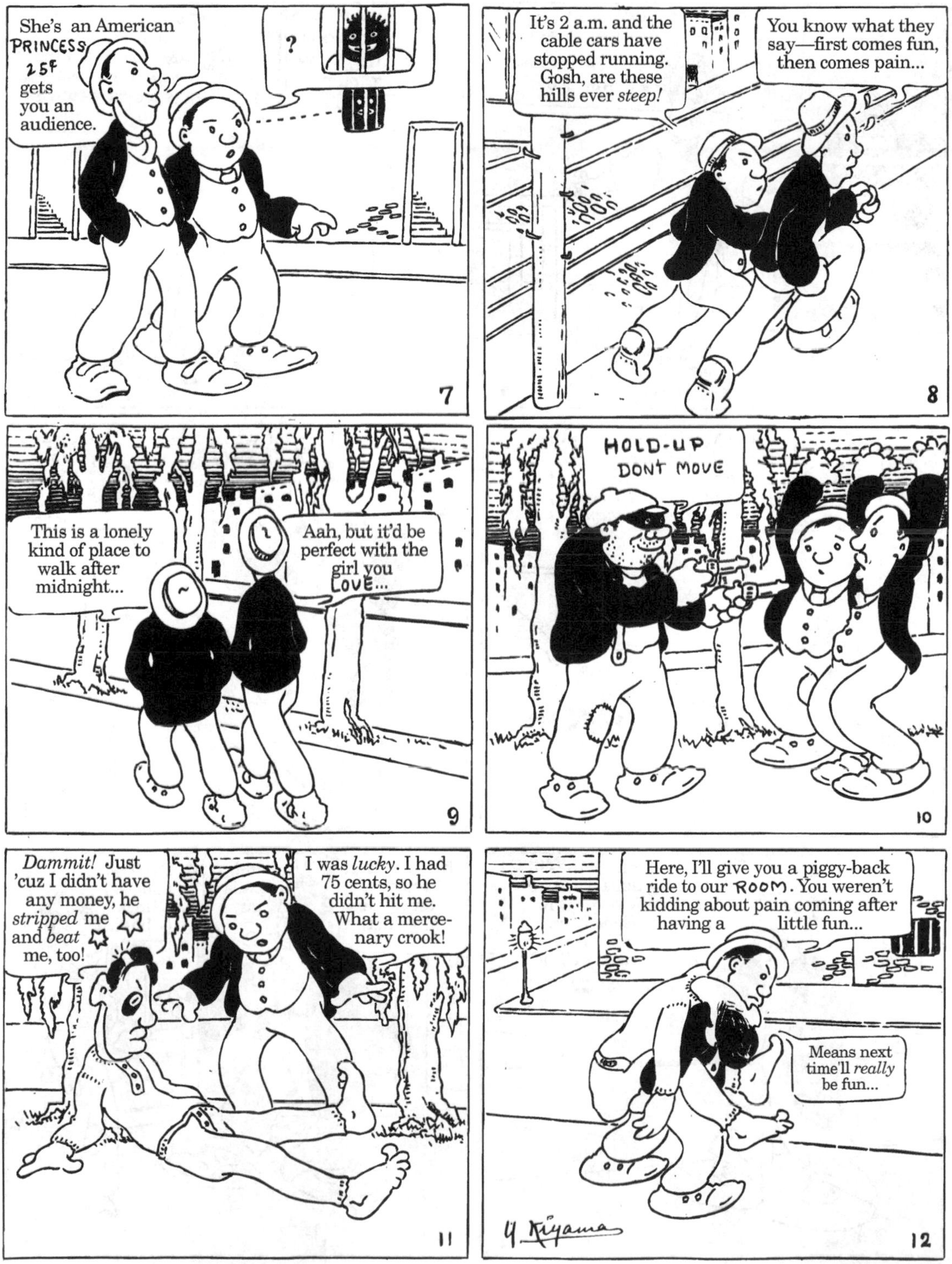
She's an American PRINCESS 25¢ gets you an audience.
?
It's 2 a.m. and the cable cars have stopped running. Gosh, are these hills ever *steep!*
You know what they say—first comes fun, then comes pain...
This is a lonely kind of place to walk after midnight...
Aah, but it'd be perfect with the girl you LOVE...
HOLD-UP DONT MOVE
Dammit! Just 'cuz I didn't have any money, he *stripped* me and *beat* me, too!
I was *lucky*. I had 75 cents, so he didn't hit me. What a mercenary crook!
Here, I'll give you a piggy-back ride to our ROOM. You weren't kidding about pain coming after having a little fun...
Means next time'll *really* be fun...
Y. Kiyama

"Schoolboys"

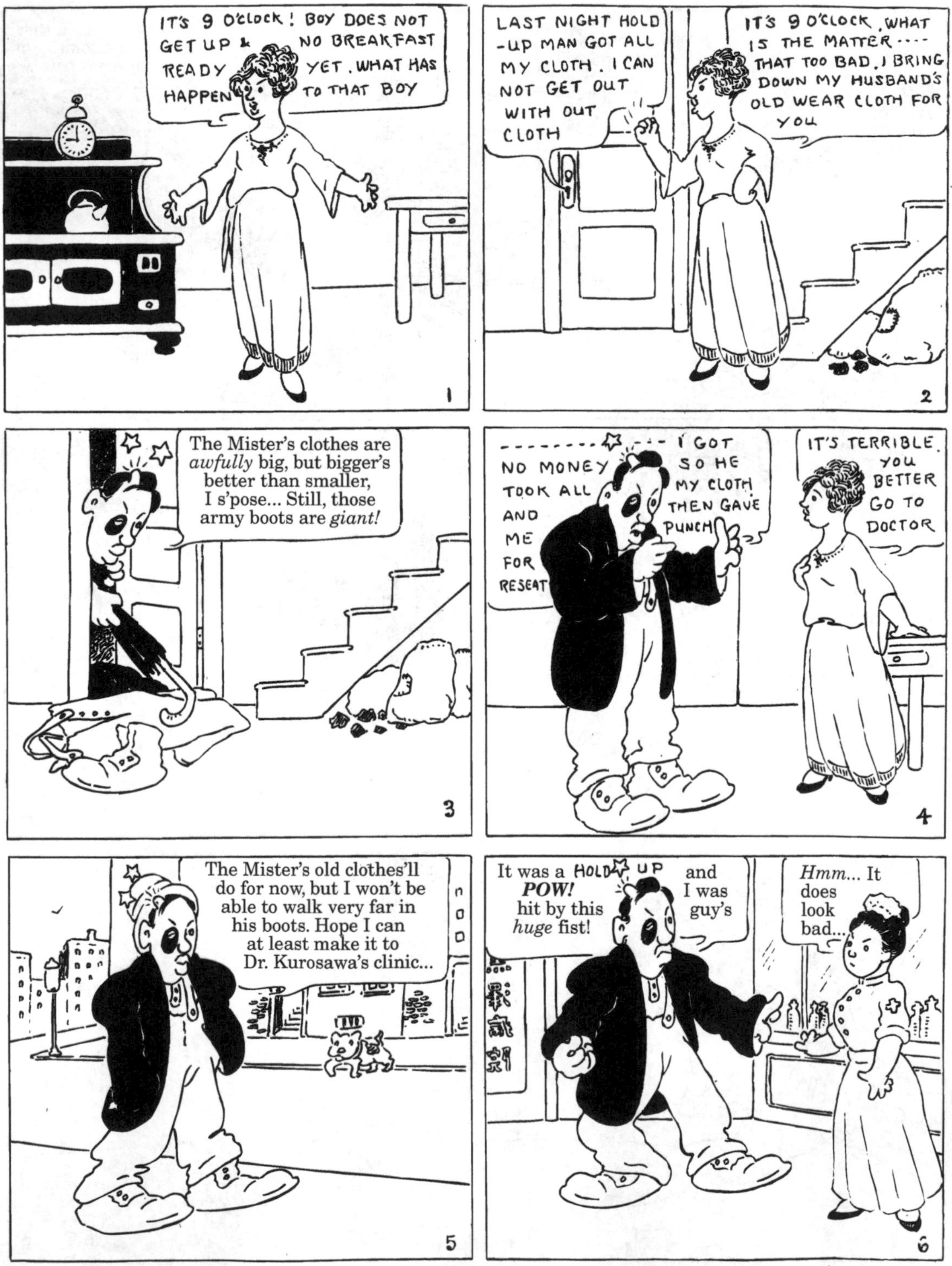
IT'S 9 O'CLOCK! BOY DOES NOT GET UP & NO BREAKFAST READY YET. WHAT HAS HAPPEN TO THAT BOY
1
LAST NIGHT HOLD-UP MAN GOT ALL MY CLOTH. I CAN NOT GET OUT WITH OUT CLOTH
IT'S 9 O'CLOCK, WHAT IS THE MATTER---- THAT TOO BAD. I BRING DOWN MY HUSBAND'S OLD WEAR CLOTH FOR YOU
2
The Mister's clothes are *awfully* big, but bigger's better than smaller, I s'pose... Still, those army boots are *giant!*
3
-------- --- I GOT NO MONEY SO HE TOOK ALL MY CLOTH AND THEN GAVE ME PUNCH FOR RESEAT
IT'S TERRIBLE. YOU BETTER GO TO DOCTOR
4
The Mister's old clothes'll do for now, but I won't be able to walk very far in his boots. Hope I can at least make it to Dr. Kurosawa's clinic...
5
It was a HOLD UP and I was hit by this guy's *huge* fist!
POW!
Hmm... It does look bad...
6

Sign (mirrored): *Kurosawa Clinic*

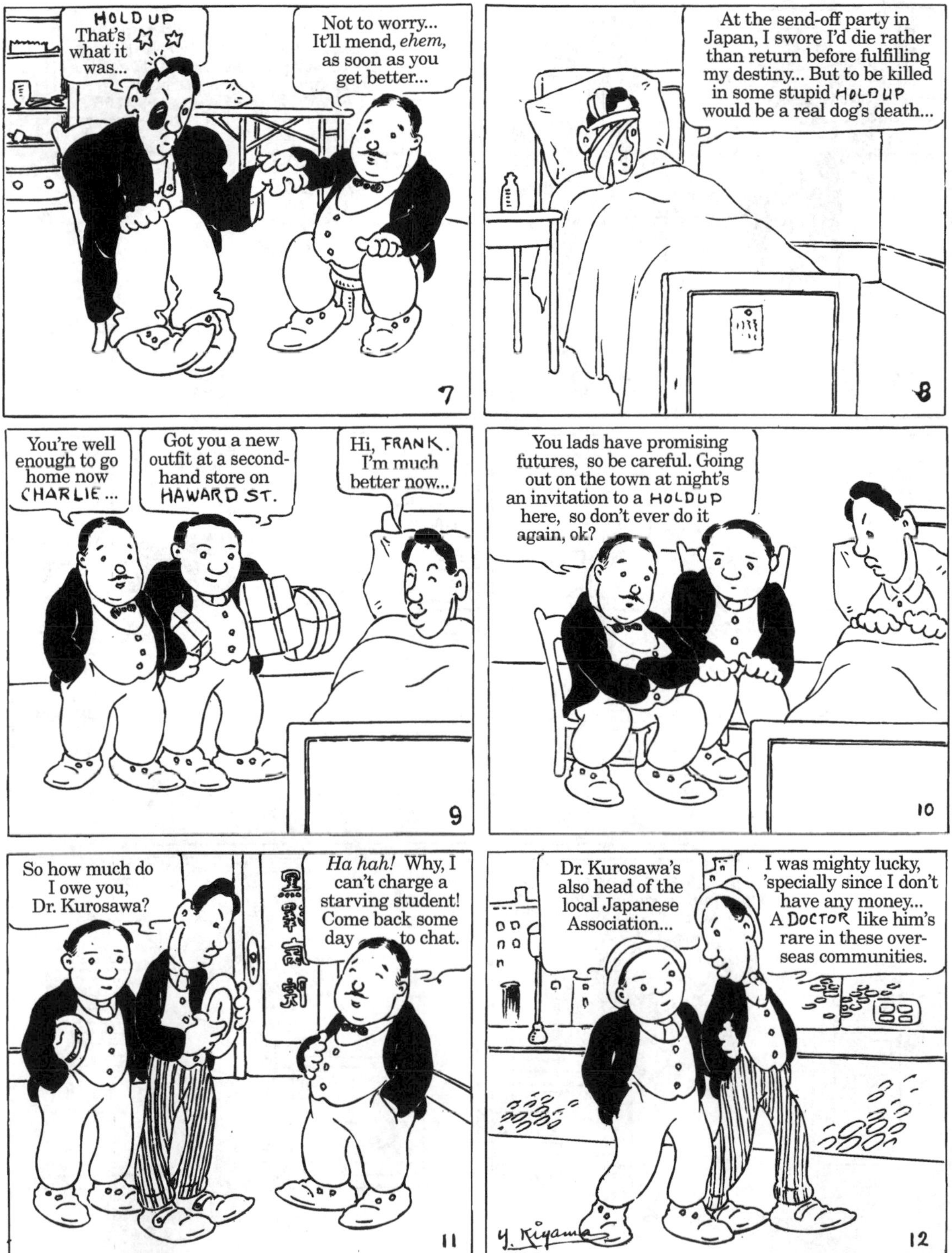
HOLDUP
That's what it was...
Not to worry... It'll mend, *ehem,* as soon as you get better...
7
At the send-off party in Japan, I swore I'd die rather than return before fulfilling my destiny... But to be killed in some stupid HOLDUP would be a real dog's death...
8
You're well enough to go home now CHARLIE...
Got you a new outfit at a second-hand store on HAWARD ST.
Hi, FRANK. I'm much better now...
9
You lads have promising futures, so be careful. Going out on the town at night's an invitation to a HOLDUP here, so don't ever do it again, ok?
10
So how much do I owe you, Dr. Kurosawa?
Ha hah! Why, I can't charge a starving student! Come back some day to chat.
11
Dr. Kurosawa's also head of the local Japanese Association...
I was mighty lucky, 'specially since I don't have any money... A DOCTOR like him's rare in these over-seas communities.
Y. Kiyama
12

"Schoolboys"

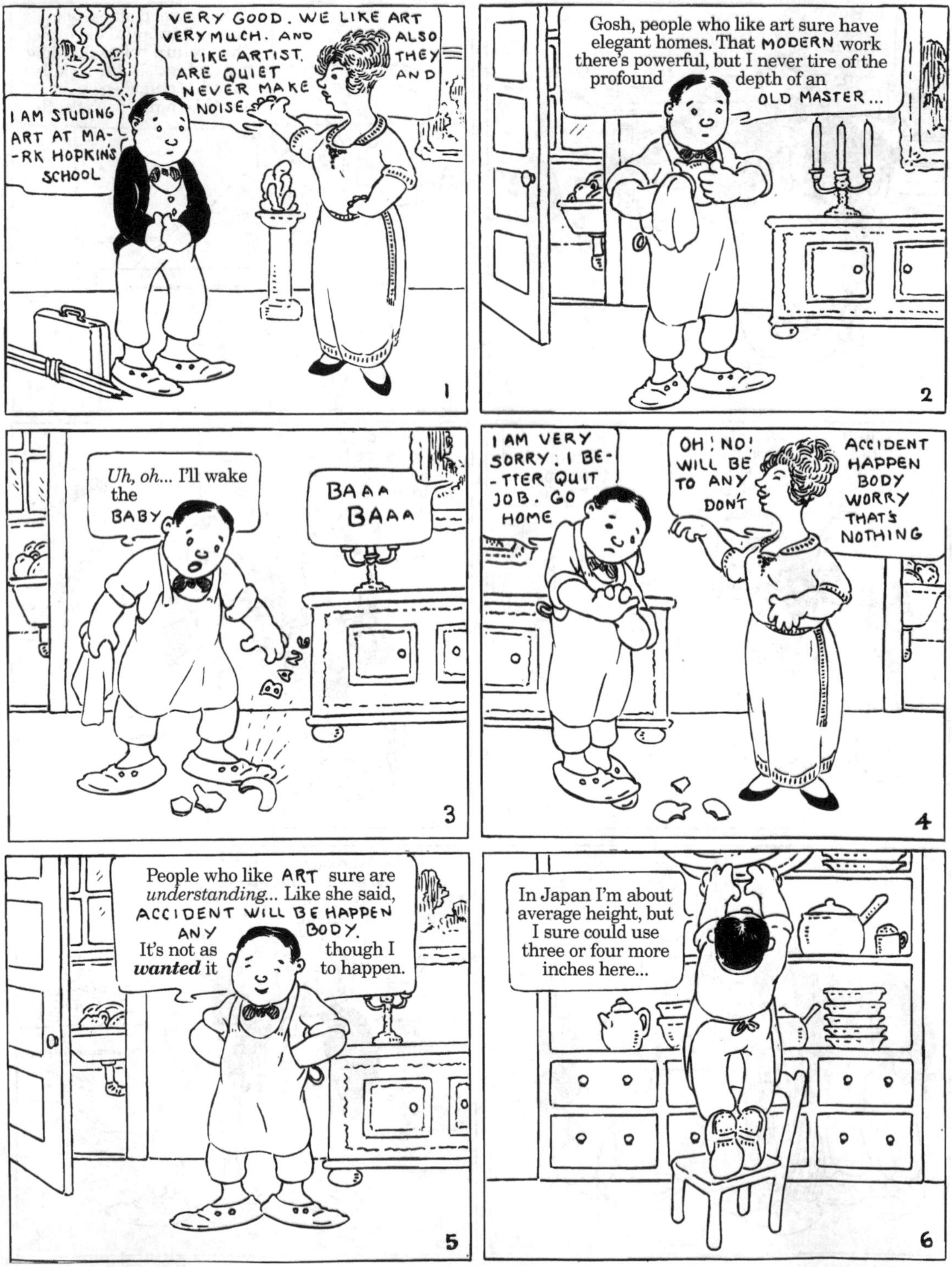
I AM STUDING ART AT MA-RK HOPKIN'S SCHOOL
VERY GOOD. WE LIKE ART VERYMUCH. AND ALSO LIKE ARTIST. THEY ARE QUIET AND NEVER MAKE NOISE
1
Gosh, people who like art sure have elegant homes. That MODERN work there's powerful, but I never tire of the profound depth of an OLD MASTER...
2
Uh, oh... I'll wake the BABY
BAAA BAAA
BANG
3
I AM VERY SORRY. I BE-TTER QUIT JOB. GO HOME
OH! NO! ACCIDENT WILL BE HAPPEN TO ANY BODY DON'T WORRY THAT'S NOTHING
4
People who like ART sure are *understanding*... Like she said, ACCIDENT WILL BE HAPPEN ANY BODY. It's not as though I ***wanted*** it to happen.
5
In Japan I'm about average height, but I sure could use three or four more inches here...
6

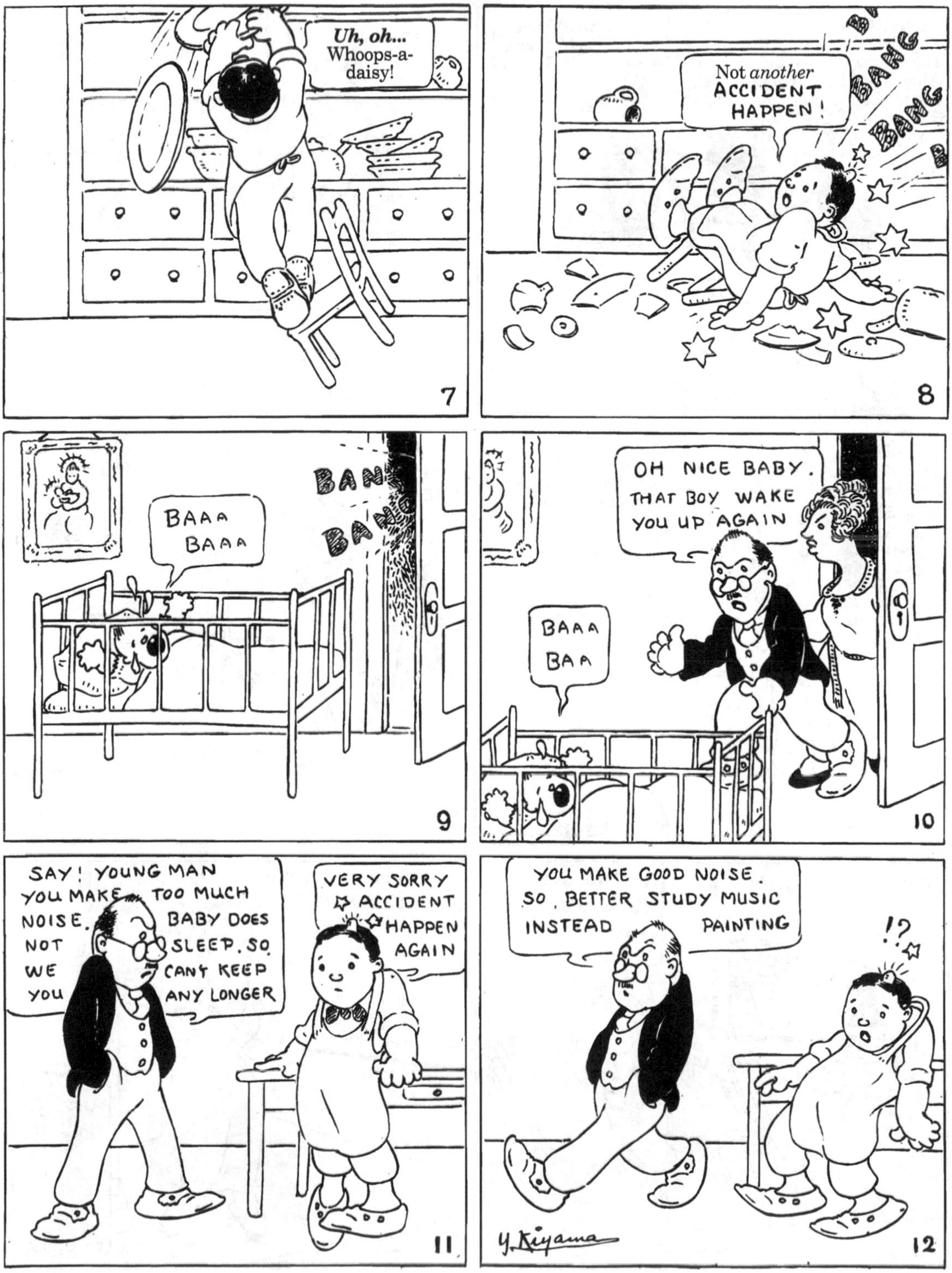
Uh, oh... Whoops-a-daisy!
7
Not *another* ACCIDENT HAPPEN!
BANG
BANG
8
BAAA BAAA
9
OH NICE BABY. THAT BOY WAKE YOU UP AGAIN
BAAA BAA
10
SAY! YOUNG MAN YOU MAKE TOO MUCH NOISE. BABY DOES NOT SLEEP. SO WE CAN'T KEEP YOU ANY LONGER
VERY SORRY ACCIDENT HAPPEN AGAIN
11
YOU MAKE GOOD NOISE. SO, BETTER STUDY MUSIC INSTEAD PAINTING
!?
Y. Kiyama
12

Mistaken Identity

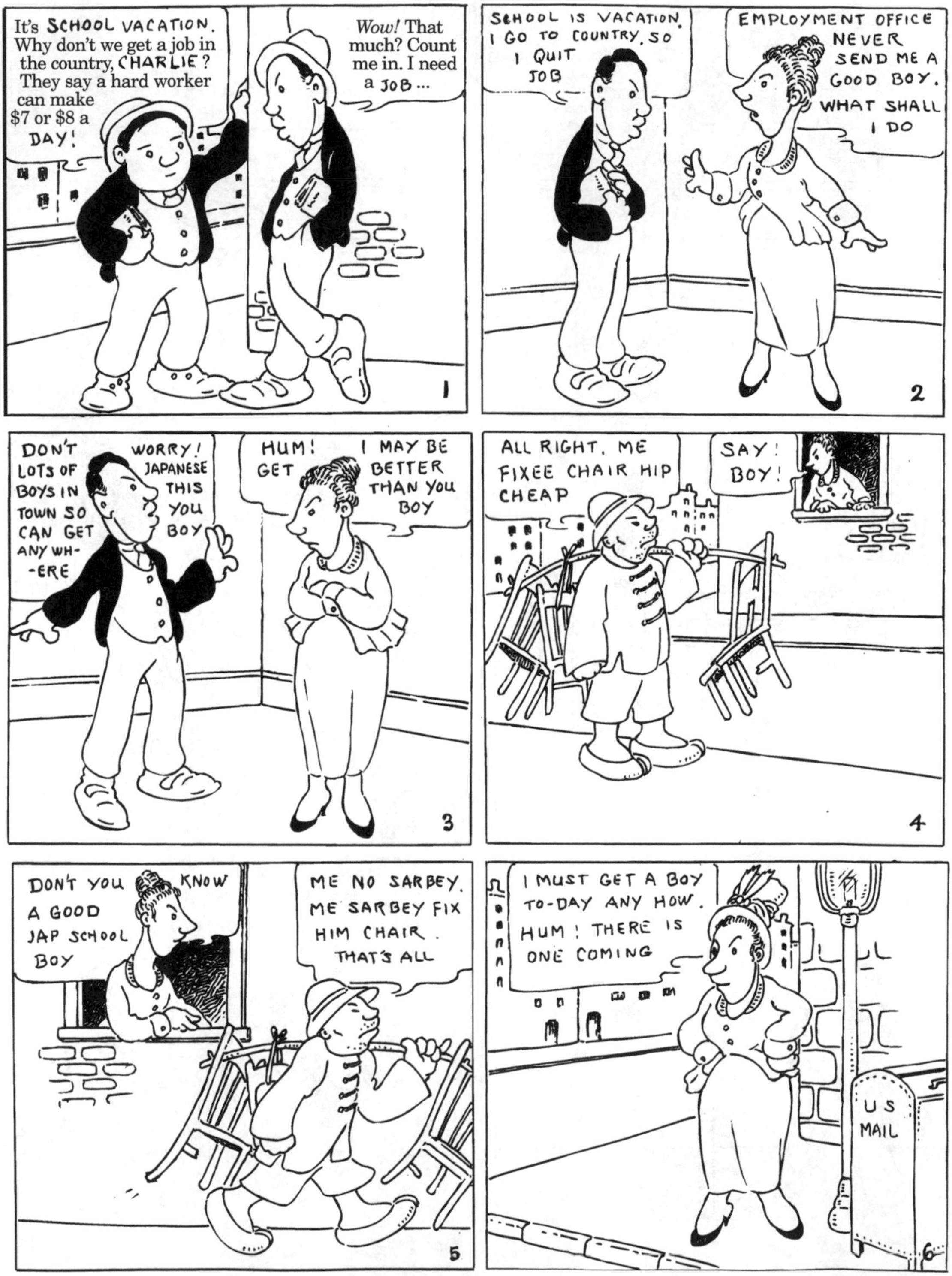
It's SCHOOL VACATION. Why don't we get a job in the country, CHARLIE? They say a hard worker can make $7 or $8 a DAY!
Wow! That much? Count me in. I need a JOB ...
1
SCHOOL IS VACATION. I GO TO COUNTRY, SO I QUIT JOB
EMPLOYMENT OFFICE NEVER SEND ME A GOOD BOY. WHAT SHALL I DO
2
DON'T WORRY! LOTS OF JAPANESE BOYS IN THIS TOWN SO YOU CAN GET BOY ANY WH-ERE
HUM! I MAY BE GET BETTER THAN YOU BOY
3
ALL RIGHT. ME FIXEE CHAIR HIP CHEAP
SAY! BOY!
4
DON'T YOU KNOW A GOOD JAP SCHOOL BOY
ME NO SARBEY. ME SARBEY FIX HIM CHAIR. THAT'S ALL
5
I MUST GET A BOY TO-DAY ANY HOW. HUM! THERE IS ONE COMING
US MAIL
6

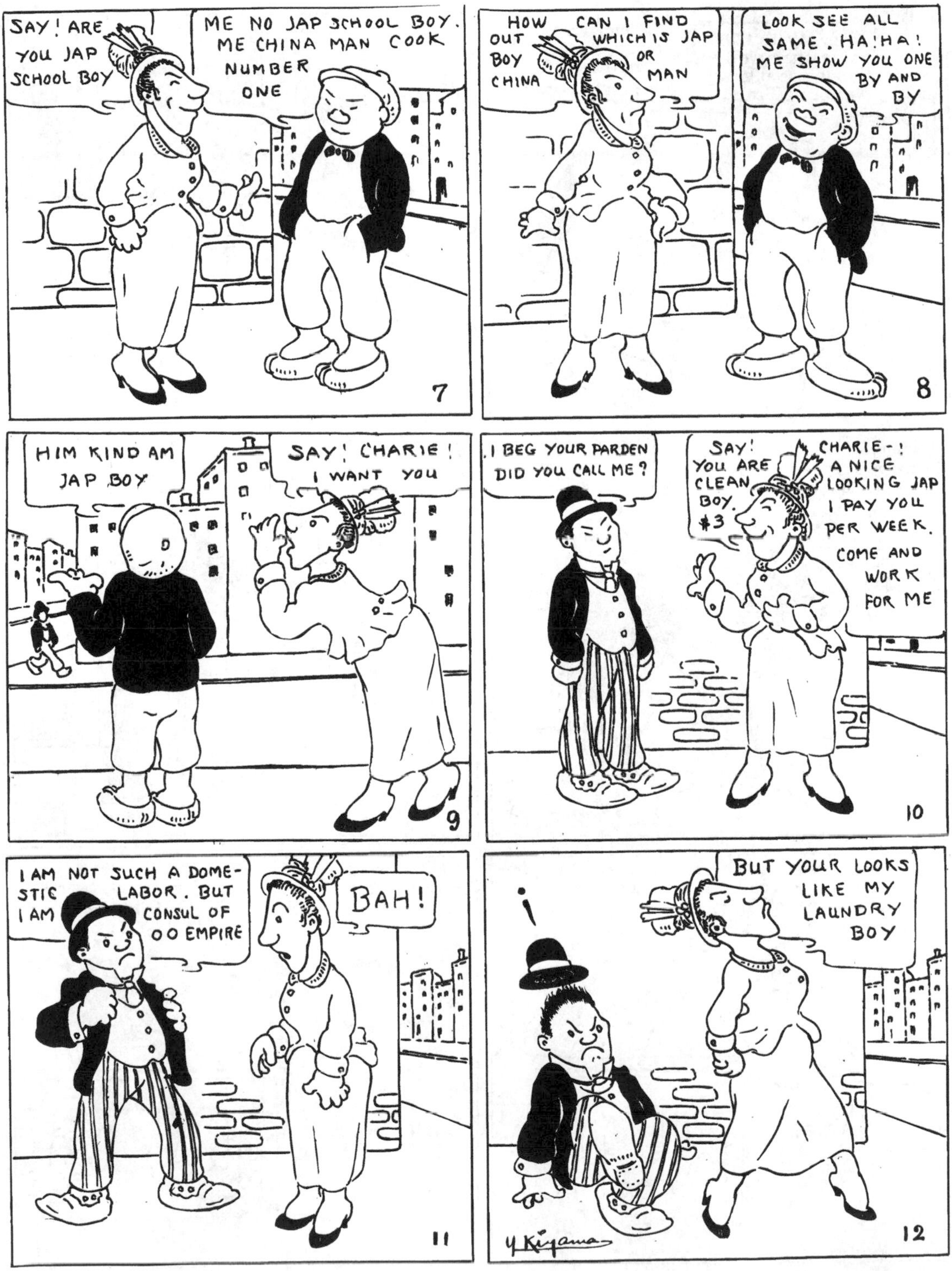
SAY! ARE YOU JAP SCHOOL BOY
ME NO JAP SCHOOL BOY. ME CHINA MAN COOK NUMBER ONE
7
HOW CAN I FIND OUT WHICH IS JAP BOY OR CHINA MAN
LOOK SEE ALL SAME. HA! HA! ME SHOW YOU ONE BY AND BY
8
HIM KIND AM JAP BOY
SAY! CHARIE! I WANT YOU
9
I BEG YOUR PARDEN DID YOU CALL ME?
SAY! CHARIE-! YOU ARE A NICE CLEAN LOOKING JAP BOY. I PAY YOU $3 PER WEEK. COME AND WORK FOR ME
10
I AM NOT SUCH A DOMESTIC LABOR. BUT I AM CONSUL OF OO EMPIRE
BAH!
11
!
BUT YOUR LOOKS LIKE MY LAUNDRY BOY
Y Kiyama
12

EPISODE 12

Working on a Farm

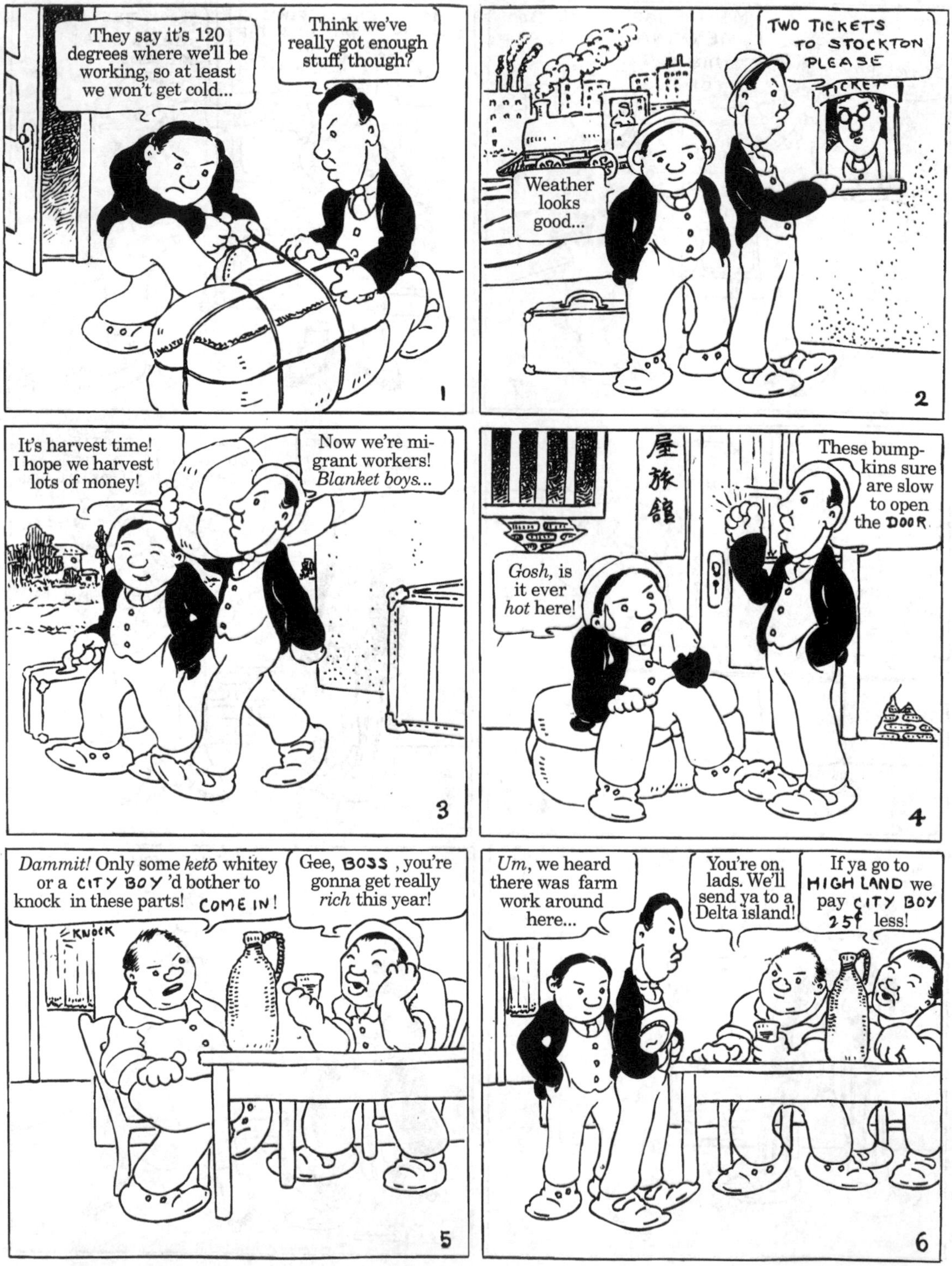

They say it's 120 degrees where we'll be working, so at least we won't get cold...
Think we've really got enough stuff, though?
1
TWO TICKETS TO STOCKTON PLEASE
TICKET
Weather looks good...
2
It's harvest time! I hope we harvest lots of money!
Now we're migrant workers! *Blanket boys...*
3
屋旅館
These bumpkins sure are slow to open the DOOR
Gosh, is it ever *hot* here!
4
Dammit! Only some *ketō* whitey or a CITY BOY 'd bother to knock in these parts! COME IN!
KNOCK
Gee, BOSS , you're gonna get really *rich* this year!
5
Um, we heard there was farm work around here...
You're on, lads. We'll send ya to a Delta island!
If ya go to HIGH LAND we pay CITY BOY 25¢ less!
6

Sign: *Humble Hotel*

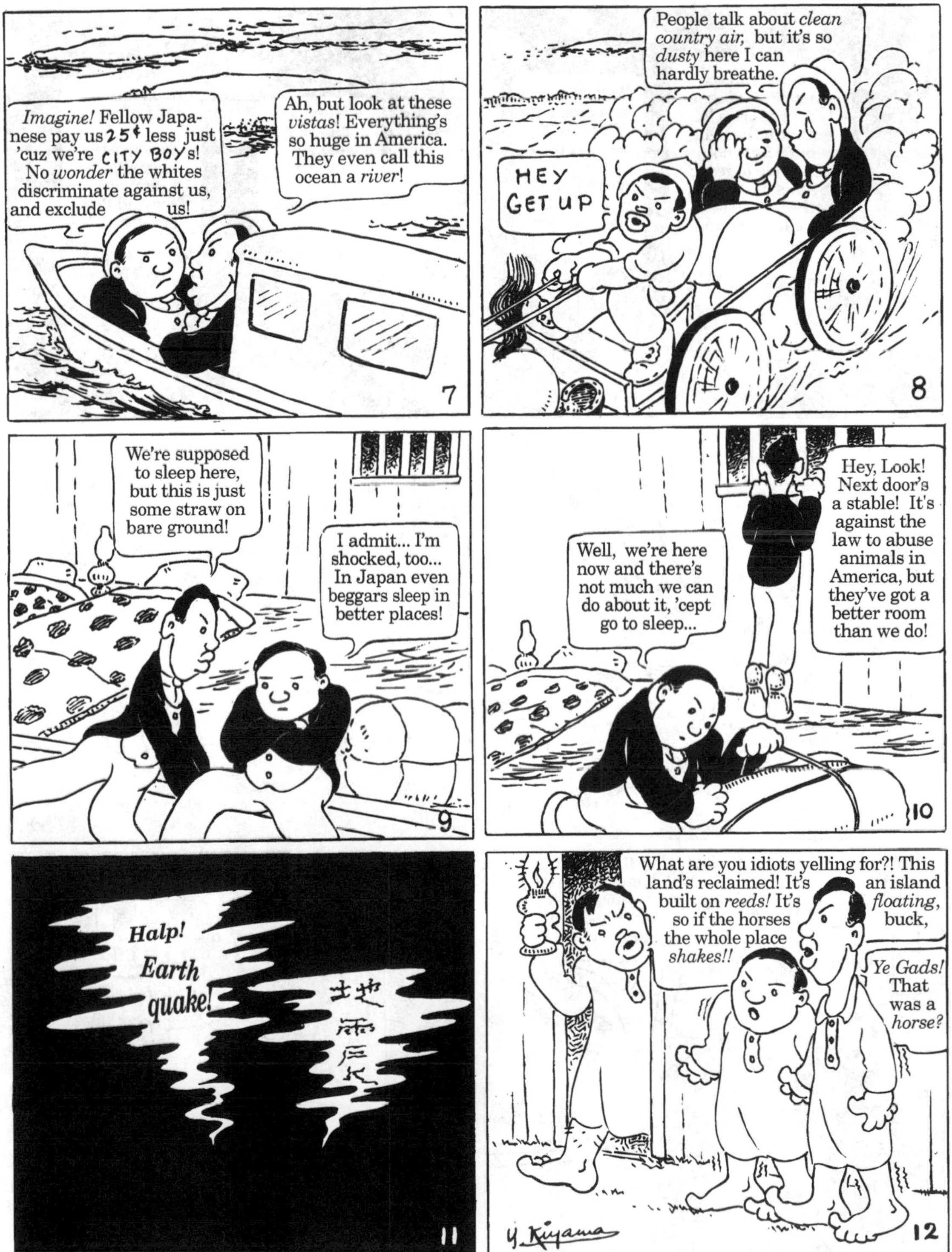

Imagine! Fellow Japanese pay us 25¢ less just 'cuz we're CITY BOYs! No *wonder* the whites discriminate against us, and exclude us!
Ah, but look at these *vistas*! Everything's so huge in America. They even call this ocean a *river*!
7
People talk about *clean country air,* but it's so *dusty* here I can hardly breathe.
HEY GET UP
8
We're supposed to sleep here, but this is just some straw on bare ground!
I admit... I'm shocked, too... In Japan even beggars sleep in better places!
9
Well, we're here now and there's not much we can do about it, 'cept go to sleep...
Hey, Look! Next door's a stable! It's against the law to abuse animals in America, but they've got a better room than we do!
10
Halp! *Earth quake!*
地震
11
What are you idiots yelling for?! This land's reclaimed! It's an island built on *reeds!* It's *floating*, so if the horses buck, the whole place *shakes!!*
Ye Gads! That was a *horse?*
Y. Kiyama
12

Japanese: *Earthquake*

Working on a Farm

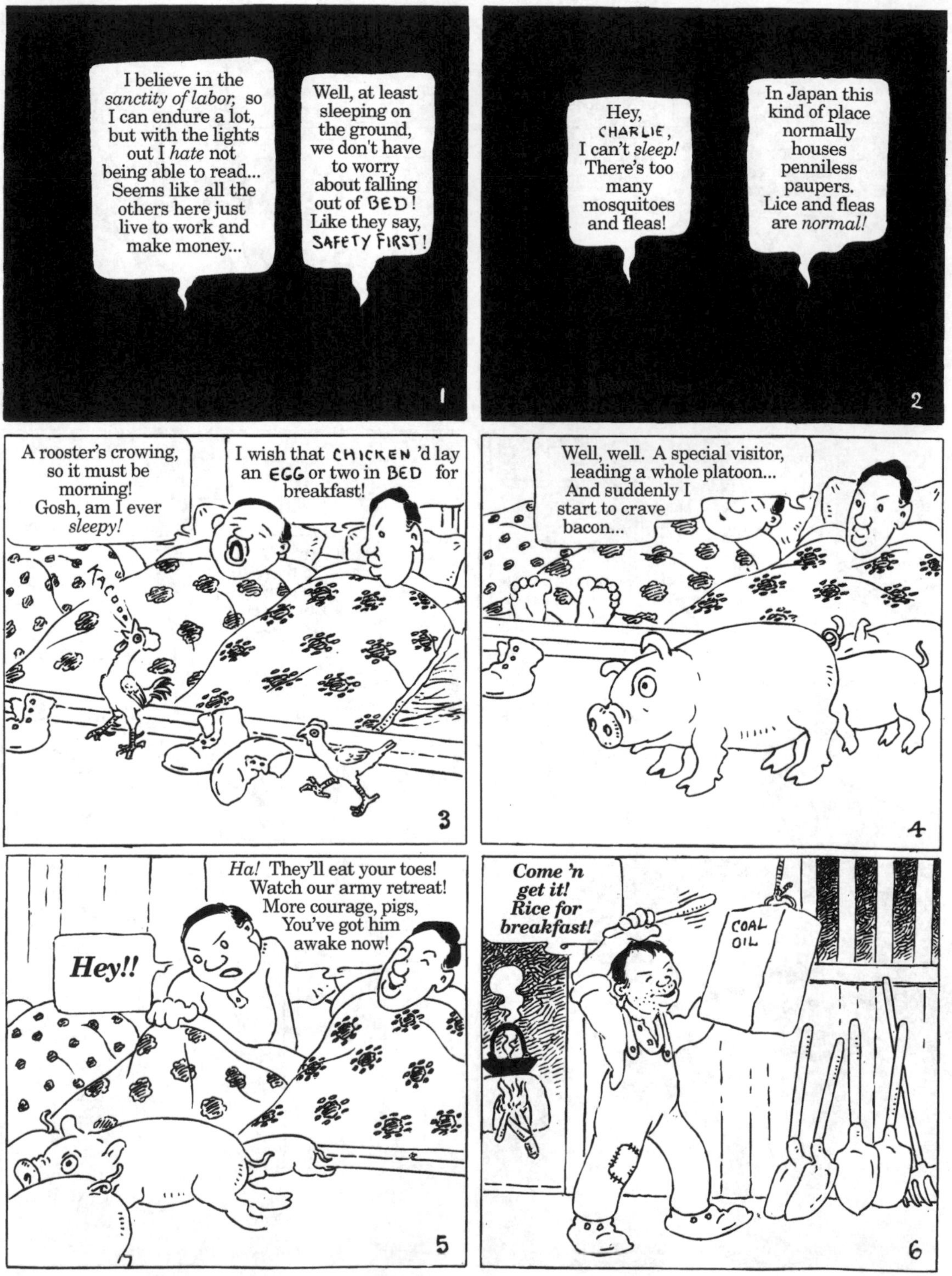
I believe in the *sanctity of labor,* so I can endure a lot, but with the lights out I *hate* not being able to read... Seems like all the others here just live to work and make money...
Well, at least sleeping on the ground, we don't have to worry about falling out of BED! Like they say, SAFETY FIRST!
1
Hey, CHARLIE, I can't *sleep!* There's too many mosquitoes and fleas!
In Japan this kind of place normally houses penniless paupers. Lice and fleas are *normal!*
2
A rooster's crowing, so it must be morning! Gosh, am I ever *sleepy!*
I wish that CHICKEN 'd lay an EGG or two in BED for breakfast!
3
Well, well. A special visitor, leading a whole platoon... And suddenly I start to crave bacon...
4
Hey!!
Ha! They'll eat your toes! Watch our army retreat! More courage, pigs, You've got him awake now!
5
Come 'n get it! Rice for breakfast!
COAL OIL
6

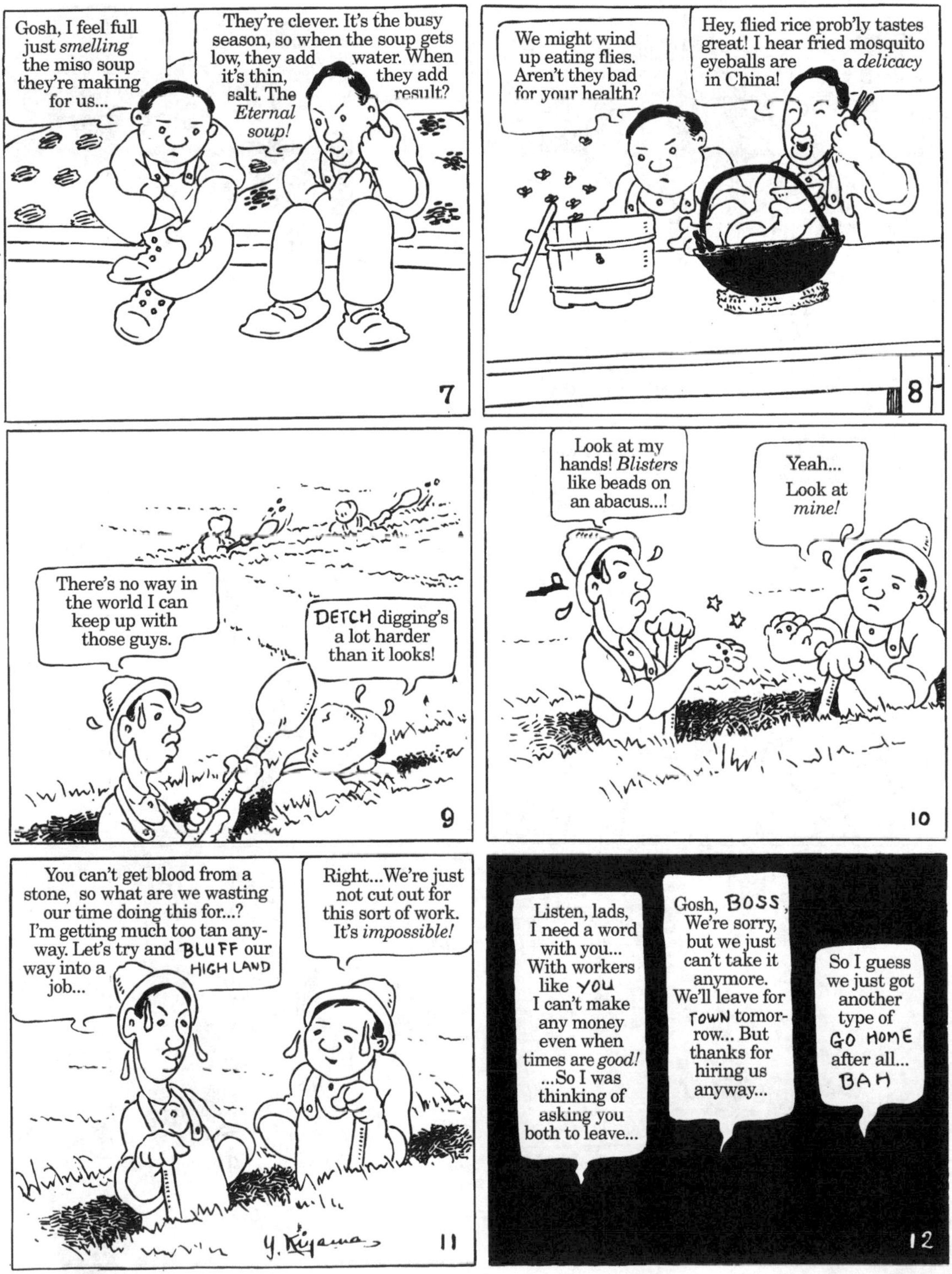
Gosh, I feel full just *smelling* the miso soup they're making for us...
They're clever. It's the busy season, so when the soup gets low, they add water. When it's thin, they add salt. The result? *Eternal soup!*
7
We might wind up eating flies. Aren't they bad for your health?
Hey, flied rice prob'ly tastes great! I hear fried mosquito eyeballs are a *delicacy* in China!
8
There's no way in the world I can keep up with those guys.
DETCH digging's a lot harder than it looks!
9
Look at my hands! *Blisters* like beads on an abacus...!
Yeah... Look at *mine!*
10
You can't get blood from a stone, so what are we wasting our time doing this for...? I'm getting much too tan any-way. Let's try and BLUFF our way into a HIGH LAND job...
Right...We're just not cut out for this sort of work. It's *impossible!*
Y. Kiyama
11
Listen, lads, I need a word with you... With workers like YOU I can't make any money even when times are *good!* ...So I was thinking of asking you both to leave...
Gosh, BOSS, We're sorry, but we just can't take it anymore. We'll leave for TOWN tomor-row... But thanks for hiring us anyway...
So I guess we just got another type of GO HOME after all... BAH
12

EPISODE 14

Working on a Farm

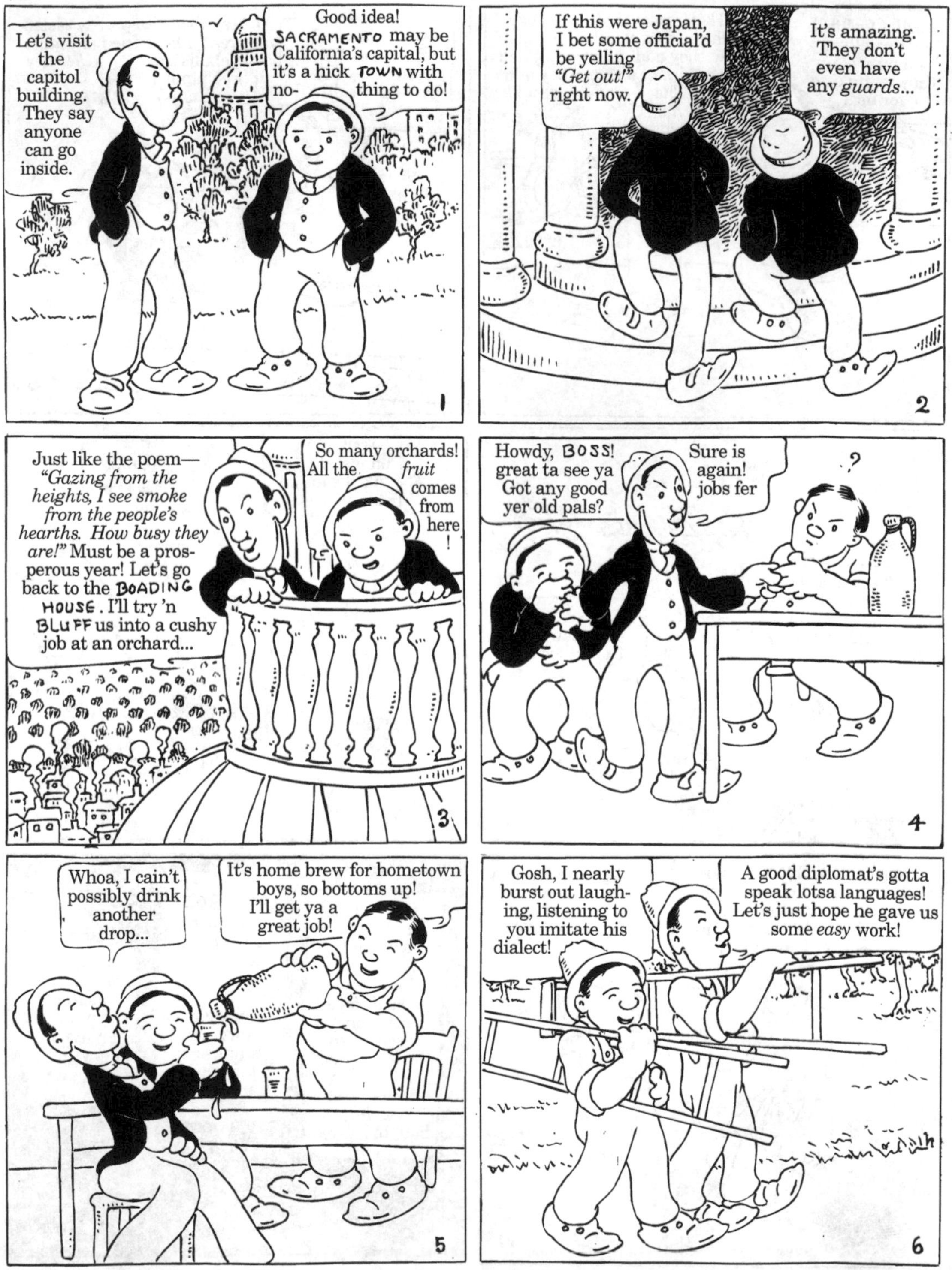

Let's visit the capitol building. They say anyone can go inside.
Good idea! SACRAMENTO may be California's capital, but it's a hick TOWN with no- thing to do!
1
If this were Japan, I bet some official'd be yelling *"Get out!"* right now.
It's amazing. They don't even have any *guards*...
2
Just like the poem—*"Gazing from the heights, I see smoke from the people's hearths. How busy they are!"* Must be a pros-perous year! Let's go back to the BOADING HOUSE. I'll try 'n BLUFF us into a cushy job at an orchard...
So many orchards! All the *fruit* comes from here !
3
Howdy, BOSS! great ta see ya Got any good yer old pals?
Sure is again! jobs fer
?
4
Whoa, I cain't possibly drink another drop...
It's home brew for hometown boys, so bottoms up! I'll get ya a great job!
5
Gosh, I nearly burst out laugh-ing, listening to you imitate his dialect!
A good diplomat's gotta speak lotsa languages! Let's just hope he gave us some *easy* work!
6

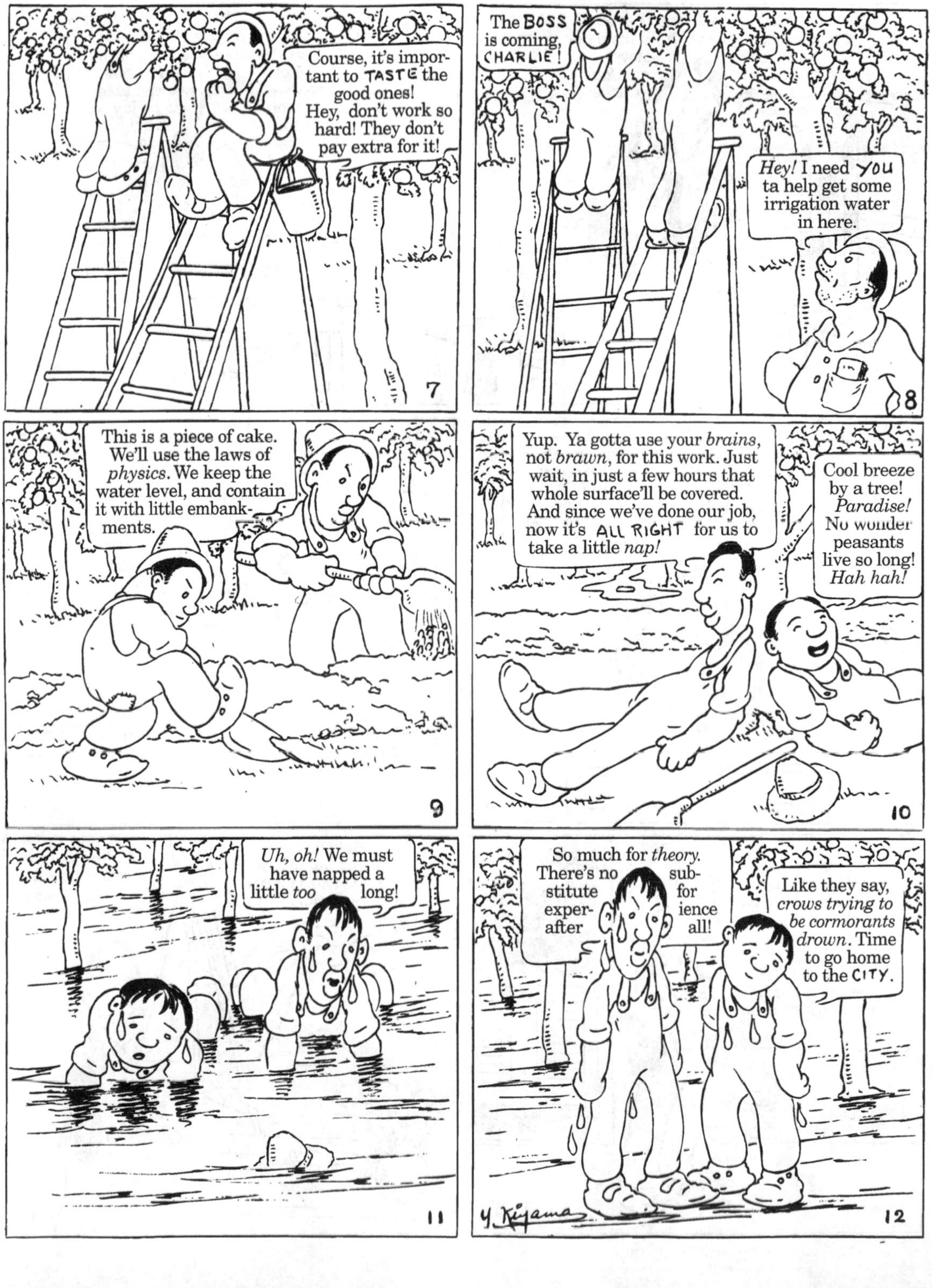
Course, it's important to TASTE the good ones! Hey, don't work so hard! They don't pay extra for it!
7
The BOSS is coming, CHARLIE!
Hey! I need YOU ta help get some irrigation water in here.
8
This is a piece of cake. We'll use the laws of *physics*. We keep the water level, and contain it with little embankments.
9
Yup. Ya gotta use your *brains*, not *brawn*, for this work. Just wait, in just a few hours that whole surface'll be covered. And since we've done our job, now it's ALL RIGHT for us to take a little *nap!*
Cool breeze by a tree! *Paradise!* No wonder peasants live so long! *Hah hah!*
10
Uh, oh! We must have napped a little *too* long!
11
So much for *theory.* There's no substitute for experience after all!
Like they say, *crows trying to be cormorants drown*. Time to go home to the CITY.
Y. Kiyama
12

News of a Parent's Death

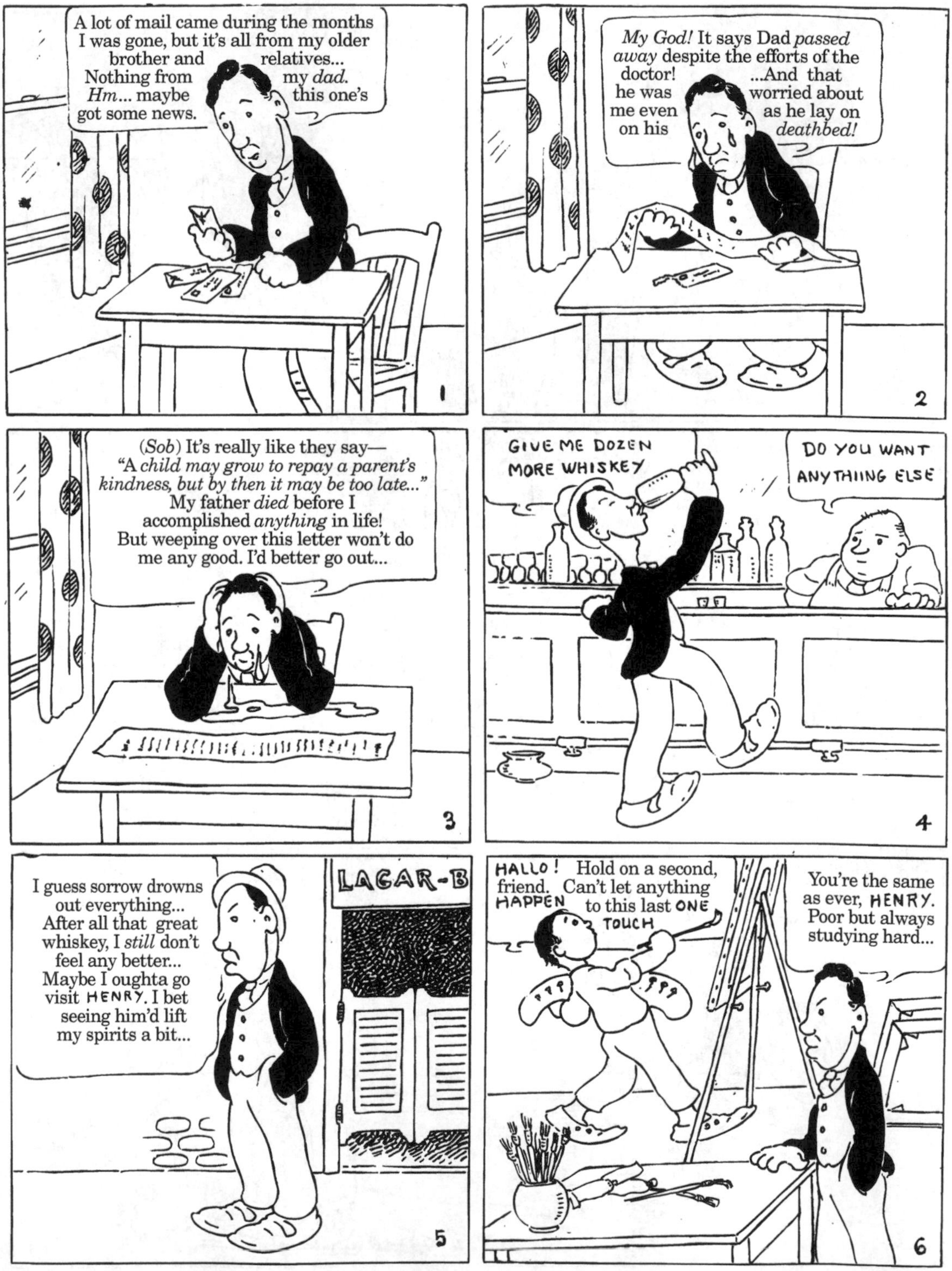
A lot of mail came during the months I was gone, but it's all from my older brother and relatives... Nothing from my *dad*. *Hm*... maybe this one's got some news.
My God! It says Dad *passed away* despite the efforts of the doctor! ...And that he was worried about me even as he lay on on his *deathbed!*
(*Sob*) It's really like they say— "A *child may grow to repay a parent's kindness, but by then it may be too late...*" My father *died* before I accomplished *anything* in life! But weeping over this letter won't do me any good. I'd better go out...
GIVE ME DOZEN MORE WHISKEY
DO YOU WANT ANYTHIING ELSE
I guess sorrow drowns out everything... After all that great whiskey, I *still* don't feel any better... Maybe I oughta go visit HENRY. I bet seeing him'd lift my spirits a bit...
LAGAR-B
HALLO! Hold on a second, friend. Can't let anything HAPPEN to this last ONE TOUCH
You're the same as ever, HENRY. Poor but always studying hard...

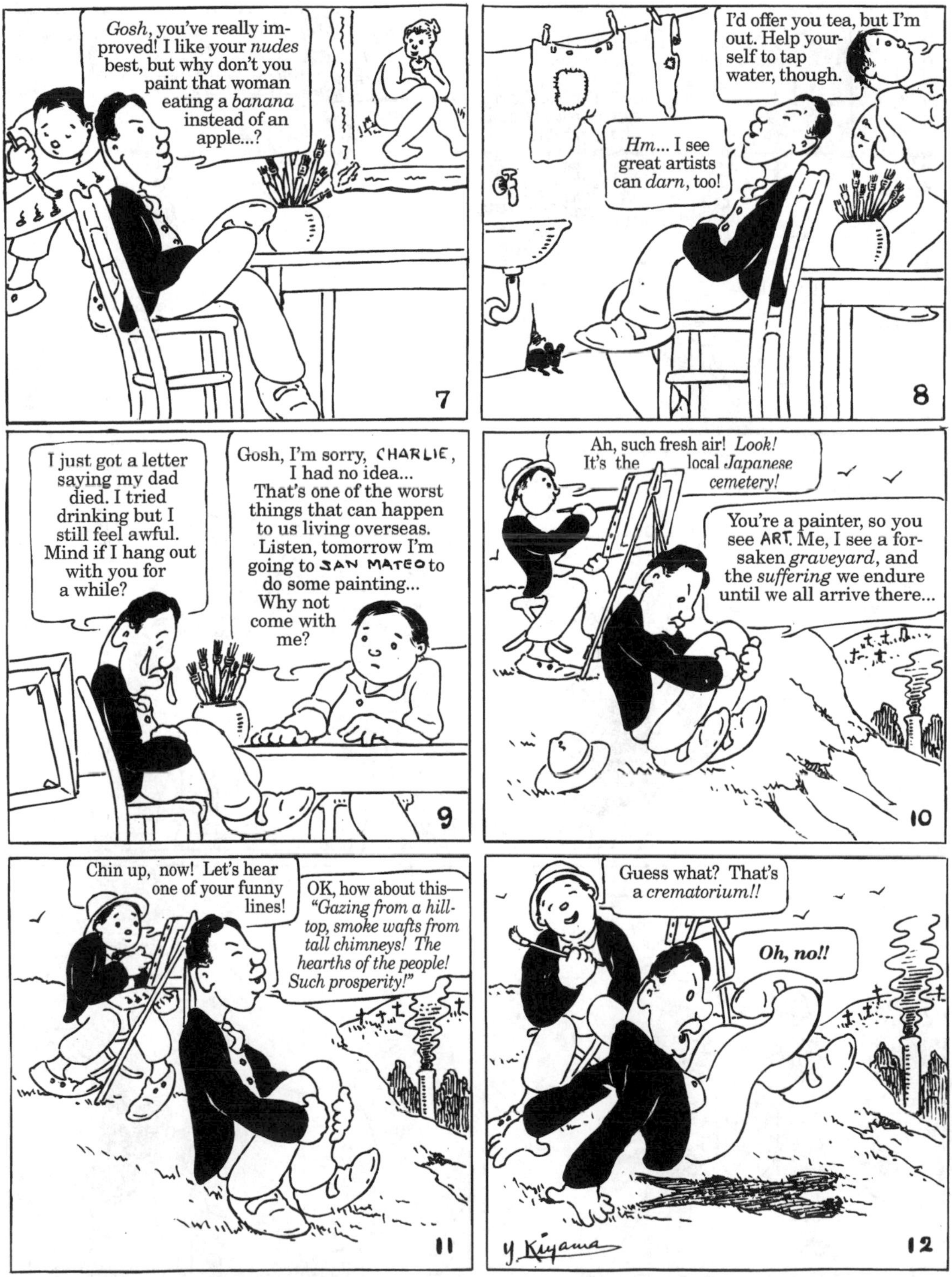
Gosh, you've really improved! I like your nudes best, but why don't you paint that woman eating a banana instead of an apple...?
7
I'd offer you tea, but I'm out. Help yourself to tap water, though.
Hm... I see great artists can darn, too!
8
I just got a letter saying my dad died. I tried drinking but I still feel awful. Mind if I hang out with you for a while?
Gosh, I'm sorry, CHARLIE, I had no idea... That's one of the worst things that can happen to us living overseas. Listen, tomorrow I'm going to SAN MATEO to do some painting... Why not come with me?
9
Ah, such fresh air! Look! It's the local Japanese cemetery!
You're a painter, so you see ART. Me, I see a forsaken graveyard, and the suffering we endure until we all arrive there...
10
Chin up, now! Let's hear one of your funny lines!
OK, how about this—"Gazing from a hilltop, smoke wafts from tall chimneys! The hearths of the people! Such prosperity!"
11
Guess what? That's a crematorium!!
Oh, no!!
Y. Kiyama
12

Decadence

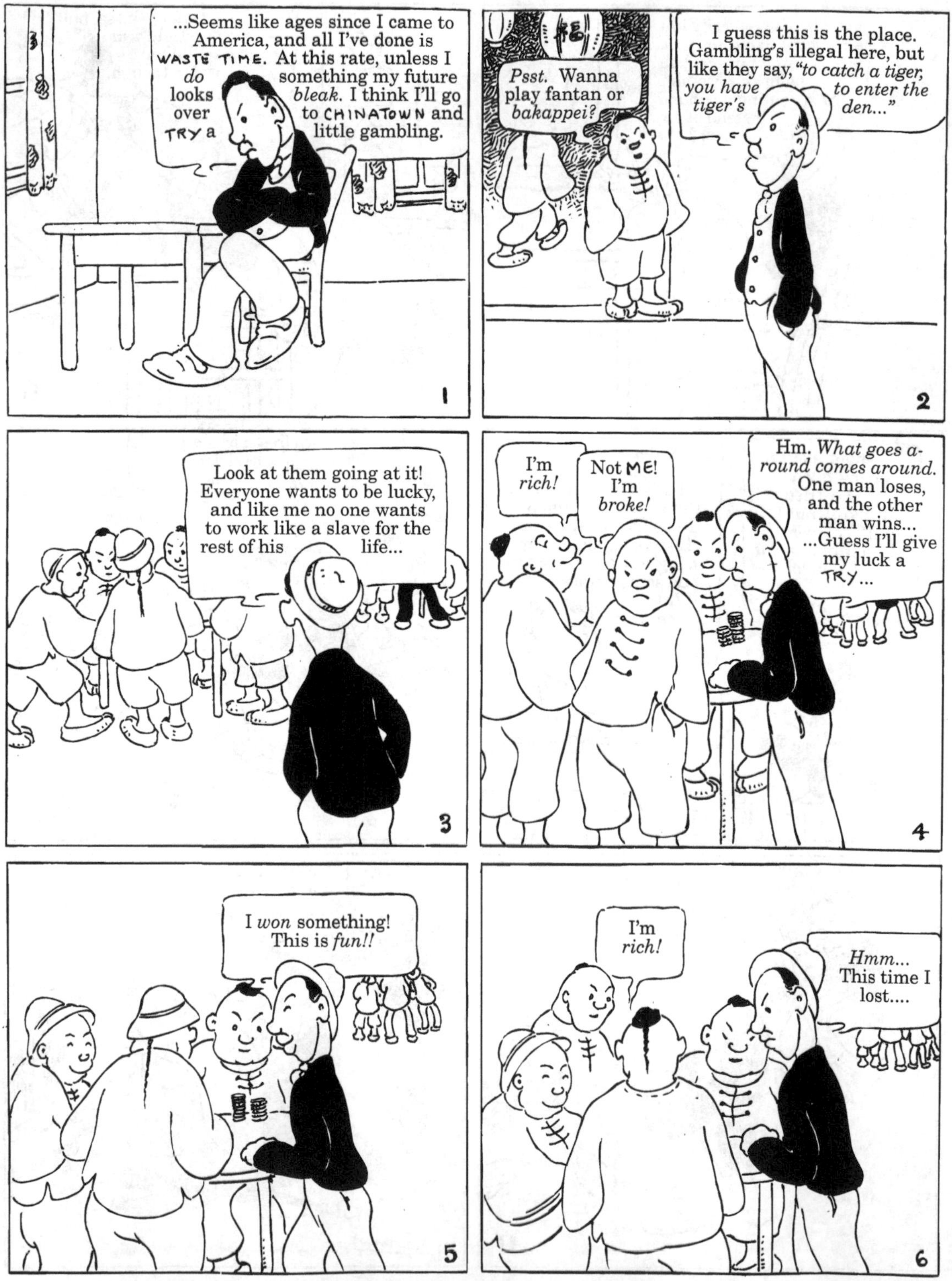
...Seems like ages since I came to America, and all I've done is WASTE TIME. At this rate, unless I *do* something my future looks *bleak.* I think I'll go over to CHINATOWN and TRY a little gambling.
Psst. Wanna play fantan or *bakappei?*
I guess this is the place. Gambling's illegal here, but like they say, *"to catch a tiger, you have to enter the tiger's den..."*
Look at them going at it! Everyone wants to be lucky, and like me no one wants to work like a slave for the rest of his life...
I'm *rich!*
Not ME! I'm *broke!*
Hm. *What goes a-round comes around.* One man loses, and the other man wins... ...Guess I'll give my luck a TRY...
I *won* something! This is *fun!!*
I'm *rich!*
Hmm... This time I lost....

Character on lantern: *Happiness*

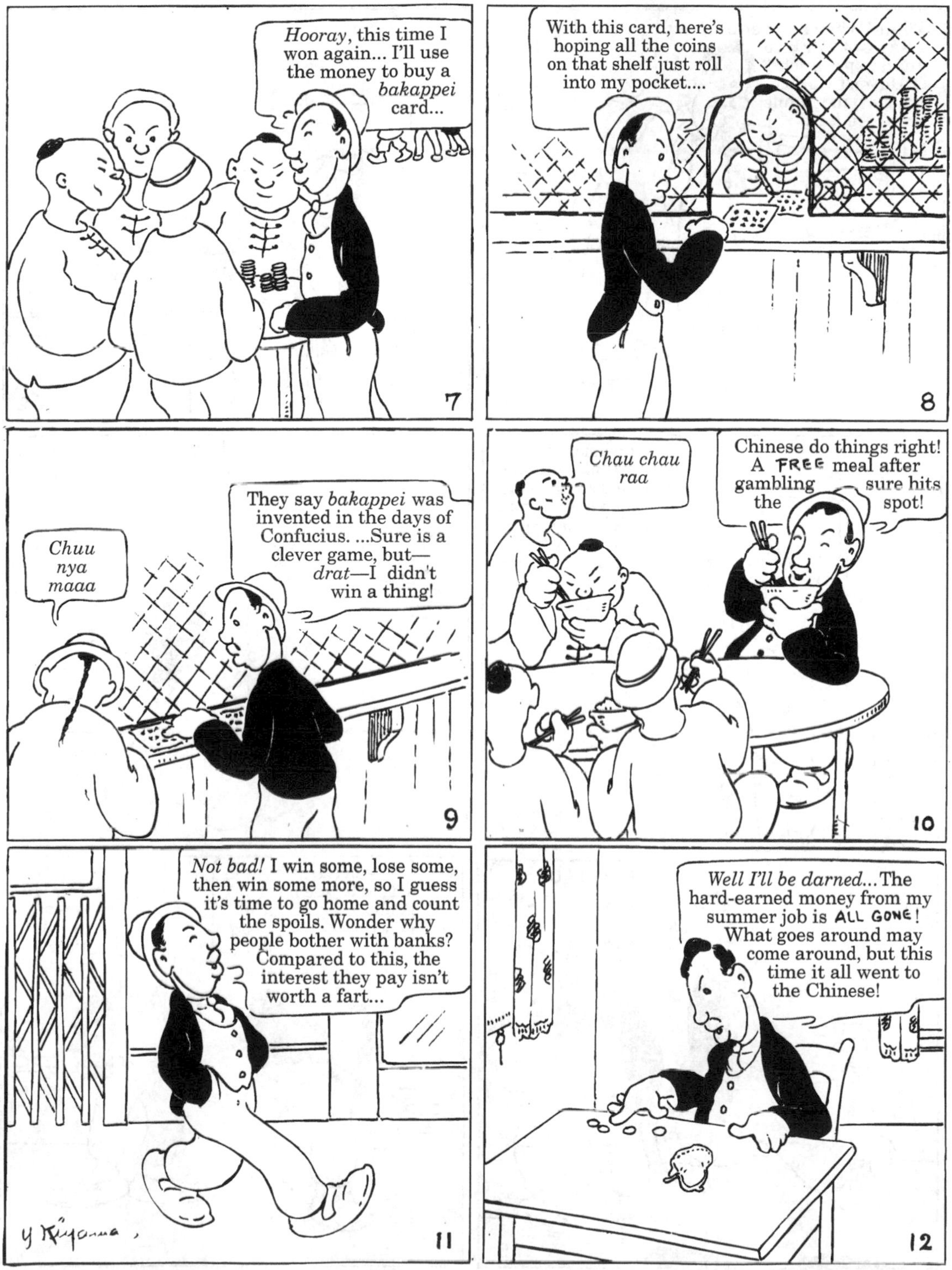
Hooray, this time I won again... I'll use the money to buy a *bakappei* card...
With this card, here's hoping all the coins on that shelf just roll into my pocket....
Chuu nya maaa
They say *bakappei* was invented in the days of Confucius. ...Sure is a clever game, but— *drat*—I didn't win a thing!
Chau chau raa
Chinese do things right! A FREE meal after gambling sure hits the spot!
Not bad! I win some, lose some, then win some more, so I guess it's time to go home and count the spoils. Wonder why people bother with banks? Compared to this, the interest they pay isn't worth a fart...
Y Kiyama,
Well I'll be darned... The hard-earned money from my summer job is ALL GONE! What goes around may come around, but this time it all went to the Chinese!

EPISODE 17

Decadence

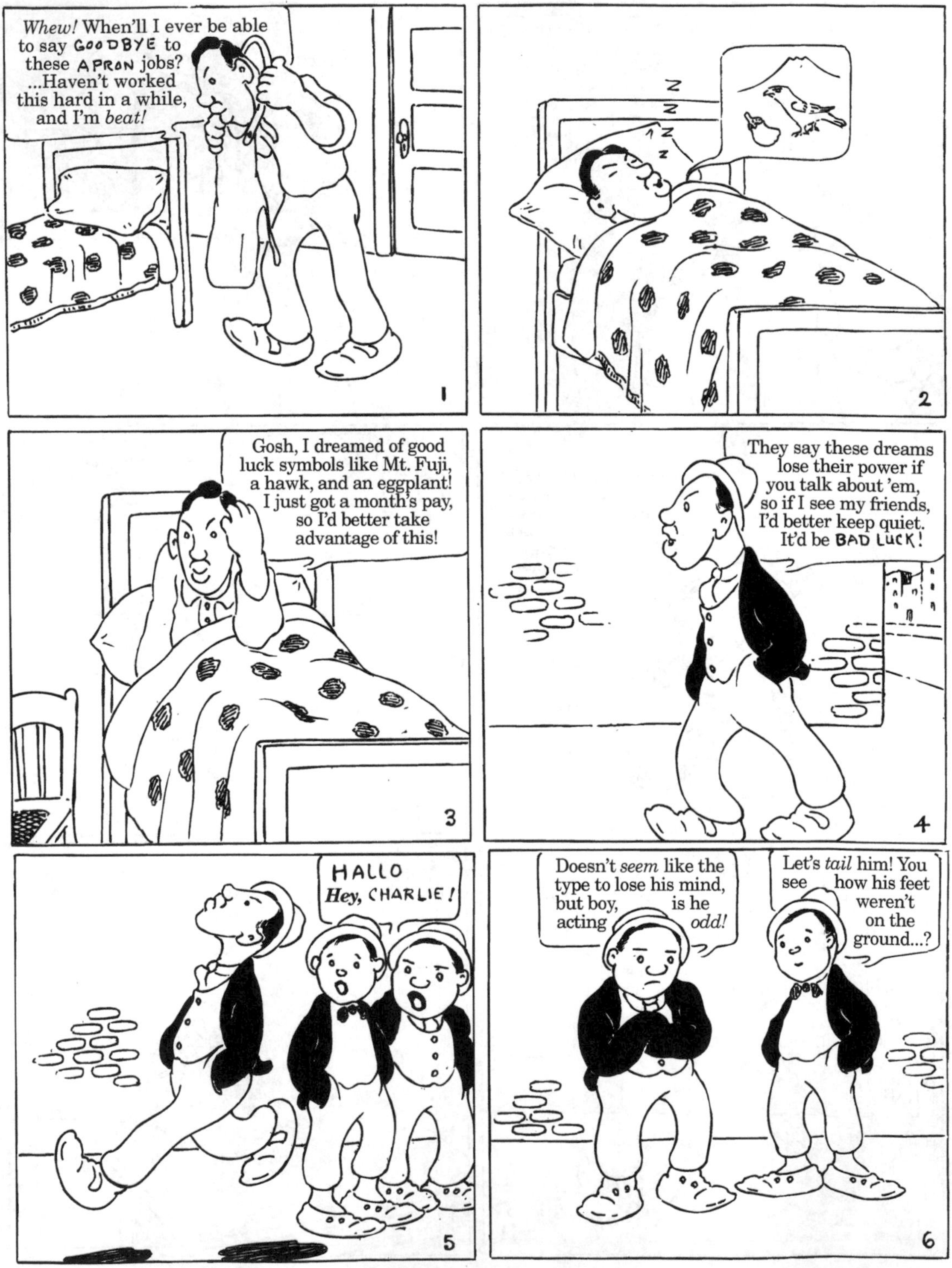
Whew! When'll I ever be able to say GOODBYE to these APRON jobs? ...Haven't worked this hard in a while, and I'm beat!
Z Z Z Z
Gosh, I dreamed of good luck symbols like Mt. Fuji, a hawk, and an eggplant! I just got a month's pay, so I'd better take advantage of this!
They say these dreams lose their power if you talk about 'em, so if I see my friends, I'd better keep quiet. It'd be BAD LUCK!
HALLO
Hey, CHARLIE!
Doesn't seem like the type to lose his mind, but boy, is he acting odd!
Let's tail him! You see how his feet weren't on the ground...?

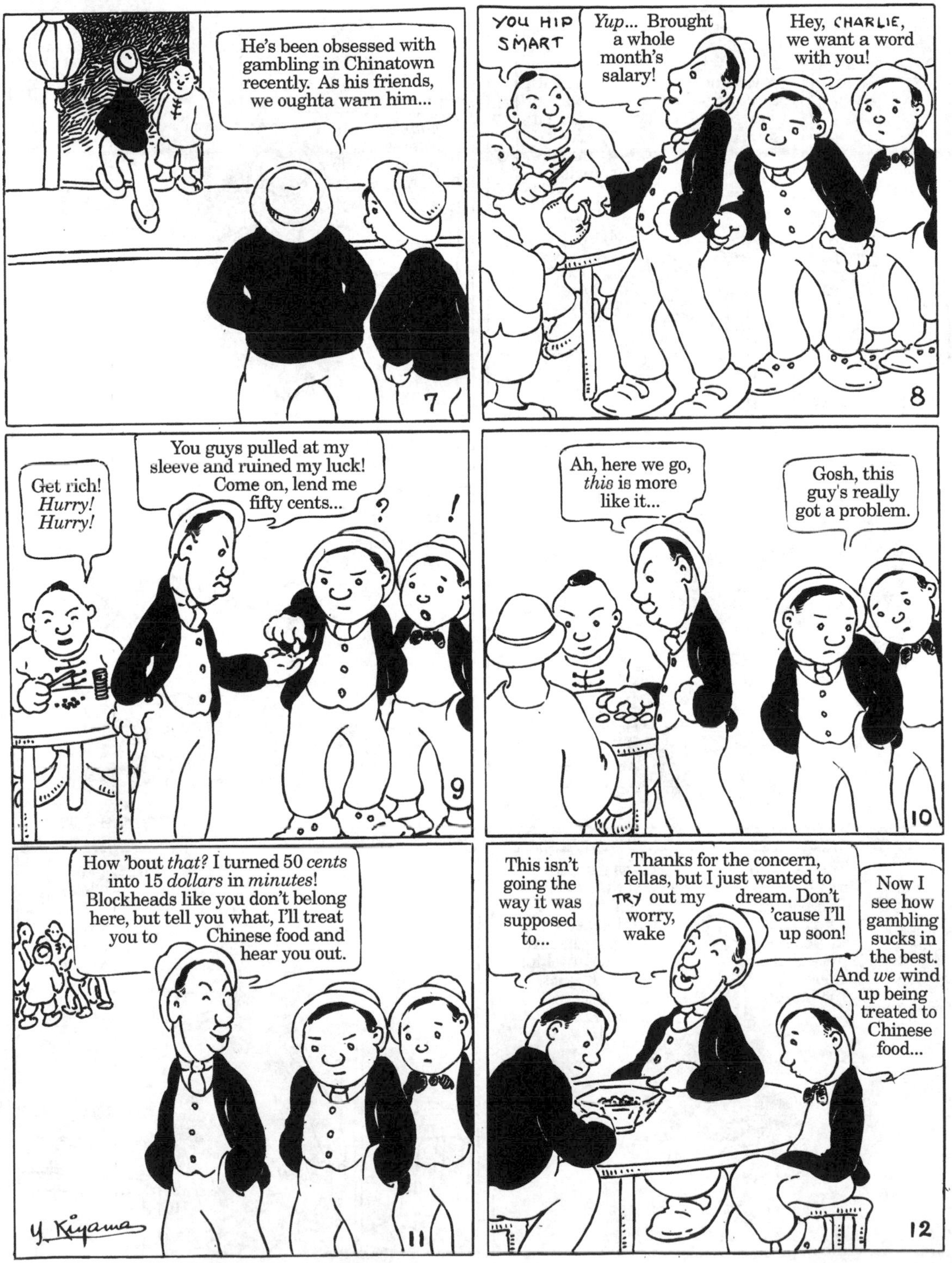
He's been obsessed with gambling in Chinatown recently. As his friends, we oughta warn him...
7
YOU HIP SMART
Yup... Brought a whole month's salary!
Hey, CHARLIE, we want a word with you!
8
Get rich! *Hurry! Hurry!*
You guys pulled at my sleeve and ruined my luck! Come on, lend me fifty cents...
?
!
9
Ah, here we go, *this* is more like it...
Gosh, this guy's really got a problem.
10
How 'bout *that?* I turned 50 *cents* into 15 *dollars* in *minutes*! Blockheads like you don't belong here, but tell you what, I'll treat you to Chinese food and hear you out.
Y. Kiyama
11
This isn't going the way it was supposed to...
Thanks for the concern, fellas, but I just wanted to TRY out my dream. Don't worry, 'cause I'll wake up soon!
Now I see how gambling sucks in the best. And *we* wind up being treated to Chinese food...
12

Decadence

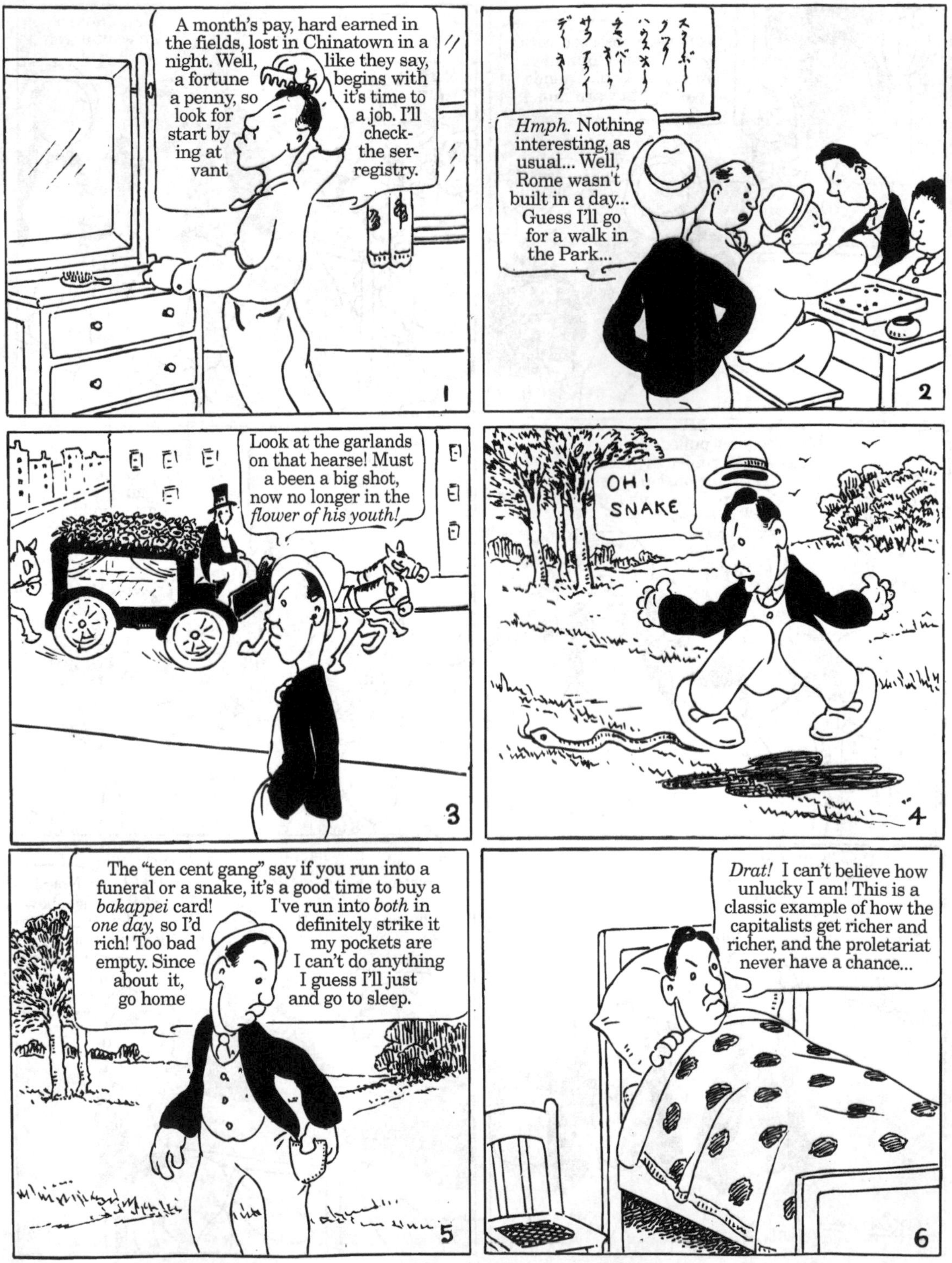
A month's pay, hard earned in the fields, lost in Chinatown in a night. Well, like they say, a fortune begins with a penny, so it's time to look for a job. I'll start by check- ing at the ser- vant registry.
Hmph. Nothing interesting, as usual... Well, Rome wasn't built in a day... Guess I'll go for a walk in the Park...
Look at the garlands on that hearse! Must a been a big shot, now no longer in the *flower of his youth!*
OH! SNAKE
The "ten cent gang" say if you run into a funeral or a snake, it's a good time to buy a *bakappei* card! I've run into *both* in *one day,* so I'd definitely strike it rich! Too bad my pockets are empty. Since I can't do anything about it, I guess I'll just go home and go to sleep.
Drat! I can't believe how unlucky I am! This is a classic example of how the capitalists get richer and richer, and the proletariat never have a chance...

Sign: *Openings for "schoolboy," cook, housekeeper, chamber work, dishwasher, day worker.*

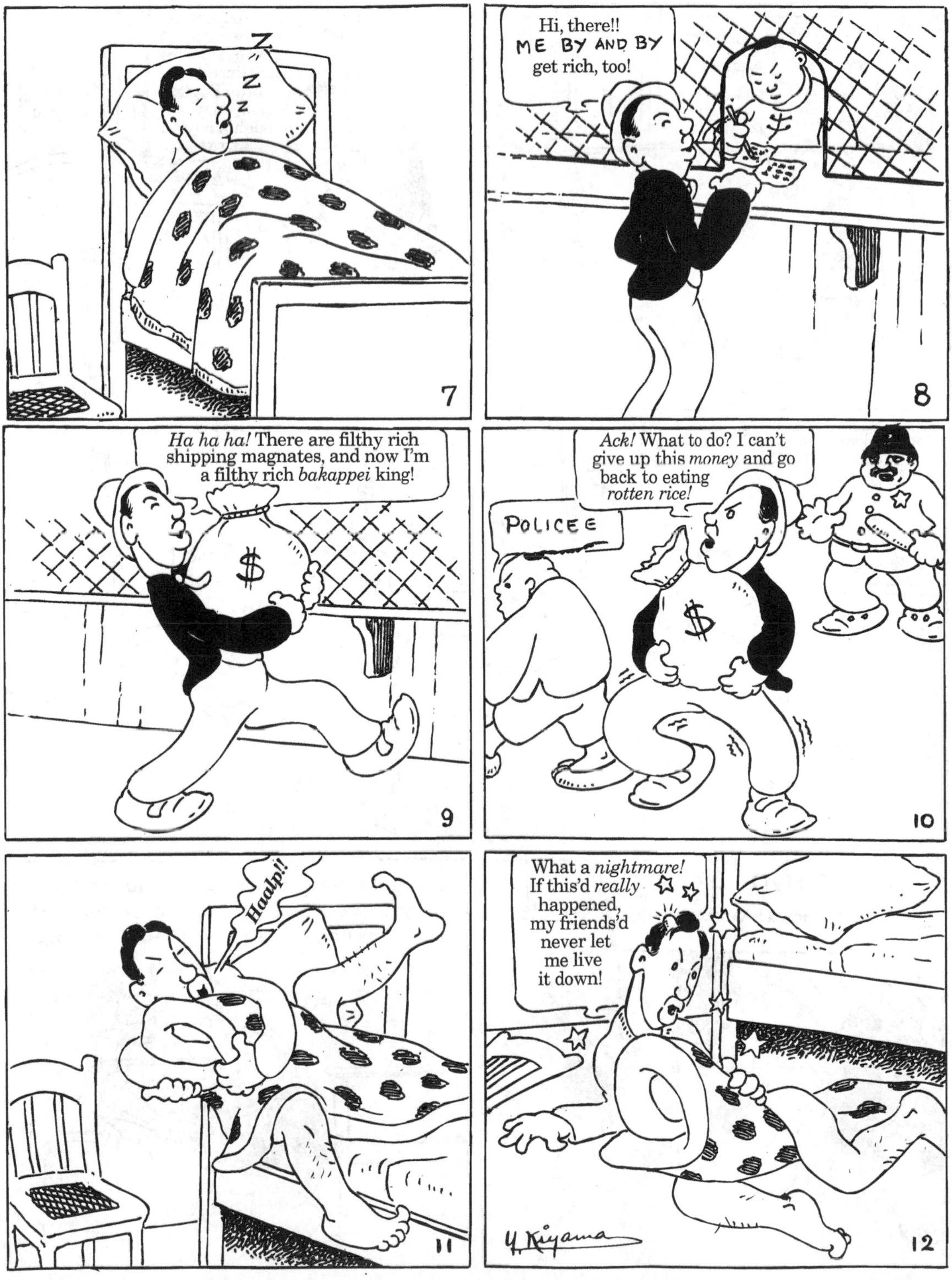
Z
Z
Z
7
Hi, there!! ME BY AND BY get rich, too!
8
Ha ha ha! There are filthy rich shipping magnates, and now I'm a filthy rich *bakappei* king!
$
9
Ack! What to do? I can't give up this *money* and go back to eating *rotten rice!*
POLICEE
$
10
Haalp!!
11
What a *nightmare!* If this'd *really* happened, my friends'd never let me live it down!
Y. Kiyama
12

EPISODE 19

The Shoe Salesman

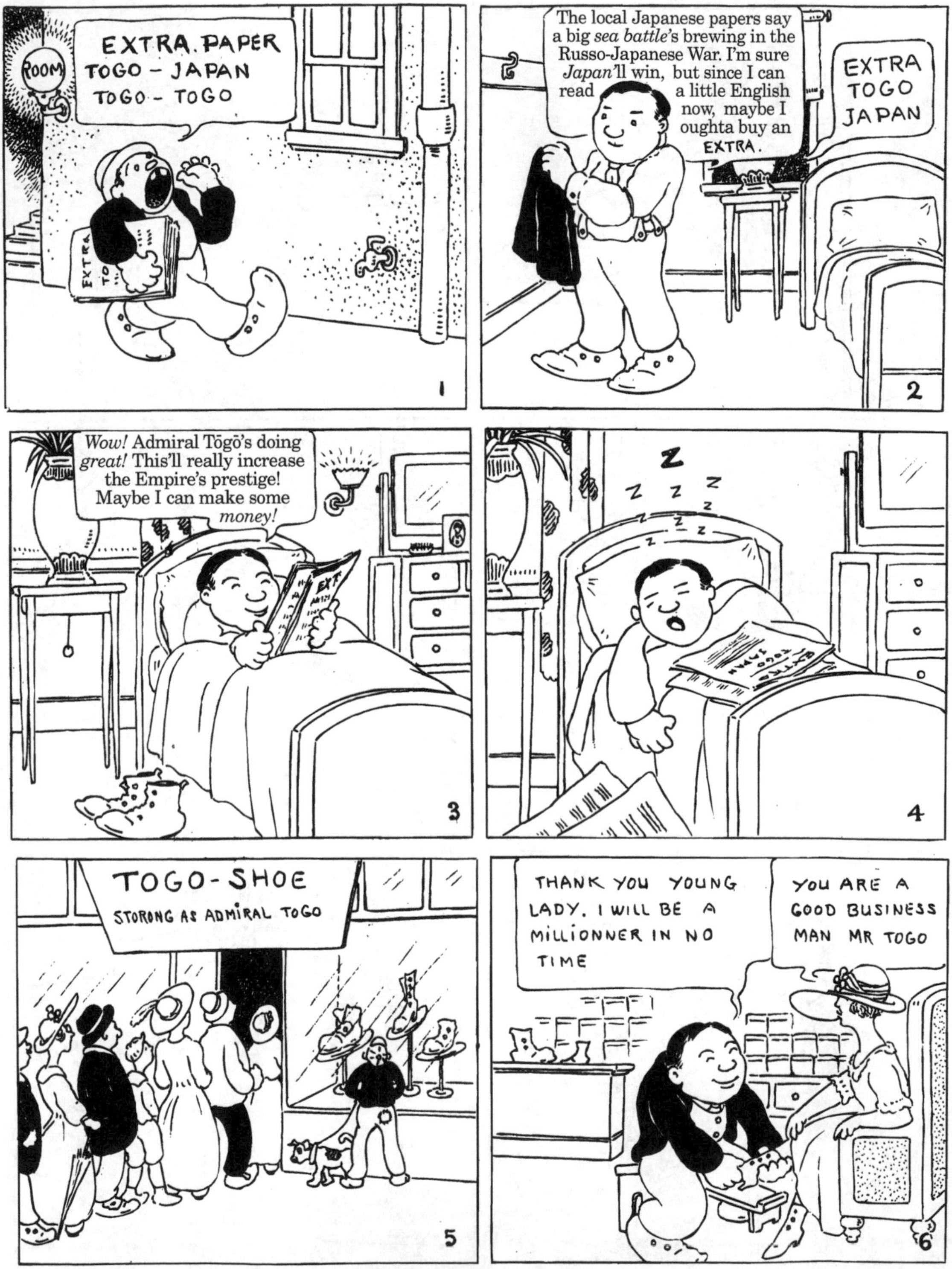
ROOM
EXTRA. PAPER TOGO - JAPAN TOGO - TOGO
EXTRA TO
1
The local Japanese papers say a big *sea battle*'s brewing in the Russo-Japanese War. I'm sure *Japan*'ll win, but since I can read a little English now, maybe I oughta buy an EXTRA.
EXTRA TOGO JAPAN
2
Wow! Admiral Tōgō's doing *great!* This'll really increase the Empire's prestige! Maybe I can make some *money!*
3
Z Z Z Z Z Z Z Z
4
TOGO-SHOE STORONG AS ADMIRAL TOGO
5
THANK YOU YOUNG LADY. I WILL BE A MILLIONNER IN NO TIME
YOU ARE A GOOD BUSINESS MAN MR TOGO
6

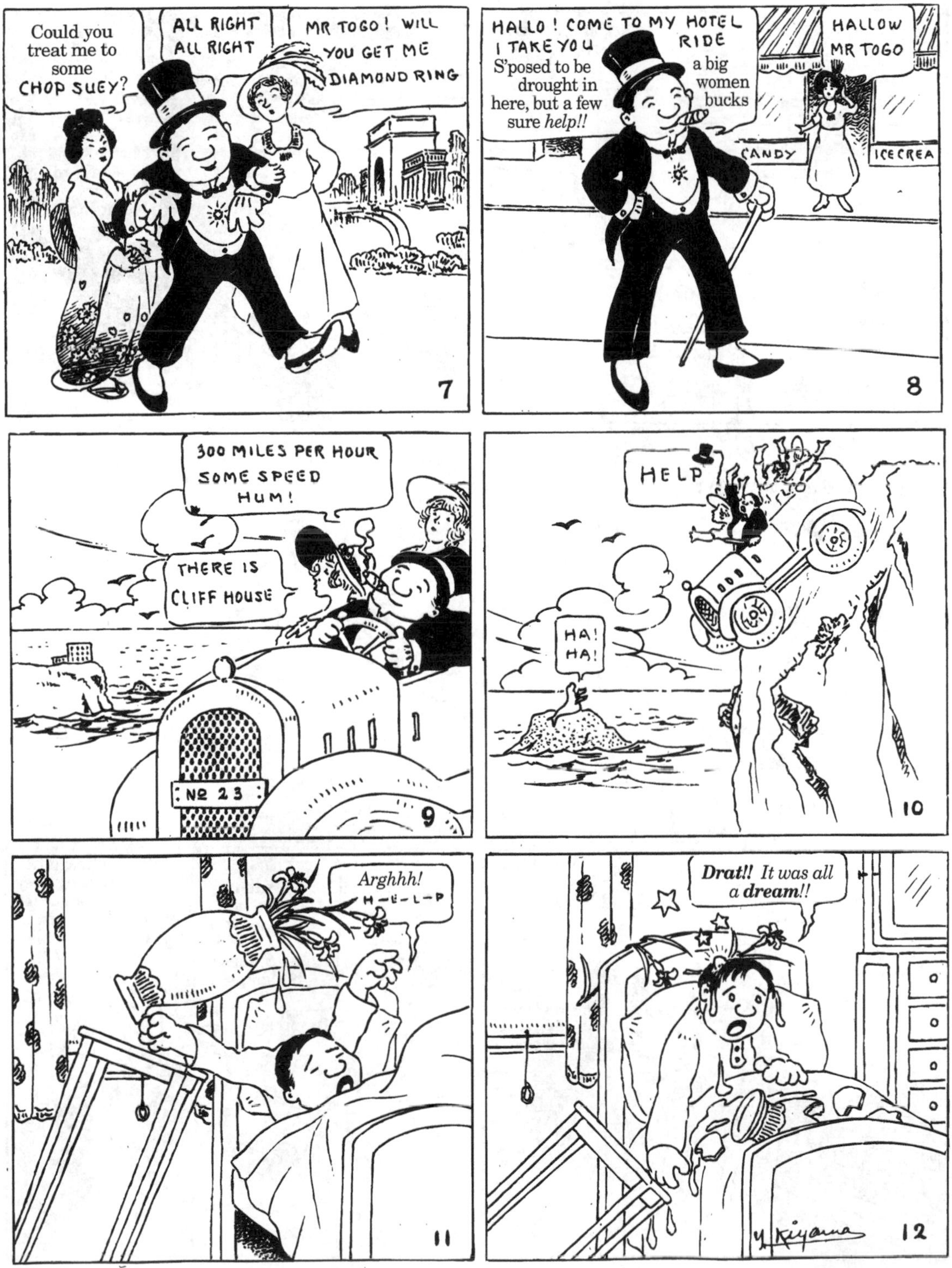
Could you treat me to some CHOP SUEY?
ALL RIGHT ALL RIGHT
MR TOGO! WILL YOU GET ME DIAMOND RING
7
HALLO! COME TO MY HOTEL I TAKE YOU RIDE
S'posed to be drought in here, but a few sure *help!!*
a big women bucks
HALLOW MR TOGO
CANDY
ICECREA
8
300 MILES PER HOUR SOME SPEED HUM!
THERE IS CLIFF HOUSE
№ 23
9
HELP
HA! HA!
10
Arghhh! H-E-L-P
11
Drat!! *It was all a **dream!!***
Y. Kiyama
12

The Great San Francisco Quake

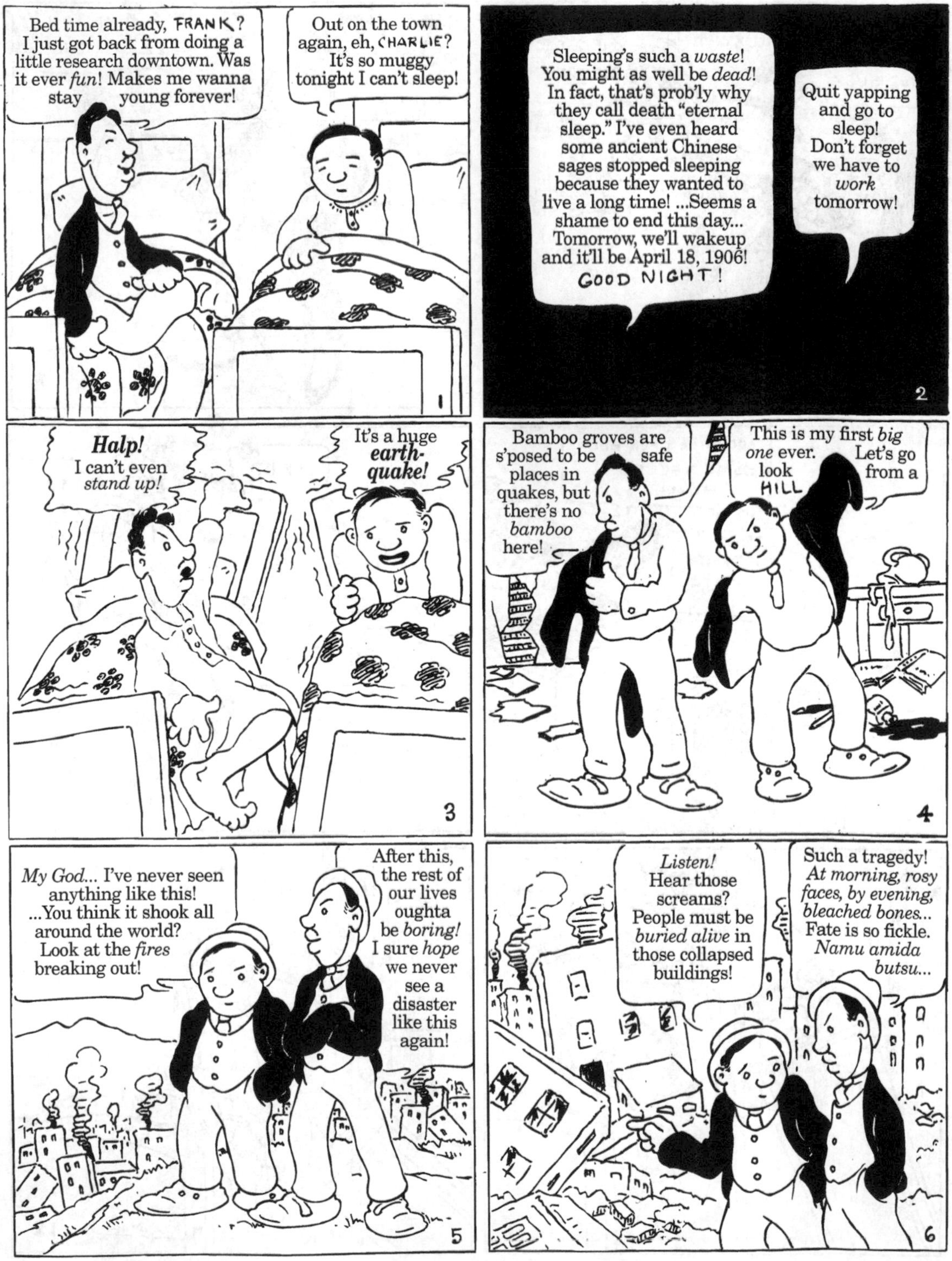
Bed time already, FRANK? I just got back from doing a little research downtown. Was it ever *fun*! Makes me wanna stay young forever!
Out on the town again, eh, CHARLIE? It's so muggy tonight I can't sleep!
1
Sleeping's such a *waste*! You might as well be *dead*! In fact, that's prob'ly why they call death "eternal sleep." I've even heard some ancient Chinese sages stopped sleeping because they wanted to live a long time! ...Seems a shame to end this day... Tomorrow, we'll wakeup and it'll be April 18, 1906! GOOD NIGHT!
Quit yapping and go to sleep! Don't forget we have to *work* tomorrow!
2
Halp! I can't even *stand up!*
It's a huge ***earth-quake!***
3
Bamboo groves are s'posed to be safe places in quakes, but there's no *bamboo* here!
This is my first *big one* ever. Let's go look from a HILL
4
My God... I've never seen anything like this! ...You think it shook all around the world? Look at the *fires* breaking out!
After this, the rest of our lives oughta be *boring!* I sure *hope* we never see a disaster like this again!
5
Listen! Hear those screams? People must be *buried alive* in those collapsed buildings!
Such a tragedy! *At morning, rosy faces, by evening, bleached bones...* Fate is so fickle. *Namu amida butsu...*
6

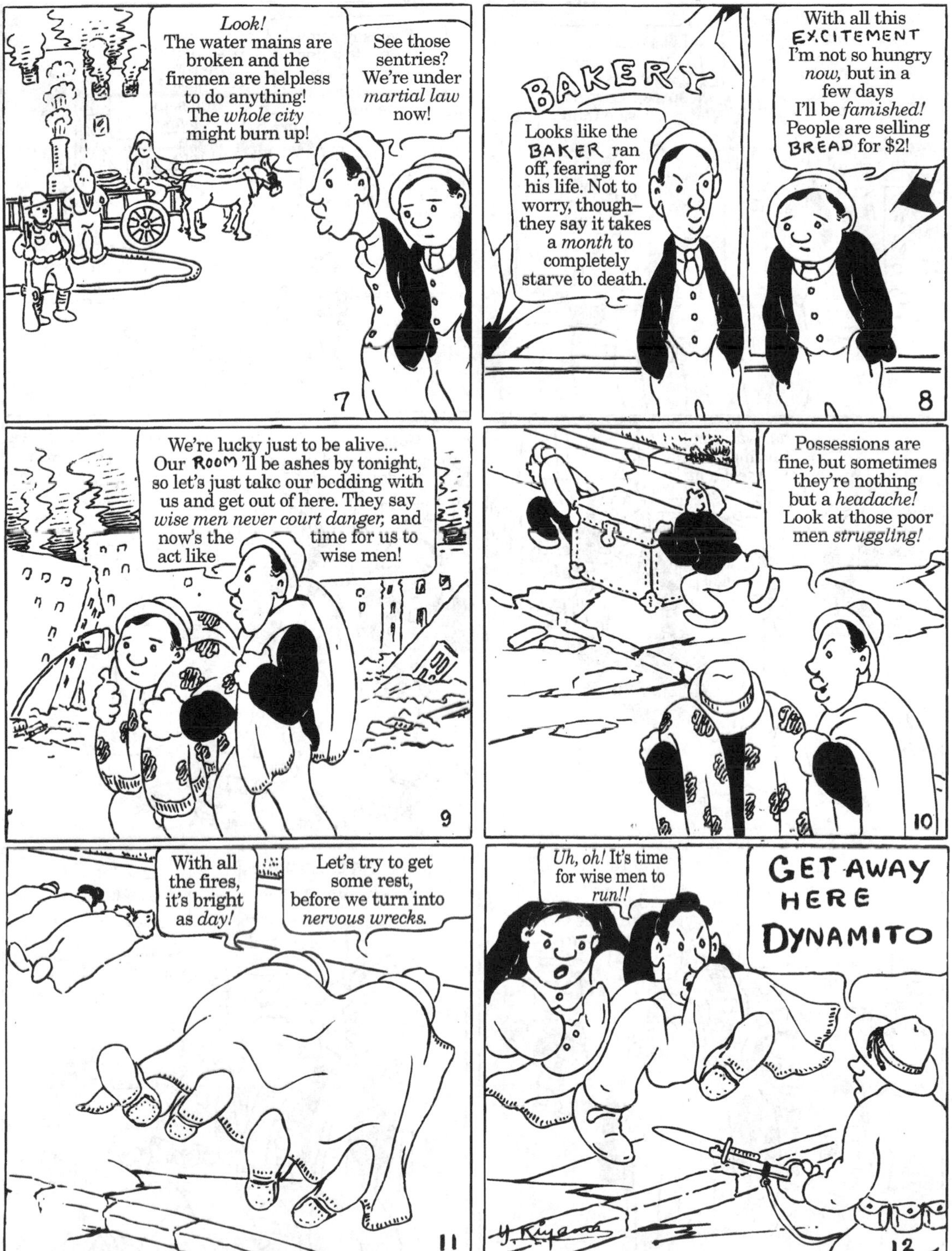

Look! The water mains are broken and the firemen are helpless to do anything! The *whole city* might burn up!
See those sentries? We're under *martial law* now!
7
BAKERY
Looks like the BAKER ran off, fearing for his life. Not to worry, though– they say it takes a *month* to completely starve to death.
With all this EXCITEMENT I'm not so hungry *now,* but in a few days I'll be *famished!* People are selling BREAD for $2!
8
We're lucky just to be alive... Our ROOM 'll be ashes by tonight, so let's just take our bedding with us and get out of here. They say *wise men never court danger,* and now's the time for us to act like wise men!
9
Possessions are fine, but sometimes they're nothing but a *headache!* Look at those poor men *struggling!*
10
With all the fires, it's bright as *day!*
Let's try to get some rest, before we turn into *nervous wrecks.*
11
Uh, oh! It's time for wise men to *run!!*
GET AWAY HERE DYNAMITO
Y. Kiyama
12

EPISODE 21

The Great San Francisco Quake

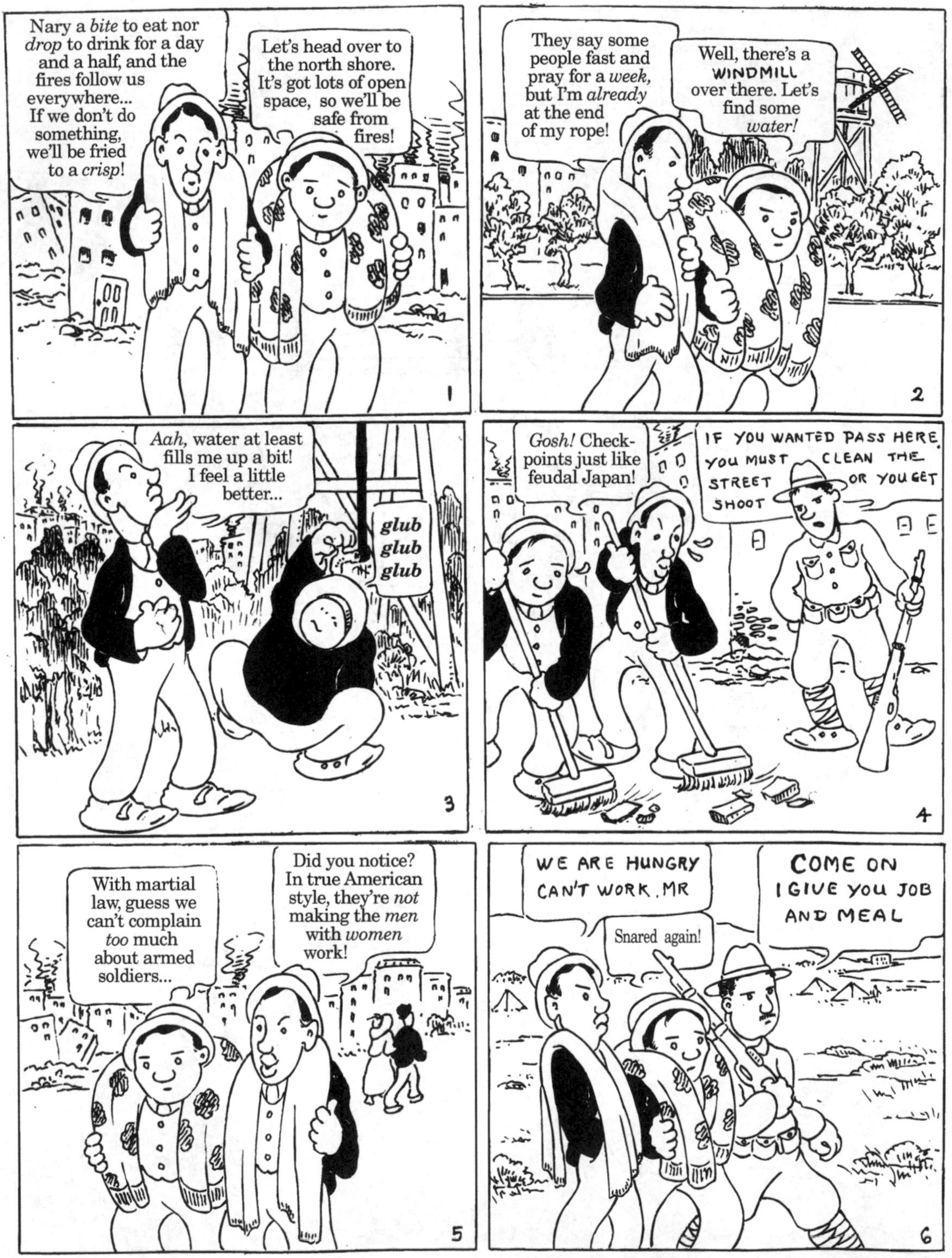
Nary a *bite* to eat nor *drop* to drink for a day and a half, and the fires follow us everywhere... If we don't do something, we'll be fried to a *crisp*!
Let's head over to the north shore. It's got lots of open space, so we'll be safe from fires!
1
They say some people fast and pray for a *week*, but I'm *already* at the end of my rope!
Well, there's a WINDMILL over there. Let's find some *water!*
2
Aah, water at least fills me up a bit! I feel a little better...
glub glub glub
3
Gosh! Check-points just like feudal Japan!
IF YOU WANTED PASS HERE YOU MUST CLEAN THE STREET OR YOU GET SHOOT
4
With martial law, guess we can't complain *too* much about armed soldiers...
Did you notice? In true American style, they're *not* making the *men* with *women* work!
5
WE ARE HUNGRY CAN'T WORK, MR
Snared again!
COME ON I GIVE YOU JOB AND MEAL
6

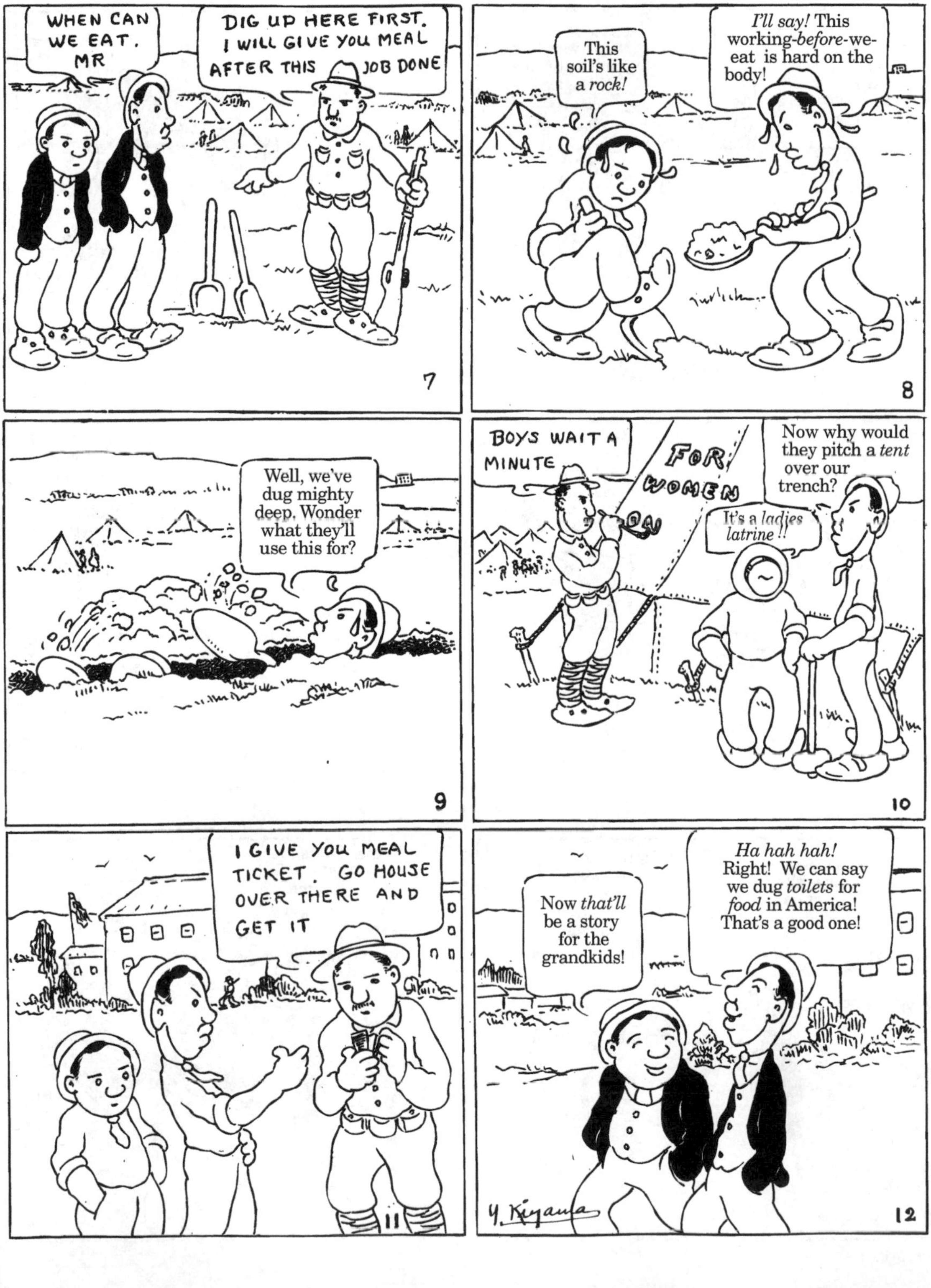
WHEN CAN WE EAT. MR
DIG UP HERE FIRST. I WILL GIVE YOU MEAL AFTER THIS JOB DONE
7
This soil's like a *rock!*
I'll say! This working-*before*-we-eat is hard on the body!
8
Well, we've dug mighty deep. Wonder what they'll use this for?
9
BOYS WAIT A MINUTE
FOR WOMEN
Now why would they pitch a *tent* over our trench?
It's a *ladies latrine* !!
10
I GIVE YOU MEAL TICKET. GO HOUSE OVER THERE AND GET IT
11
Now *that'll* be a story for the grandkids!
Ha hah hah! Right! We can say we dug *toilets* for *food* in America! That's a good one!
Y. Kiyama
12

EPISODE 22

The Great San Francisco Quake

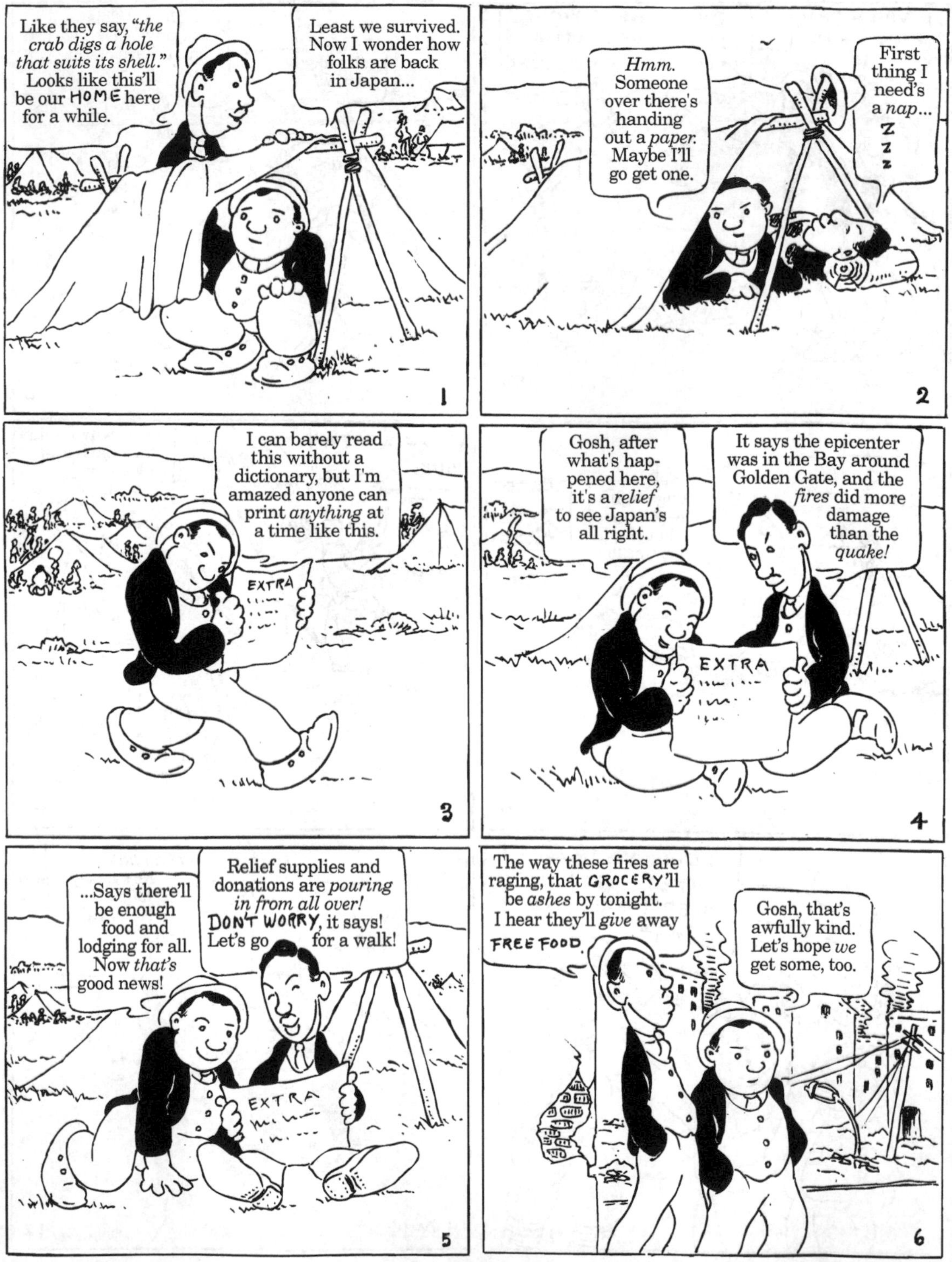
Like they say, "*the crab digs a hole that suits its shell.*" Looks like this'll be our HOME here for a while.
Least we survived. Now I wonder how folks are back in Japan...
1
Hmm. Someone over there's handing out a *paper.* Maybe I'll go get one.
First thing I need's a *nap*...
Z Z Z
2
I can barely read this without a dictionary, but I'm amazed anyone can print *anything* at a time like this.
EXTRA
3
Gosh, after what's happened here, it's a *relief* to see Japan's all right.
It says the epicenter was in the Bay around Golden Gate, and the *fires* did more damage than the *quake!*
EXTRA
4
...Says there'll be enough food and lodging for all. Now *that's* good news!
Relief supplies and donations are *pouring in from all over!* DON'T WORRY, it says! Let's go for a walk!
EXTRA
5
The way these fires are raging, that GROCERY'll be *ashes* by tonight. I hear they'll *give* away FREE FOOD.
Gosh, that's awfully kind. Let's hope *we* get some, too.
6

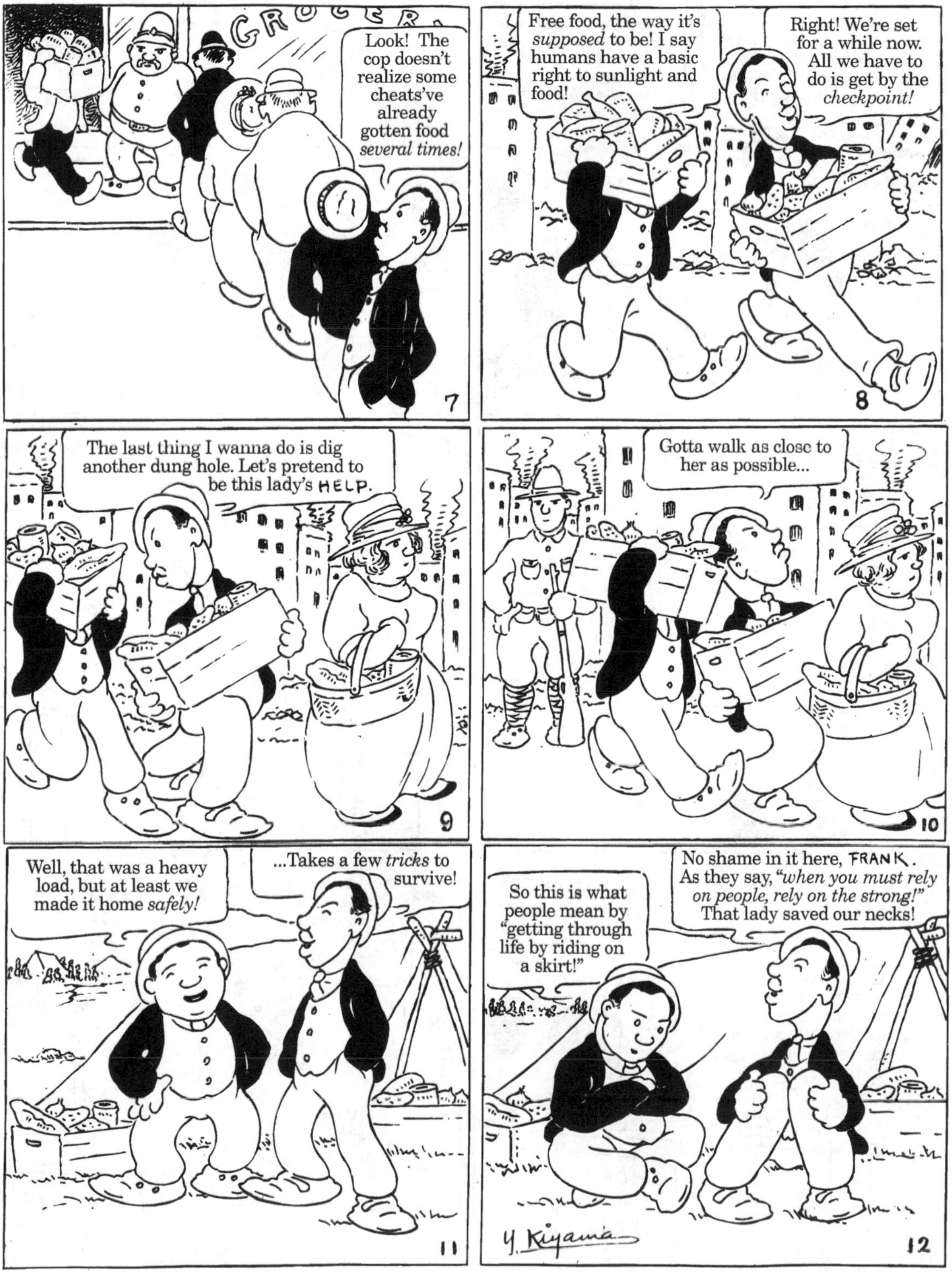
GROCER
Look! The cop doesn't realize some cheats've already gotten food *several times!*
7
Free food, the way it's *supposed* to be! I say humans have a basic right to sunlight and food!
Right! We're set for a while now. All we have to do is get by the *checkpoint!*
8
The last thing I wanna do is dig another dung hole. Let's pretend to be this lady's HELP.
9
Gotta walk as close to her as possible...
10
Well, that was a heavy load, but at least we made it home *safely!*
...Takes a few *tricks* to survive!
11
So this is what people mean by "getting through life by riding on a skirt!"
No shame in it here, FRANK. As they say, "*when you must rely on people, rely on the strong!*" That lady saved our necks!
Y. Kiyama
12

EPISODE 23

The Great San Francisco Quake

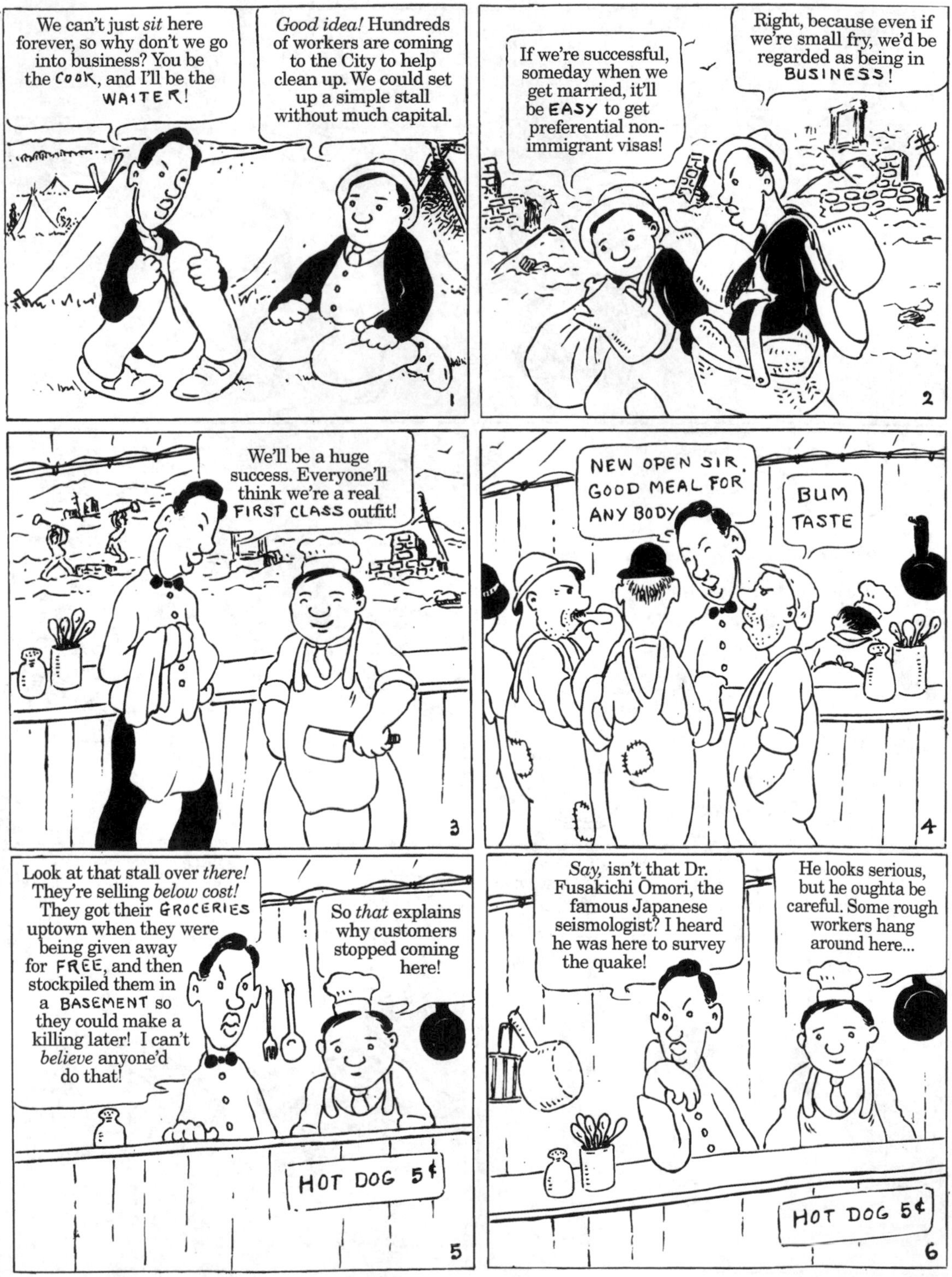

We can't just *sit* here forever, so why don't we go into business? You be the COOK, and I'll be the WAITER!
Good idea! Hundreds of workers are coming to the City to help clean up. We could set up a simple stall without much capital.
1
If we're successful, someday when we get married, it'll be EASY to get preferential non-immigrant visas!
Right, because even if we're small fry, we'd be regarded as being in BUSINESS!
2
We'll be a huge success. Everyone'll think we're a real FIRST CLASS outfit!
3
NEW OPEN SIR. GOOD MEAL FOR ANY BODY
BUM TASTE
4
Look at that stall over *there!* They're selling *below cost!* They got their GROCERIES uptown when they were being given away for FREE, and then stockpiled them in a BASEMENT so they could make a killing later! I can't *believe* anyone'd do that!
So *that* explains why customers stopped coming here!
HOT DOG 5¢
5
Say, isn't that Dr. Fusakichi Ōmori, the famous Japanese seismologist? I heard he was here to survey the quake!
He looks serious, but he oughta be careful. Some rough workers hang around here...
HOT DOG 5¢
6

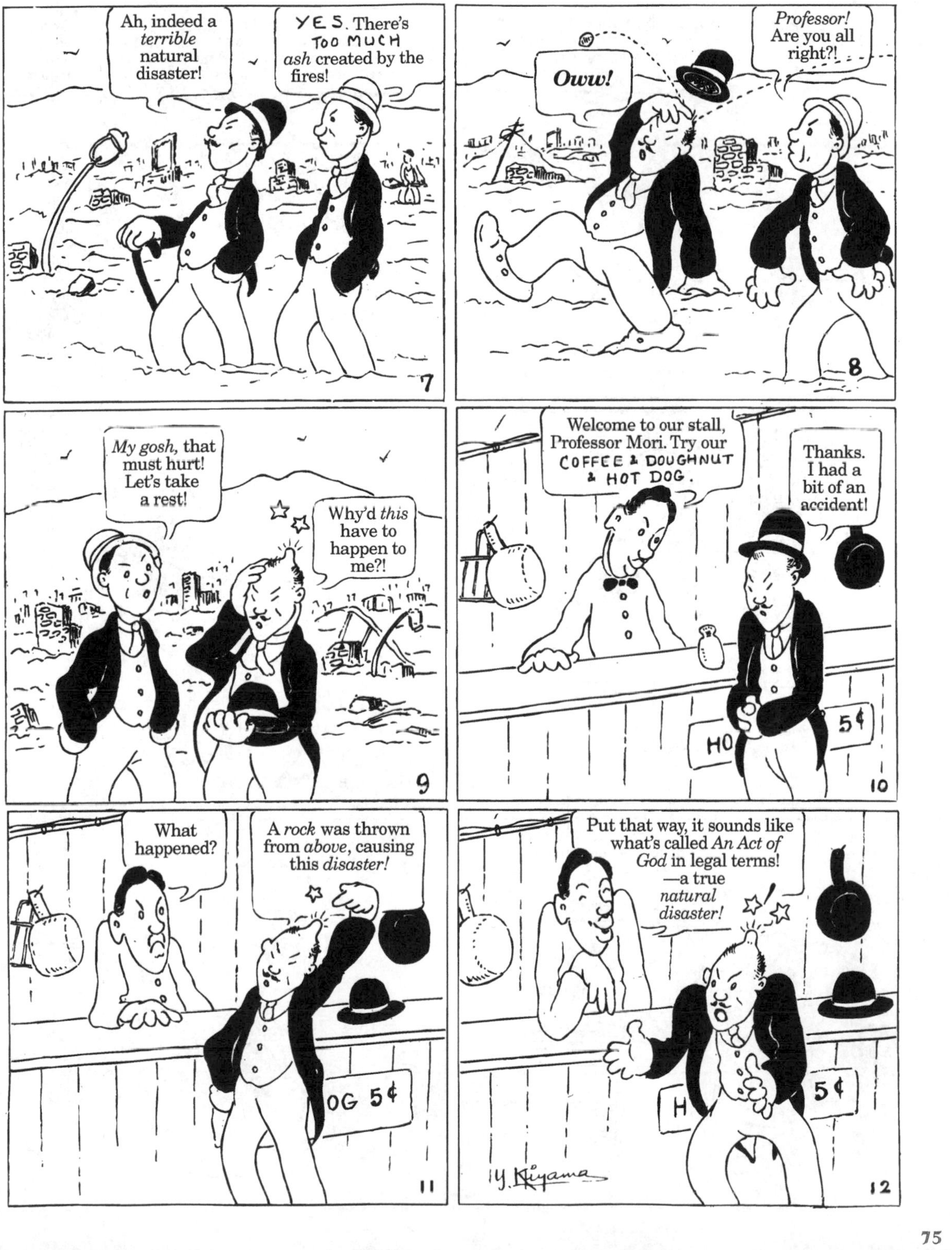
Ah, indeed a *terrible* natural disaster!
YES. There's TOO MUCH *ash* created by the fires!
7
Oww!
Professor! Are you all right?!
8
My gosh, that must hurt! Let's take a rest!
Why'd *this* have to happen to me?!
9
Welcome to our stall, Professor Mori. Try our COFFEE & DOUGHNUT & HOT DOG.
Thanks. I had a bit of an accident!
HO
5¢
10
What happened?
A *rock* was thrown from *above*, causing this *disaster!*
OG 5¢
11
Put that way, it sounds like what's called *An Act of God* in legal terms! —a true *natural disaster!*
H
5¢
Y. Kiyama
12

Plain Cook

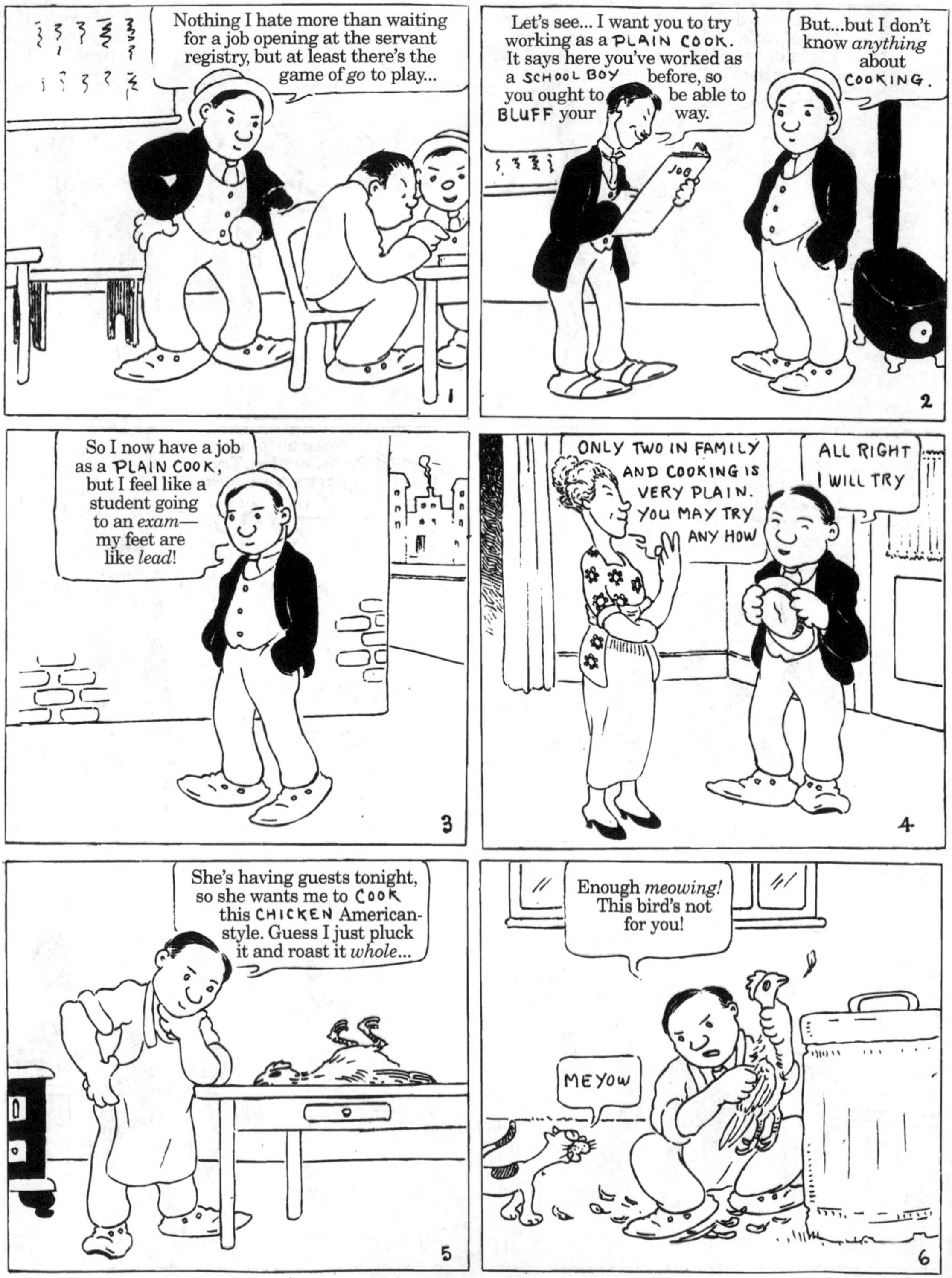
Nothing I hate more than waiting for a job opening at the servant registry, but at least there's the game of *go* to play...
Let's see... I want you to try working as a PLAIN COOK. It says here you've worked as a SCHOOL BOY before, so you ought to be able to BLUFF your way.
JOB
But...but I don't know *anything* about COOKING.
So I now have a job as a PLAIN COOK, but I feel like a student going to an *exam*—my feet are like *lead*!
ONLY TWO IN FAMILY AND COOKING IS VERY PLAIN. YOU MAY TRY ANY HOW
ALL RIGHT I WILL TRY
She's having guests tonight, so she wants me to COOK this CHICKEN American-style. Guess I just pluck it and roast it *whole*...
Enough *meowing!* This bird's not for you!
MEYOW

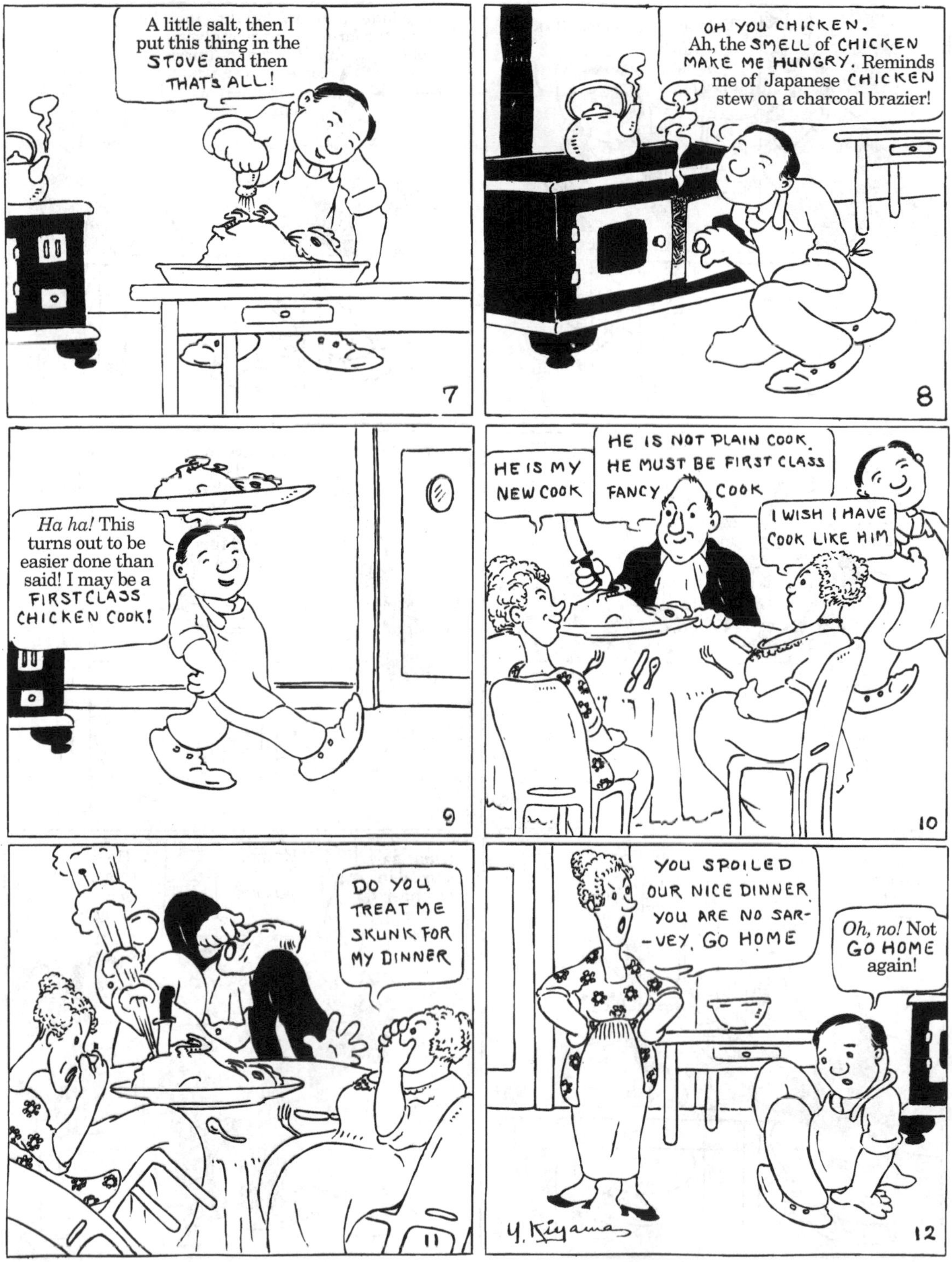
A little salt, then I put this thing in the STOVE and then THAT'S ALL!
7
OH YOU CHICKEN. Ah, the SMELL of CHICKEN MAKE ME HUNGRY. Reminds me of Japanese CHICKEN stew on a charcoal brazier!
8
Ha ha! This turns out to be easier done than said! I may be a FIRSTCLASS CHICKEN COOK!
9
HE IS MY NEW COOK
HE IS NOT PLAIN COOK. HE MUST BE FIRST CLASS FANCY COOK
I WISH I HAVE COOK LIKE HIM
10
DO YOU TREAT ME SKUNK FOR MY DINNER
11
YOU SPOILED OUR NICE DINNER YOU ARE NO SAR-VEY. GO HOME
Oh, no! Not GO HOME again!
Y. Kiyama
12

EPISODE 25

Working in a Store

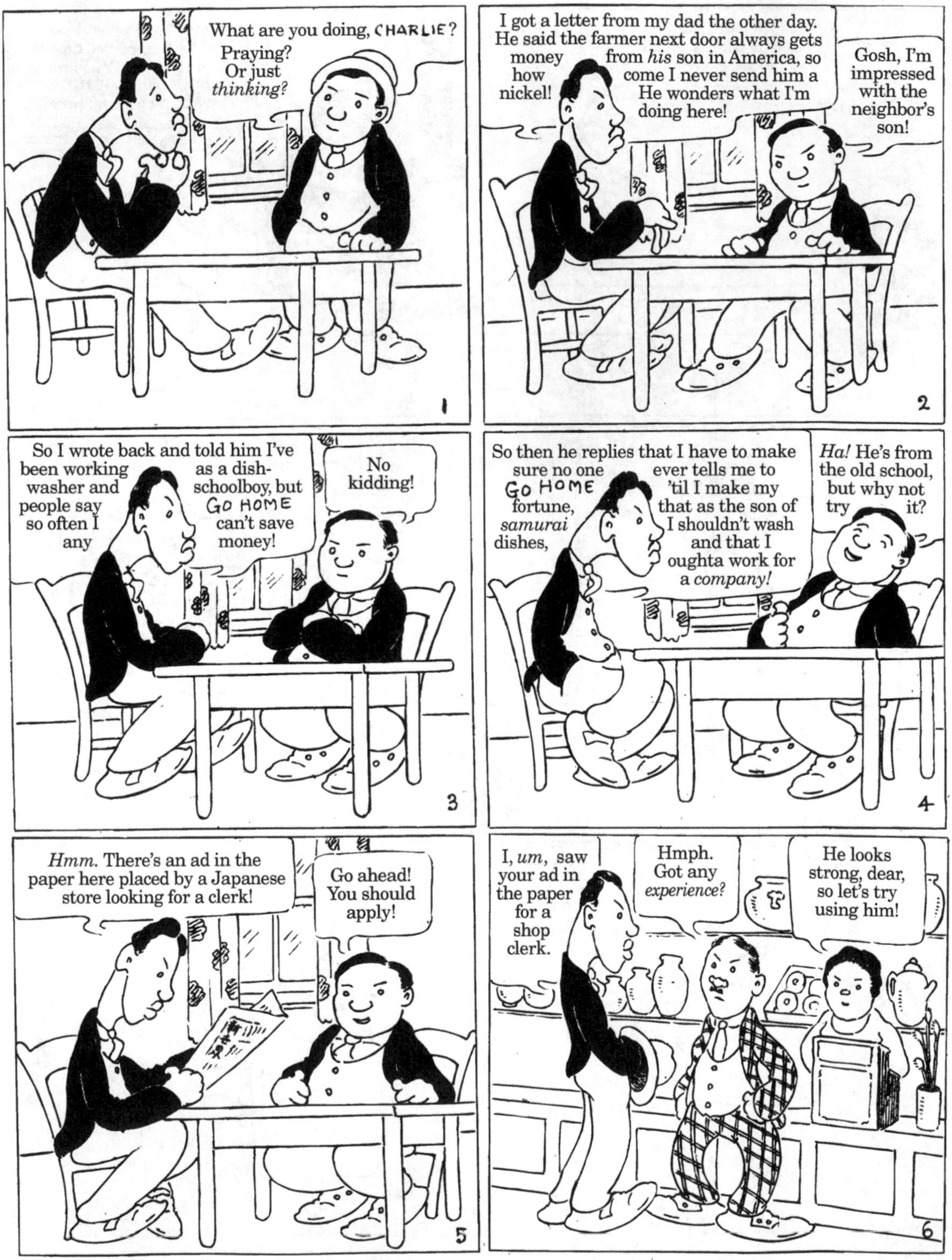

What are you doing, CHARLIE? Praying? Or just *thinking?*
I got a letter from my dad the other day. He said the farmer next door always gets money from *his* son in America, so how come I never send him a nickel! He wonders what I'm doing here!
Gosh, I'm impressed with the neighbor's son!
So I wrote back and told him I've been working as a dish-washer and schoolboy, but people say GO HOME so often I can't save any money!
No kidding!
So then he replies that I have to make sure no one ever tells me to GO HOME 'til I make my fortune, that as the son of *samurai* I shouldn't wash dishes, and that I oughta work for a *company!*
Ha! He's from the old school, but why not try it?
Hmm. There's an ad in the paper here placed by a Japanese store looking for a clerk!
Go ahead! You should apply!
I, *um,* saw your ad in the paper for a shop clerk.
Hmph. Got any *experience?*
He looks strong, dear, so let's try using him!

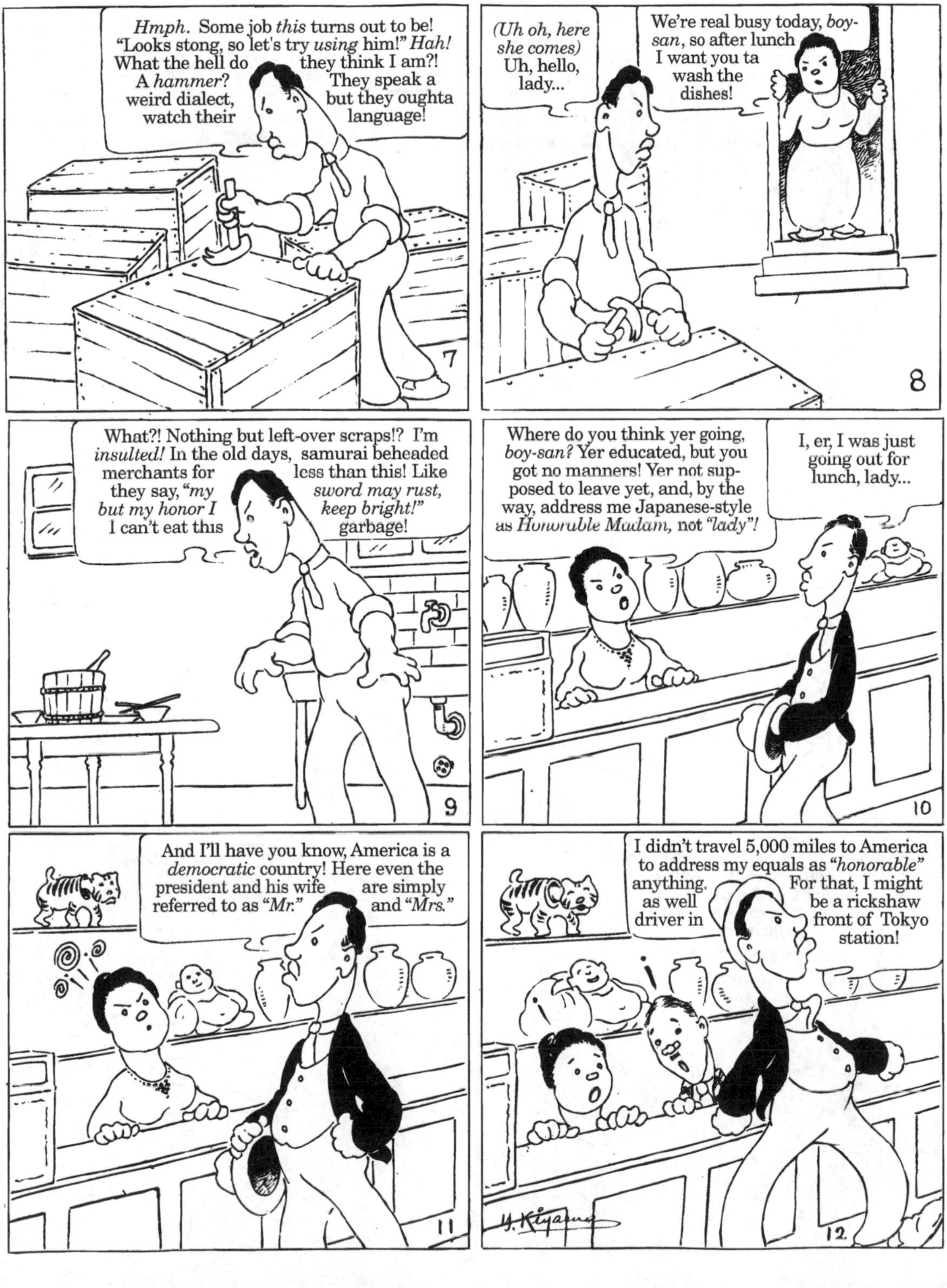

Hmph. Some job *this* turns out to be! "Looks stong, so let's try *using* him!" *Hah!* What the hell do they think I am?! A *hammer*? They speak a weird dialect, but they oughta watch their language!
(Uh oh, here she comes) Uh, hello, lady...
We're real busy today, *boy-san*, so after lunch I want you ta wash the dishes!
What?! Nothing but left-over scraps!? I'm *insulted!* In the old days, samurai beheaded merchants for less than this! Like they say, *"my sword may rust, but my honor I keep bright!"* I can't eat this garbage!
Where do you think yer going, *boy-san?* Yer educated, but you got no manners! Yer not supposed to leave yet, and, by the way, address me Japanese-style as *Honorable Madam,* not *"lady"*!
I, er, I was just going out for lunch, lady...
And I'll have you know, America is a *democratic* country! Here even the president and his wife are simply referred to as *"Mr."* and *"Mrs."*
I didn't travel 5,000 miles to America to address my equals as *"honorable"* anything. For that, I might as well be a rickshaw driver in front of Tokyo station!
Y. Kiyama

A Crisis over Japanese School Children

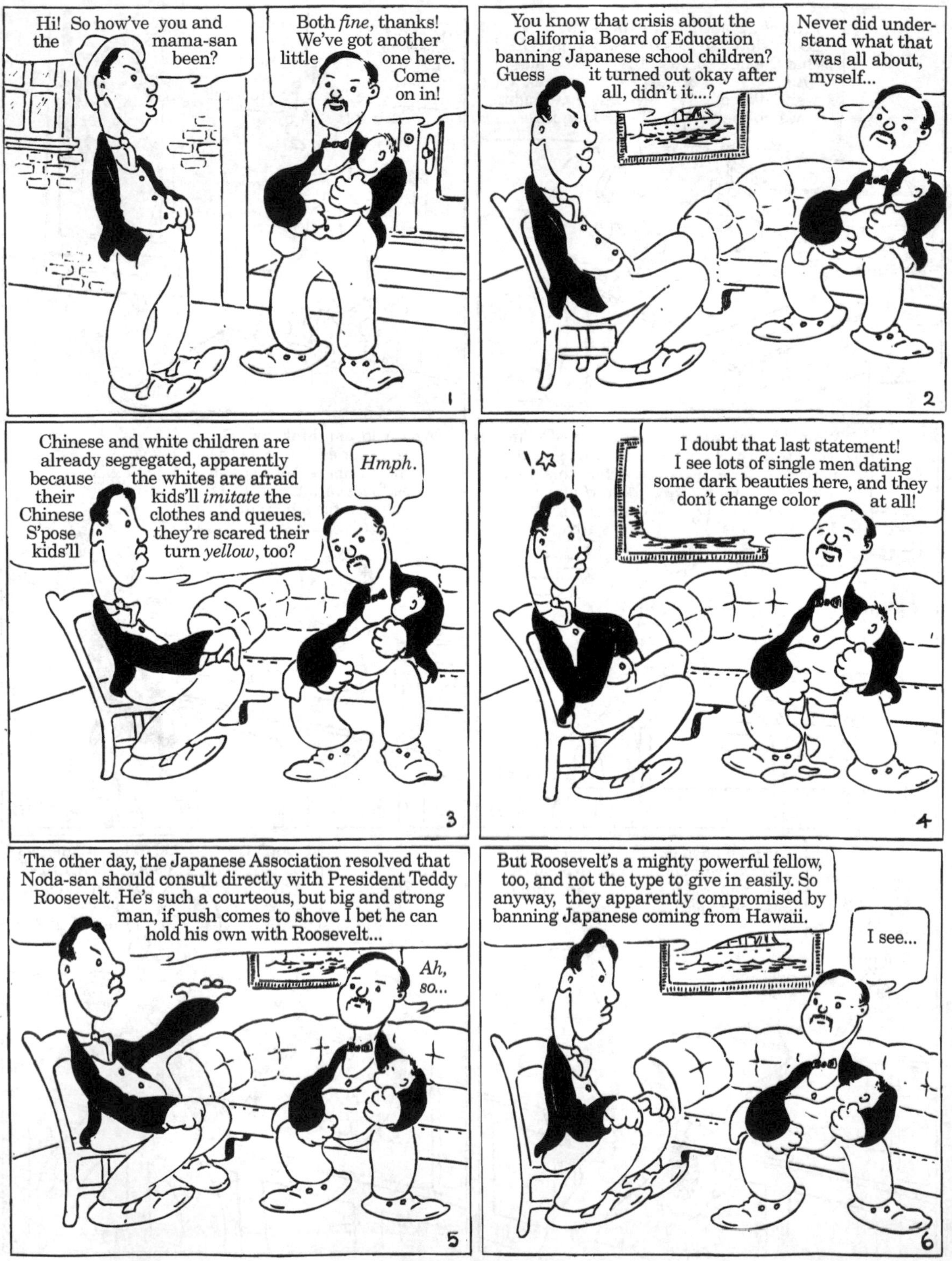

Hi! So how've you and the mama-san been?
Both *fine*, thanks! We've got another little one here. Come on in!
1
You know that crisis about the California Board of Education banning Japanese school children? Guess it turned out okay after all, didn't it...?
Never did understand what that was all about, myself...
2
Chinese and white children are already segregated, apparently because the whites are afraid their kids'll *imitate* the Chinese clothes and queues. S'pose they're scared their kids'll turn *yellow*, too?
Hmph.
3
I doubt that last statement! I see lots of single men dating some dark beauties here, and they don't change color at all!
4
The other day, the Japanese Association resolved that Noda-san should consult directly with President Teddy Roosevelt. He's such a courteous, but big and strong man, if push comes to shove I bet he can hold his own with Roosevelt...
Ah, so...
5
But Roosevelt's a mighty powerful fellow, too, and not the type to give in easily. So anyway, they apparently compromised by banning Japanese coming from Hawaii.
I see...
6

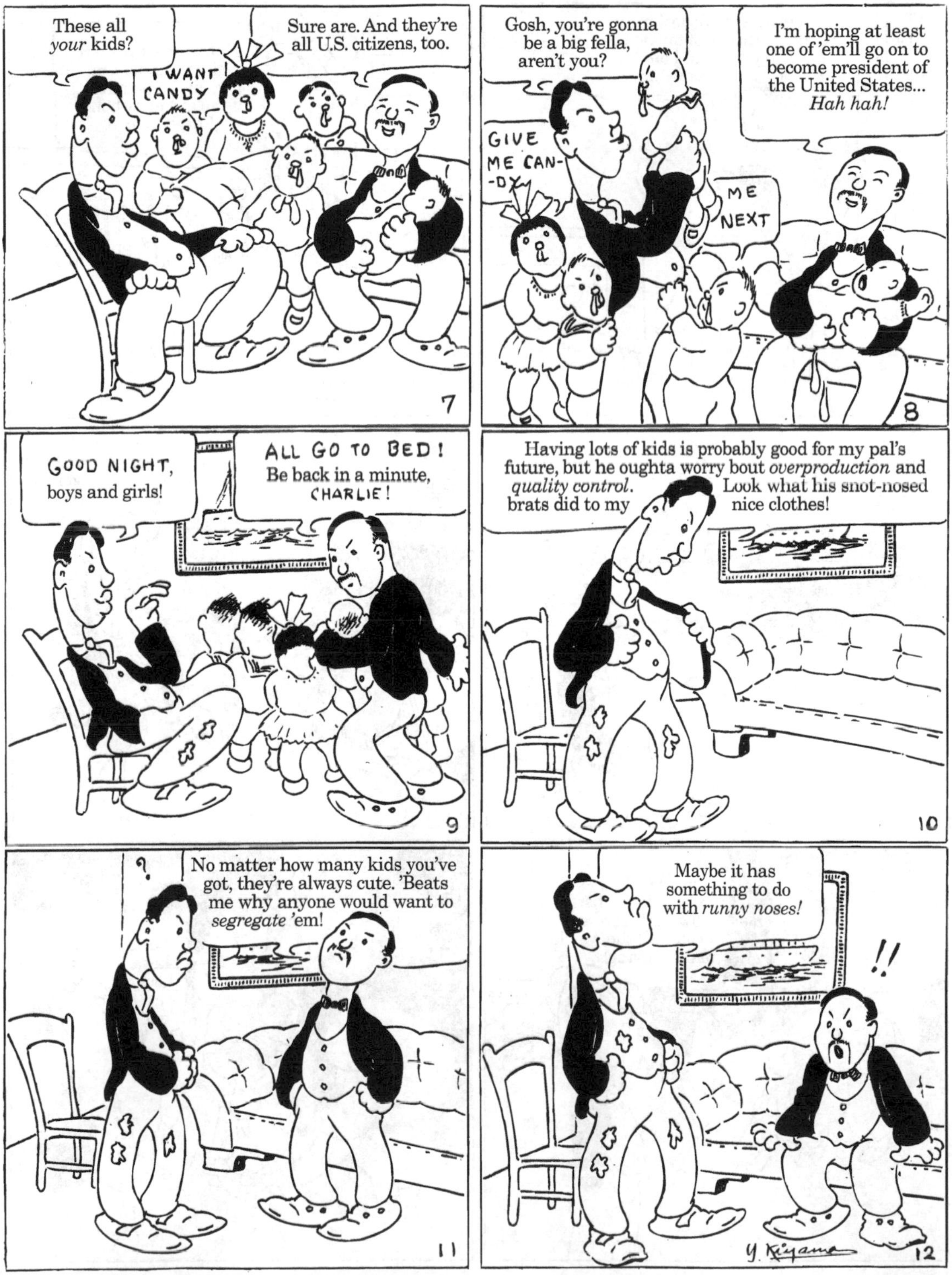
These all *your* kids?
I WANT CANDY
Sure are. And they're all U.S. citizens, too.
Gosh, you're gonna be a big fella, aren't you?
GIVE ME CAN-DY
ME NEXT
I'm hoping at least one of 'em'll go on to become president of the United States... *Hah hah!*
GOOD NIGHT, boys and girls!
ALL GO TO BED! Be back in a minute, CHARLIE!
Having lots of kids is probably good for my pal's future, but he oughta worry bout *overproduction* and *quality control*. Look what his snot-nosed brats did to my nice clothes!
?
No matter how many kids you've got, they're always cute. 'Beats me why anyone would want to *segregate* 'em!
Maybe it has something to do with *runny noses!*
!!
Y. Kiyama

Japanese Immigrants Arriving via Hawaii

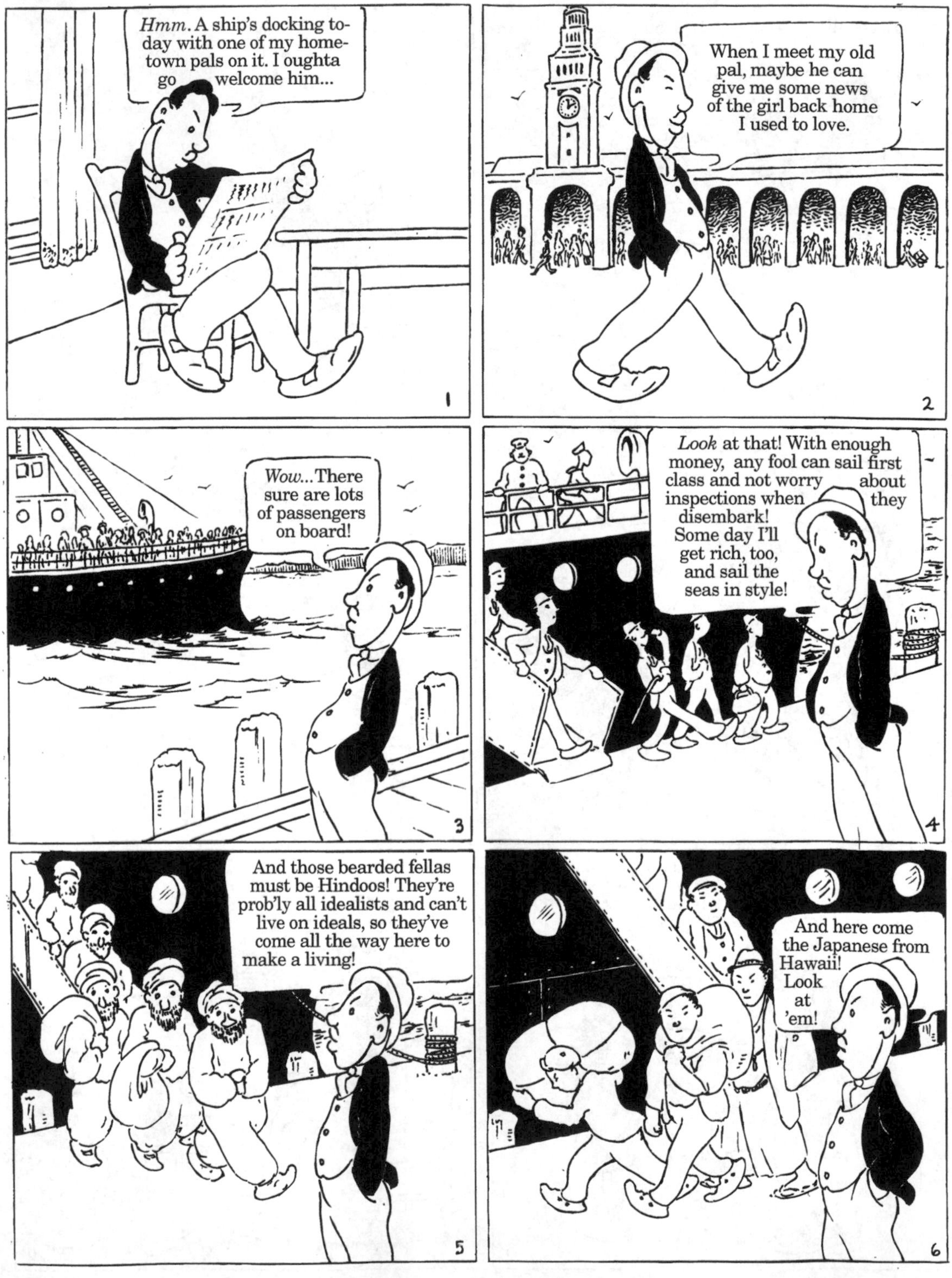
Hmm. A ship's docking today with one of my hometown pals on it. I oughta go welcome him...
1
When I meet my old pal, maybe he can give me some news of the girl back home I used to love.
2
Wow...There sure are lots of passengers on board!
3
Look at that! With enough money, any fool can sail first class and not worry about inspections when they disembark! Some day I'll get rich, too, and sail the seas in style!
4
And those bearded fellas must be Hindoos! They're prob'ly all idealists and can't live on ideals, so they've come all the way here to make a living!
5
And here come the Japanese from Hawaii! Look at 'em!
6

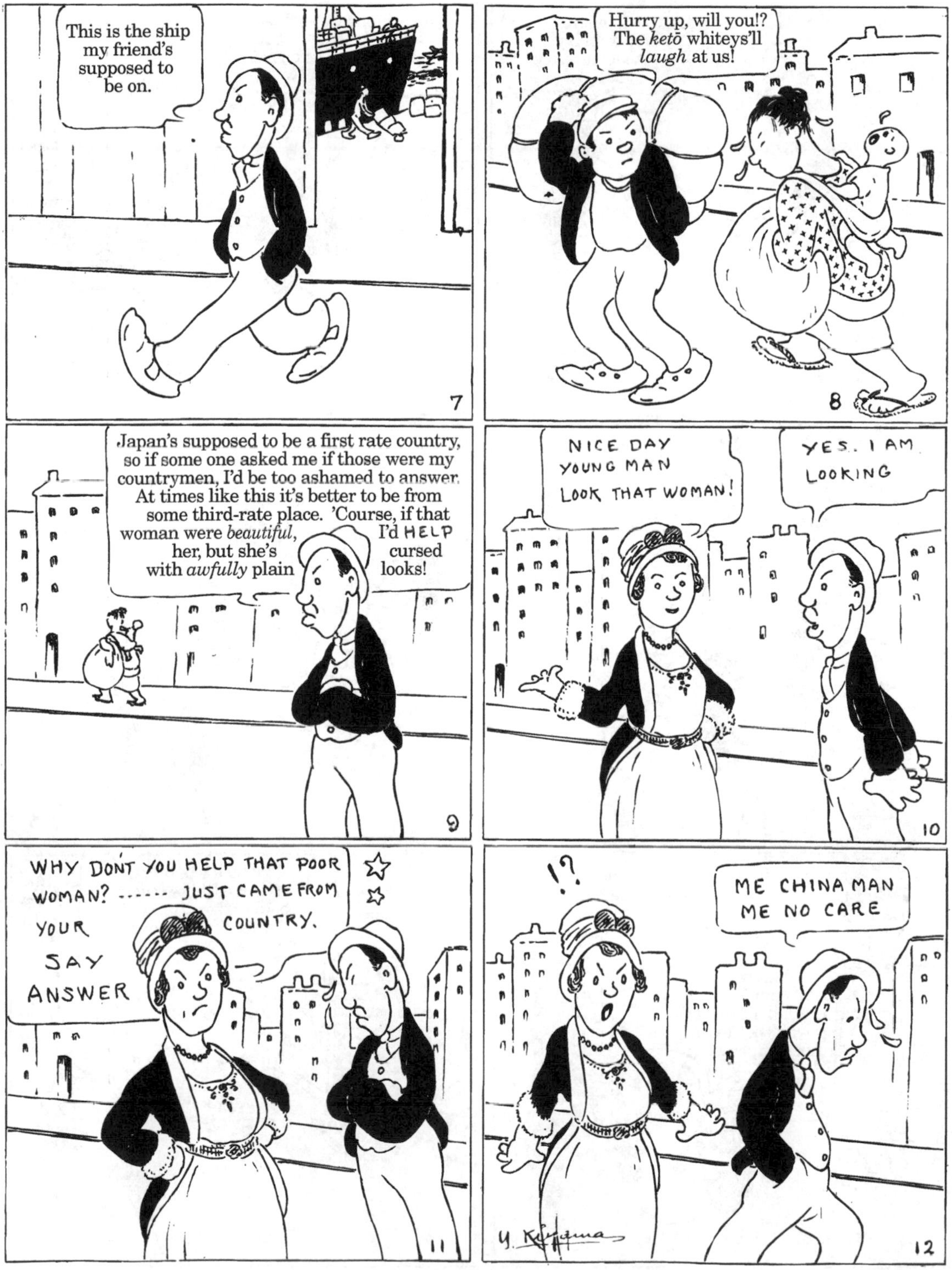

This is the ship my friend's supposed to be on.
7
Hurry up, will you!? The *ketō* whiteys'll *laugh* at us!
8
Japan's supposed to be a first rate country, so if some one asked me if those were my countrymen, I'd be too ashamed to answer. At times like this it's better to be from some third-rate place. 'Course, if that woman were *beautiful*, I'd HELP her, but she's cursed with *awfully* plain looks!
9
NICE DAY YOUNG MAN LOOK THAT WOMAN!
YES. I AM LOOKING
10
WHY DON'T YOU HELP THAT POOR WOMAN? ------ JUST CAME FROM YOUR COUNTRY. SAY ANSWER
11
!?
ME CHINA MAN ME NO CARE
12

EPISODE 28

Japanese Immigrants Arriving via Hawaii

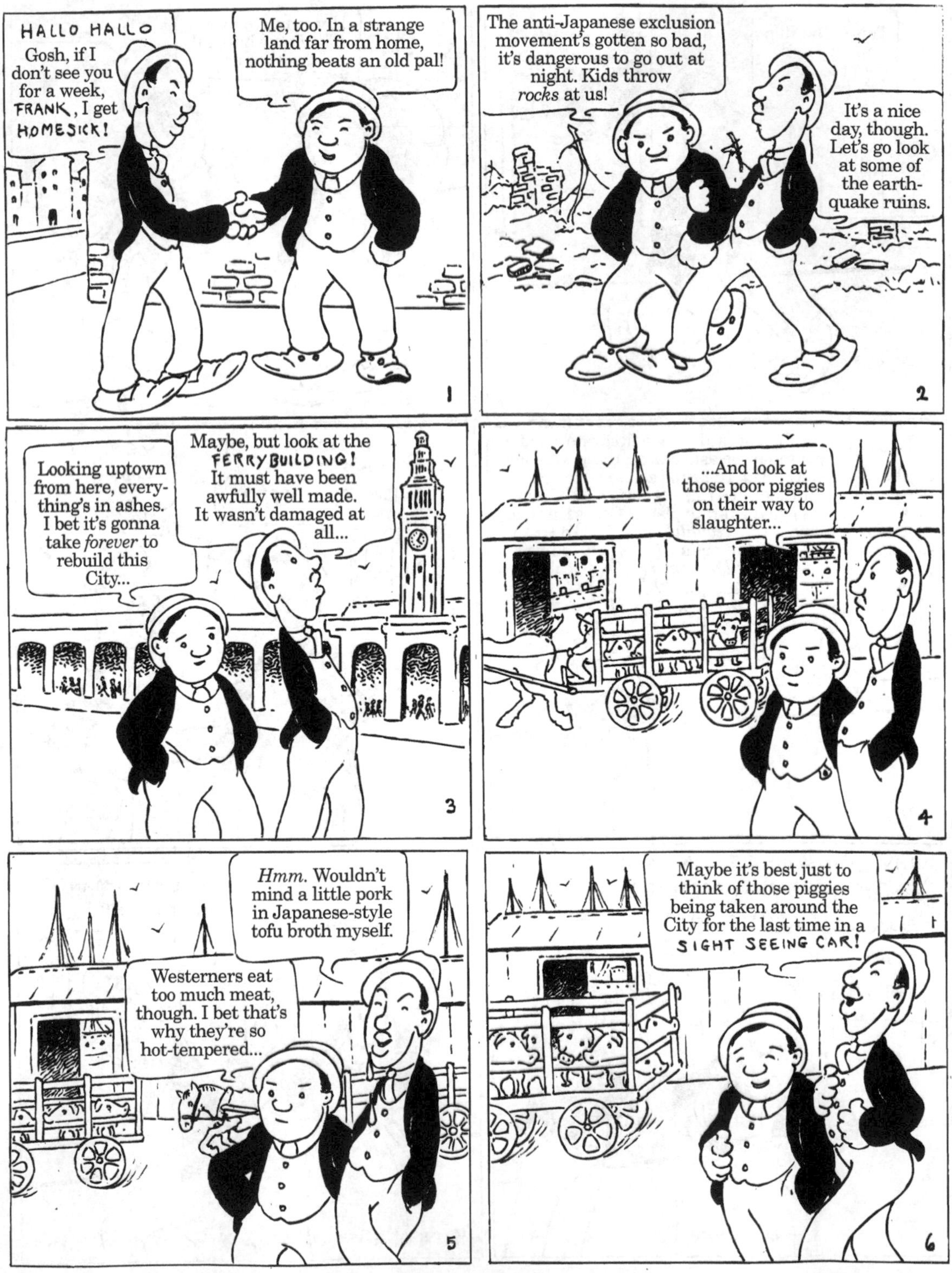
HALLO HALLO
Gosh, if I don't see you for a week, FRANK, I get HOMESICK!
Me, too. In a strange land far from home, nothing beats an old pal!
The anti-Japanese exclusion movement's gotten so bad, it's dangerous to go out at night. Kids throw *rocks* at us!
It's a nice day, though. Let's go look at some of the earth-quake ruins.
Looking uptown from here, every-thing's in ashes. I bet it's gonna take *forever* to rebuild this City...
Maybe, but look at the FERRY BUILDING! It must have been awfully well made. It wasn't damaged at all...
...And look at those poor piggies on their way to slaughter...
Westerners eat too much meat, though. I bet that's why they're so hot-tempered...
Hmm. Wouldn't mind a little pork in Japanese-style tofu broth myself.
Maybe it's best just to think of those piggies being taken around the City for the last time in a SIGHT SEEING CAR!

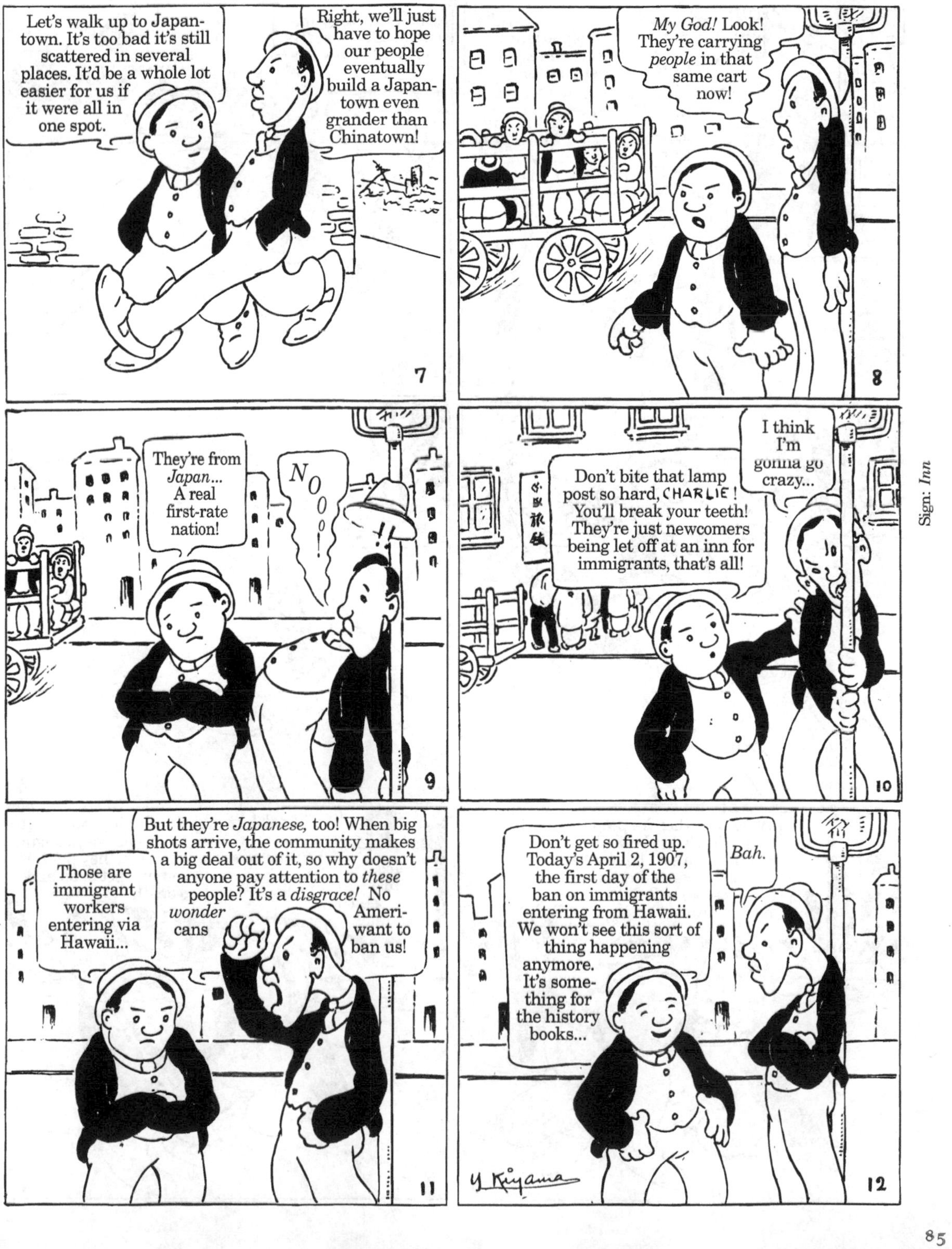

Let's walk up to Japantown. It's too bad it's still scattered in several places. It'd be a whole lot easier for us if it were all in one spot.
Right, we'll just have to hope our people eventually build a Japantown even grander than Chinatown!
7
My God! Look! They're carrying *people* in that same cart now!
8
They're from *Japan*... A real first-rate nation!
Nooo!
!!
9
Don't bite that lamp post so hard, CHARLIE! You'll break your teeth! They're just newcomers being let off at an inn for immigrants, that's all!
I think I'm gonna go crazy...
10
Those are immigrant workers entering via Hawaii...
But they're *Japanese,* too! When big shots arrive, the community makes a big deal out of it, so why doesn't anyone pay attention to *these* people? It's a *disgrace!* No *wonder* Americans want to ban us!
11
Don't get so fired up. Today's April 2, 1907, the first day of the ban on immigrants entering from Hawaii. We won't see this sort of thing happening anymore. It's something for the history books...
Bah.
Y. Kiyama
12

Sign: *Inn*

Enjoying an "Illumination" Show

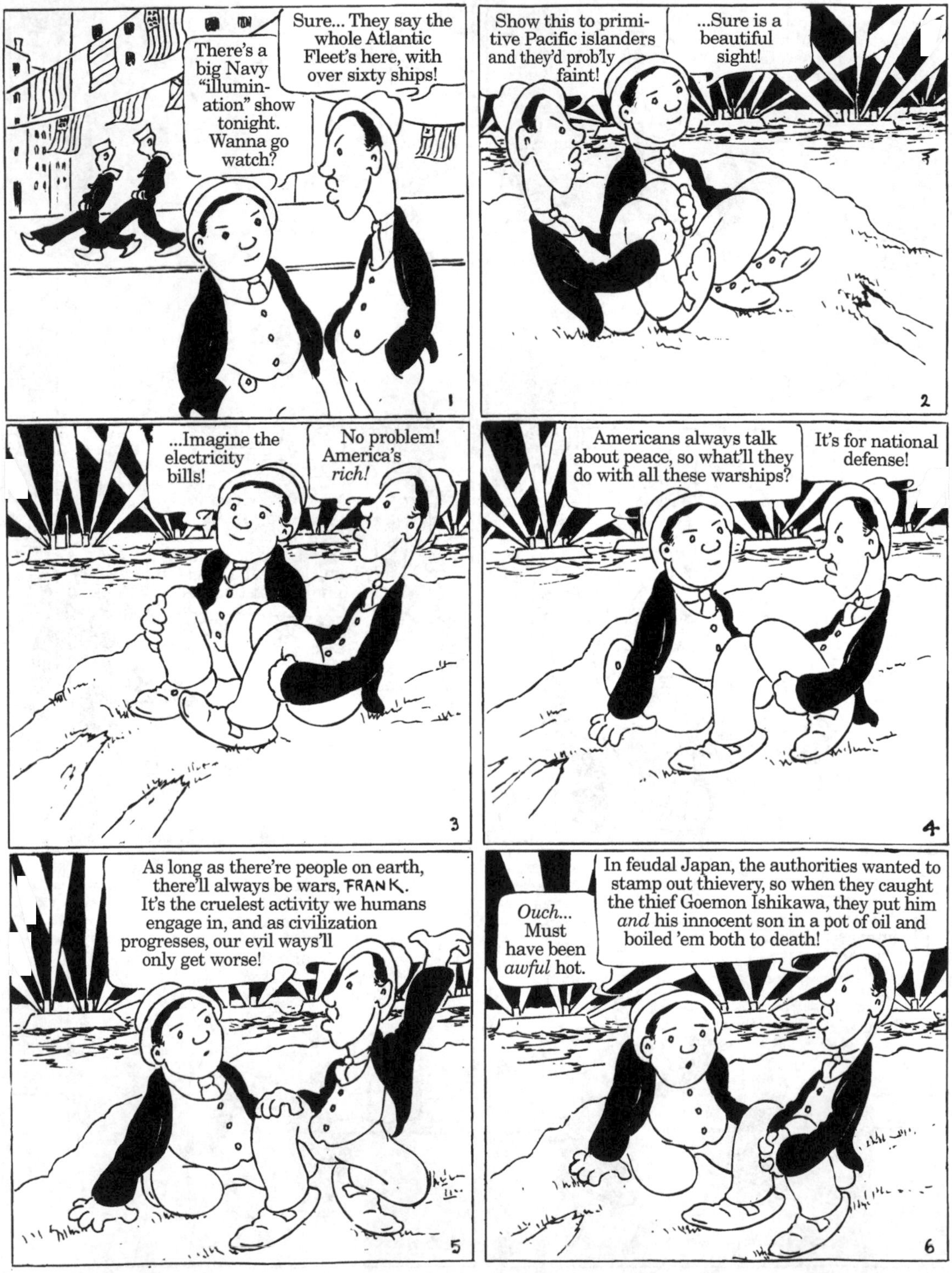
There's a big Navy "illumin-ation" show tonight. Wanna go watch?
Sure... They say the whole Atlantic Fleet's here, with over sixty ships!
1
Show this to primi-tive Pacific islanders and they'd prob'ly faint!
...Sure is a beautiful sight!
2
...Imagine the electricity bills!
No problem! America's *rich!*
3
Americans always talk about peace, so what'll they do with all these warships?
It's for national defense!
4
As long as there're people on earth, there'll always be wars, FRANK. It's the cruelest activity we humans engage in, and as civilization progresses, our evil ways'll only get worse!
5
In feudal Japan, the authorities wanted to stamp out thievery, so when they caught the thief Goemon Ishikawa, they put him *and* his innocent son in a pot of oil and boiled 'em both to death!
Ouch... Must have been *awful* hot.
6

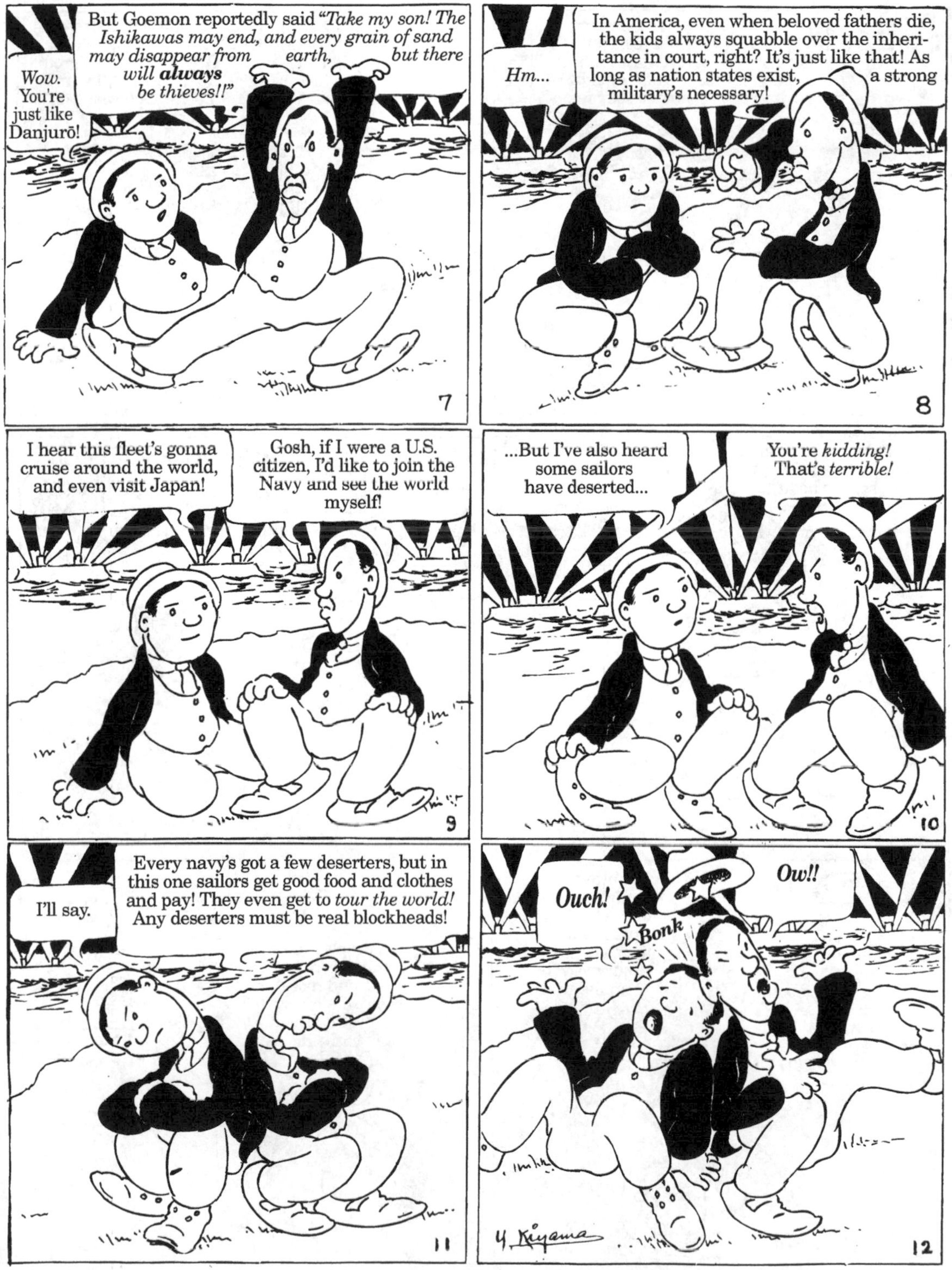
But Goemon reportedly said "*Take my son! The Ishikawas may end, and every grain of sand may disappear from earth, but there will **always** be thieves!!*"
Wow. You're just like Danjurō!
7
Hm...
In America, even when beloved fathers die, the kids always squabble over the inheritance in court, right? It's just like that! As long as nation states exist, a strong military's necessary!
8
I hear this fleet's gonna cruise around the world, and even visit Japan!
Gosh, if I were a U.S. citizen, I'd like to join the Navy and see the world myself!
9
...But I've also heard some sailors have deserted...
You're *kidding!* That's *terrible!*
10
I'll say.
Every navy's got a few deserters, but in this one sailors get good food and clothes and pay! They even get to *tour the world!* Any deserters must be real blockheads!
11
Ouch!
Ow!!
Bonk
Y. Kiyama
12

EPISODE 30

A Visit by the President

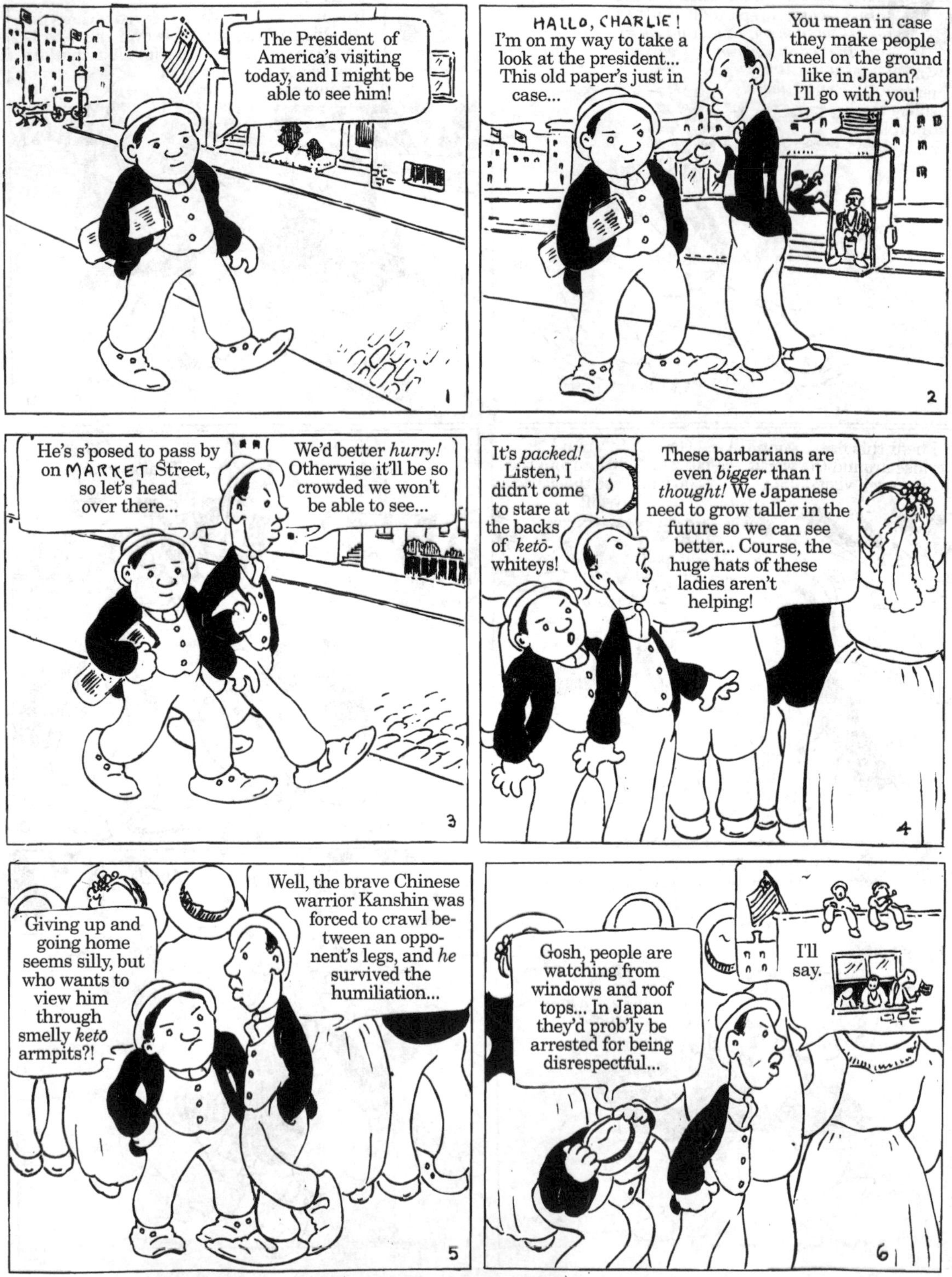
The President of America's visiting today, and I might be able to see him!
HALLO, CHARLIE! I'm on my way to take a look at the president... This old paper's just in case...
You mean in case they make people kneel on the ground like in Japan? I'll go with you!
He's s'posed to pass by on MARKET Street, so let's head over there...
We'd better *hurry!* Otherwise it'll be so crowded we won't be able to see...
It's *packed!* Listen, I didn't come to stare at the backs of *ketō*-whiteys!
These barbarians are even *bigger* than I *thought!* We Japanese need to grow taller in the future so we can see better... Course, the huge hats of these ladies aren't helping!
Giving up and going home seems silly, but who wants to view him through smelly *ketō* armpits?!
Well, the brave Chinese warrior Kanshin was forced to crawl between an opponent's legs, and *he* survived the humiliation...
Gosh, people are watching from windows and roof tops... In Japan they'd prob'ly be arrested for being disrespectful...
I'll say.

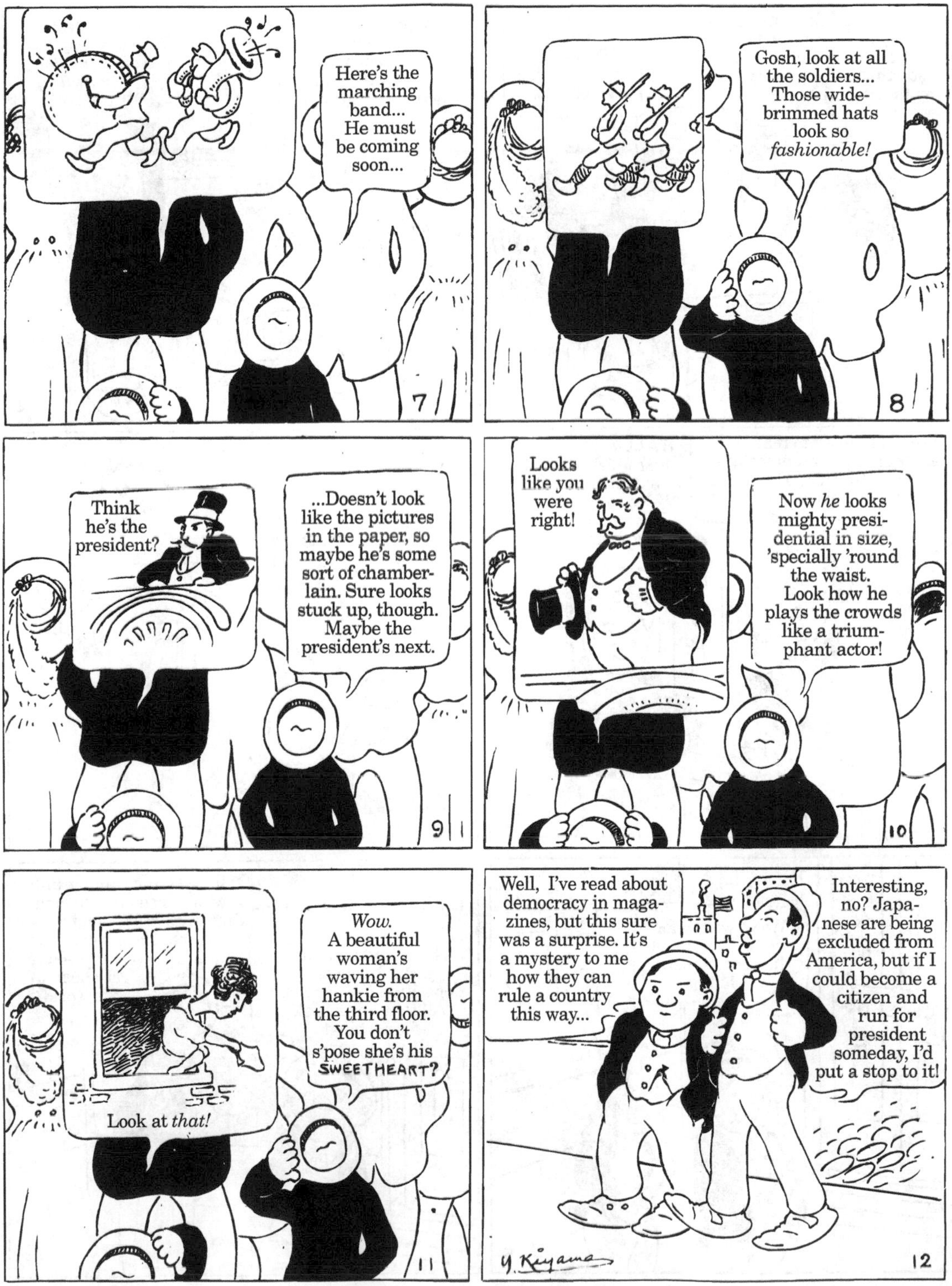
Here's the marching band... He must be coming soon...
7
Gosh, look at all the soldiers... Those wide-brimmed hats look so *fashionable!*
8
Think he's the president?
...Doesn't look like the pictures in the paper, so maybe he's some sort of chamberlain. Sure looks stuck up, though. Maybe the president's next.
9
Looks like you were right!
Now *he* looks mighty presidential in size, 'specially 'round the waist. Look how he plays the crowds like a triumphant actor!
10
Look at *that!*
Wow. A beautiful woman's waving her hankie from the third floor. You don't s'pose she's his SWEETHEART?
11
Well, I've read about democracy in magazines, but this sure was a surprise. It's a mystery to me how they can rule a country this way...
Interesting, no? Japanese are being excluded from America, but if I could become a citizen and run for president someday, I'd put a stop to it!
Y. Kiyama
12

EPISODE 31

When the Golden Gate Bank Failed

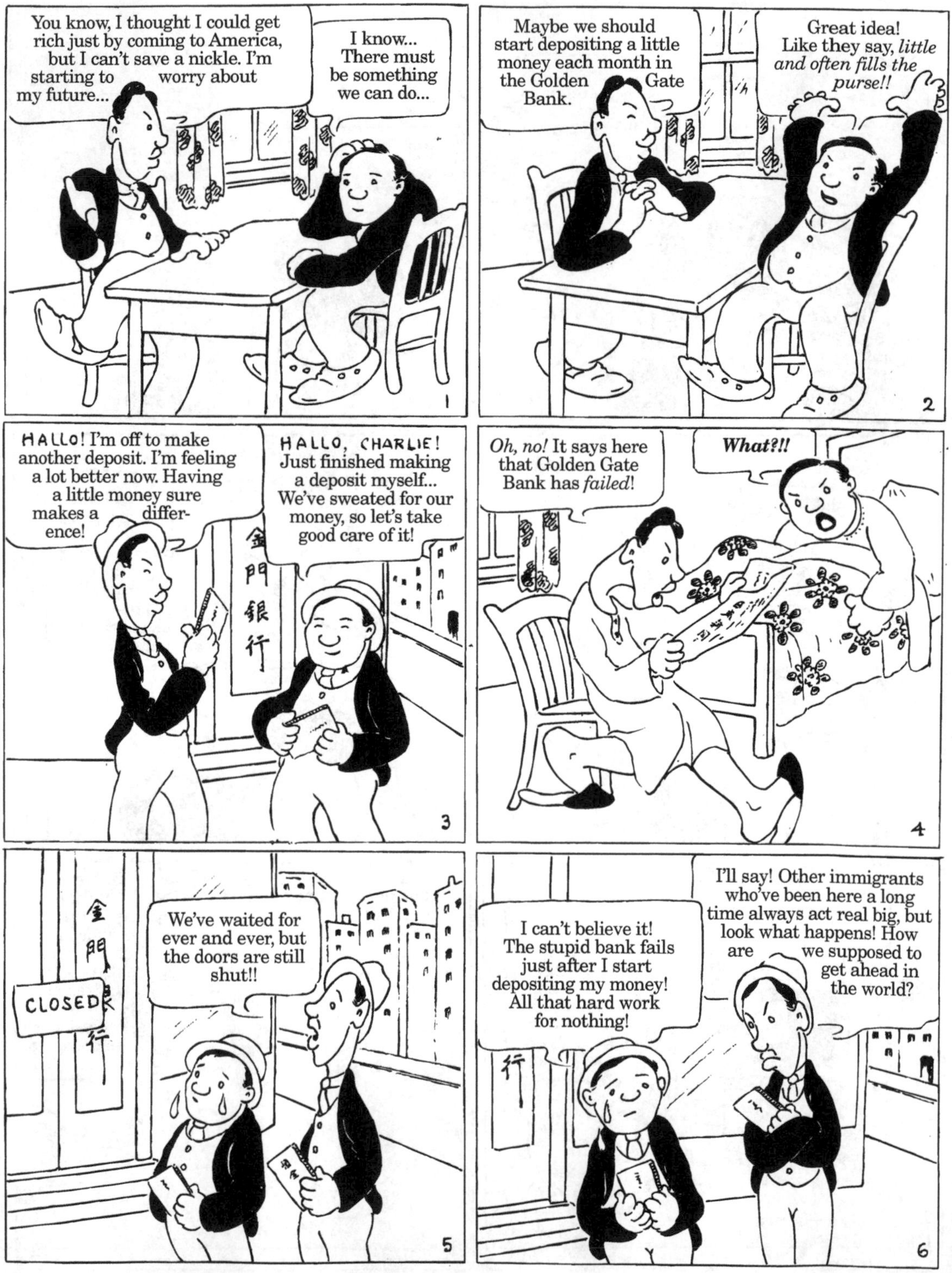

You know, I thought I could get rich just by coming to America, but I can't save a nickle. I'm starting to worry about my future...
I know... There must be something we can do...
Maybe we should start depositing a little money each month in the Golden Gate Bank.
Great idea! Like they say, *little and often fills the purse!!*
HALLO! I'm off to make another deposit. I'm feeling a lot better now. Having a little money sure makes a differ-ence!
金門銀行
HALLO, CHARLIE! Just finished making a deposit myself... We've sweated for our money, so let's take good care of it!
Oh, no! It says here that Golden Gate Bank has *failed*!
What?!!
CLOSED
We've waited for ever and ever, but the doors are still shut!!
I can't believe it! The stupid bank fails just after I start depositing my money! All that hard work for nothing!
I'll say! Other immigrants who've been here a long time always act real big, but look what happens! How are we supposed to get ahead in the world?

Sign: Golden Gate Bank

Text: *Bank Passbook*

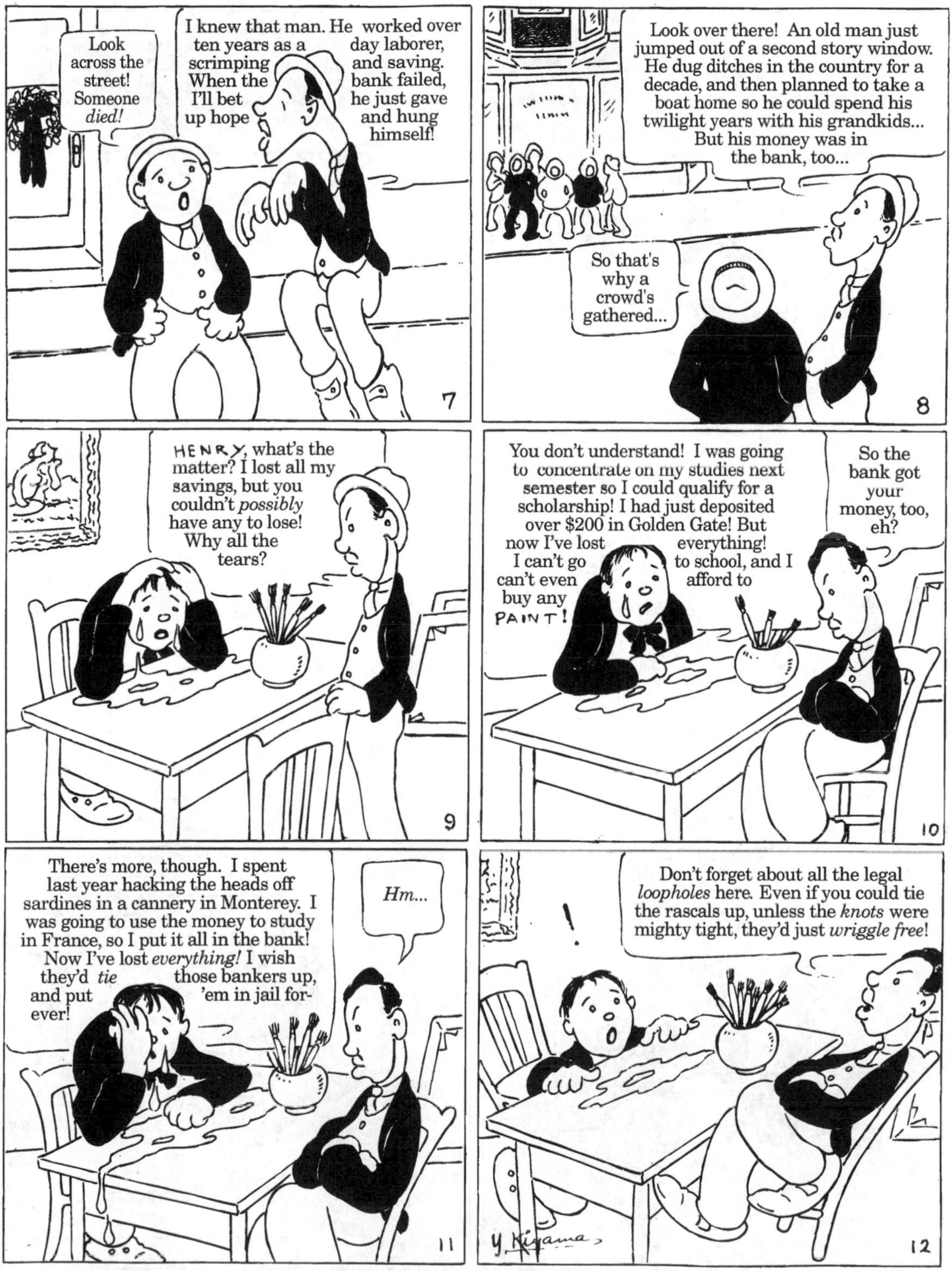
Look across the street! Someone *died!*
I knew that man. He worked over ten years as a day laborer, scrimping and saving. When the bank failed, I'll bet he just gave up hope and hung himself!
7
Look over there! An old man just jumped out of a second story window. He dug ditches in the country for a decade, and then planned to take a boat home so he could spend his twilight years with his grandkids... But his money was in the bank, too...
So that's why a crowd's gathered...
8
HENRY, what's the matter? I lost all my savings, but you couldn't *possibly* have any to lose! Why all the tears?
9
You don't understand! I was going to concentrate on my studies next semester so I could qualify for a scholarship! I had just deposited over $200 in Golden Gate! But now I've lost everything! I can't go to school, and I can't even afford to buy any PAINT!
So the bank got your money, too, eh?
10
There's more, though. I spent last year hacking the heads off sardines in a cannery in Monterey. I was going to use the money to study in France, so I put it all in the bank! Now I've lost *everything!* I wish they'd *tie* those bankers up, and put 'em in jail forever!
Hm...
11
Don't forget about all the legal *loopholes* here. Even if you could tie the rascals up, unless the *knots* were mighty tight, they'd just *wriggle free*!
Y. Kiyama
12

The Panama Pacific International Exposition

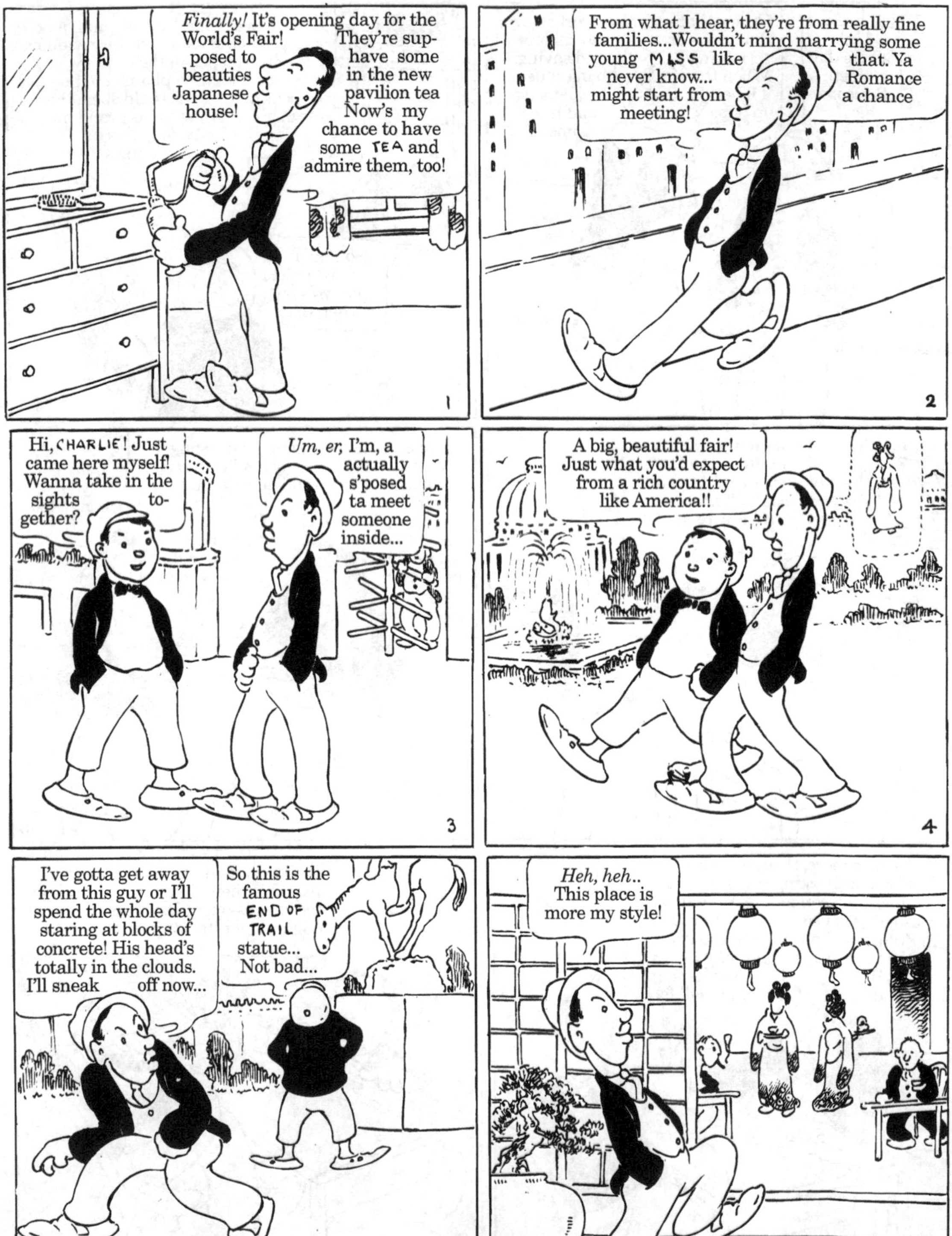
Finally! It's opening day for the World's Fair! They're supposed to have some beauties in the new Japanese pavilion tea house! Now's my chance to have some TEA and admire them, too!
From what I hear, they're from really fine families...Wouldn't mind marrying some young MISS like that. Ya never know... Romance might start from a chance meeting!
Hi, CHARLIE! Just came here myself! Wanna take in the sights together?
Um, er, I'm, a actually s'posed ta meet someone inside...
A big, beautiful fair! Just what you'd expect from a rich country like America!!
I've gotta get away from this guy or I'll spend the whole day staring at blocks of concrete! His head's totally in the clouds. I'll sneak off now...
So this is the famous END OF TRAIL statue... Not bad...
Heh, heh.. This place is more my style!

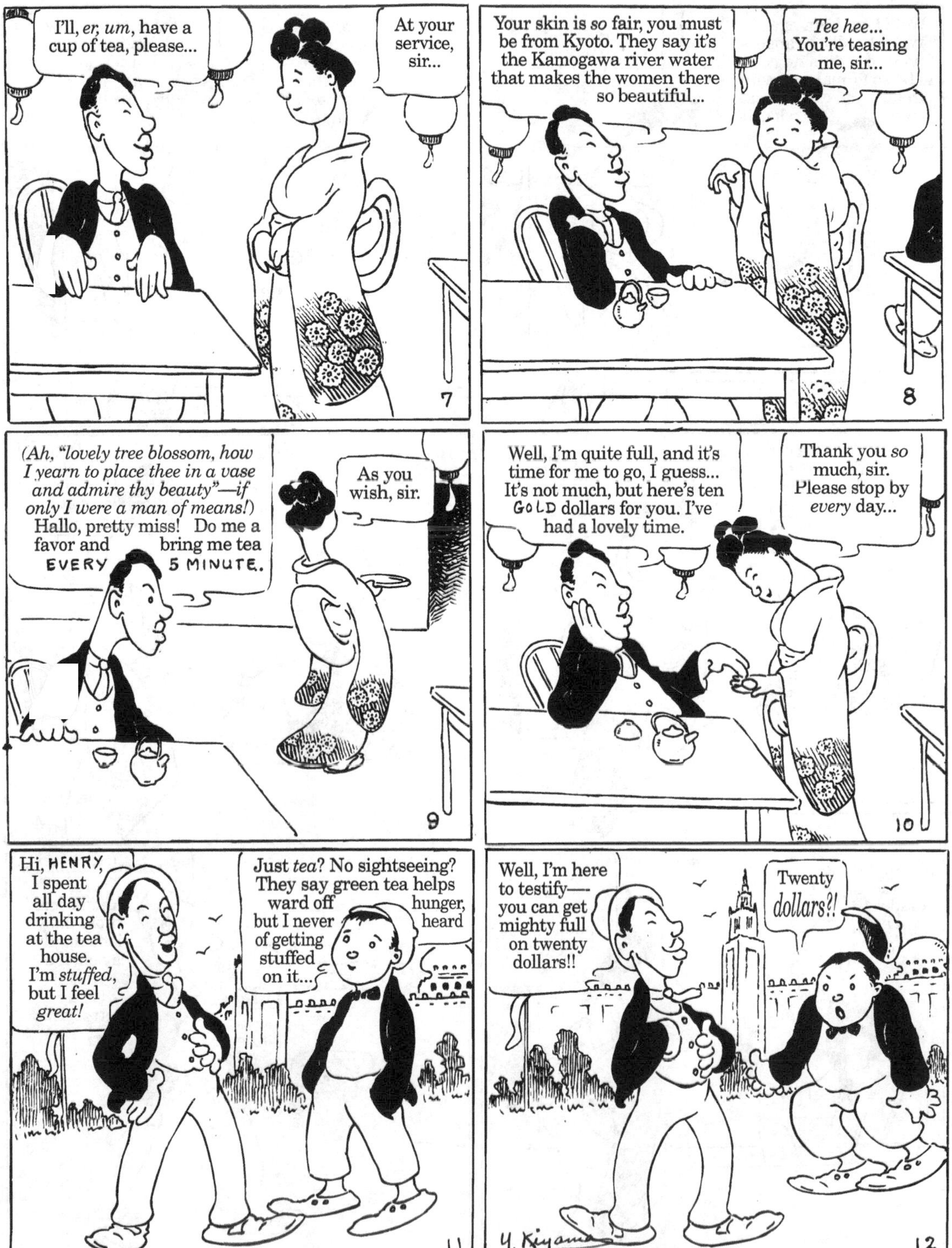
I'll, *er, um*, have a cup of tea, please...
At your service, sir...
7
Your skin is *so* fair, you must be from Kyoto. They say it's the Kamogawa river water that makes the women there so beautiful...
Tee hee... You're teasing me, sir...
8
(*Ah, "lovely tree blossom, how I yearn to place thee in a vase and admire thy beauty"—if only I were a man of means!*) Hallo, pretty miss! Do me a favor and bring me tea EVERY 5 MINUTE.
As you wish, sir.
9
Well, I'm quite full, and it's time for me to go, I guess... It's not much, but here's ten GOLD dollars for you. I've had a lovely time.
Thank you *so* much, sir. Please stop by *every* day...
10
Hi, HENRY, I spent all day drinking at the tea house. I'm *stuffed*, but I feel *great!*
Just *tea*? No sightseeing? They say green tea helps ward off hunger, but I never heard of getting stuffed on it...
11
Well, I'm here to testify— you can get mighty full on twenty dollars!!
Twenty *dollars?!*
Y. Kiyama
12

The Panama Pacific International Exposition

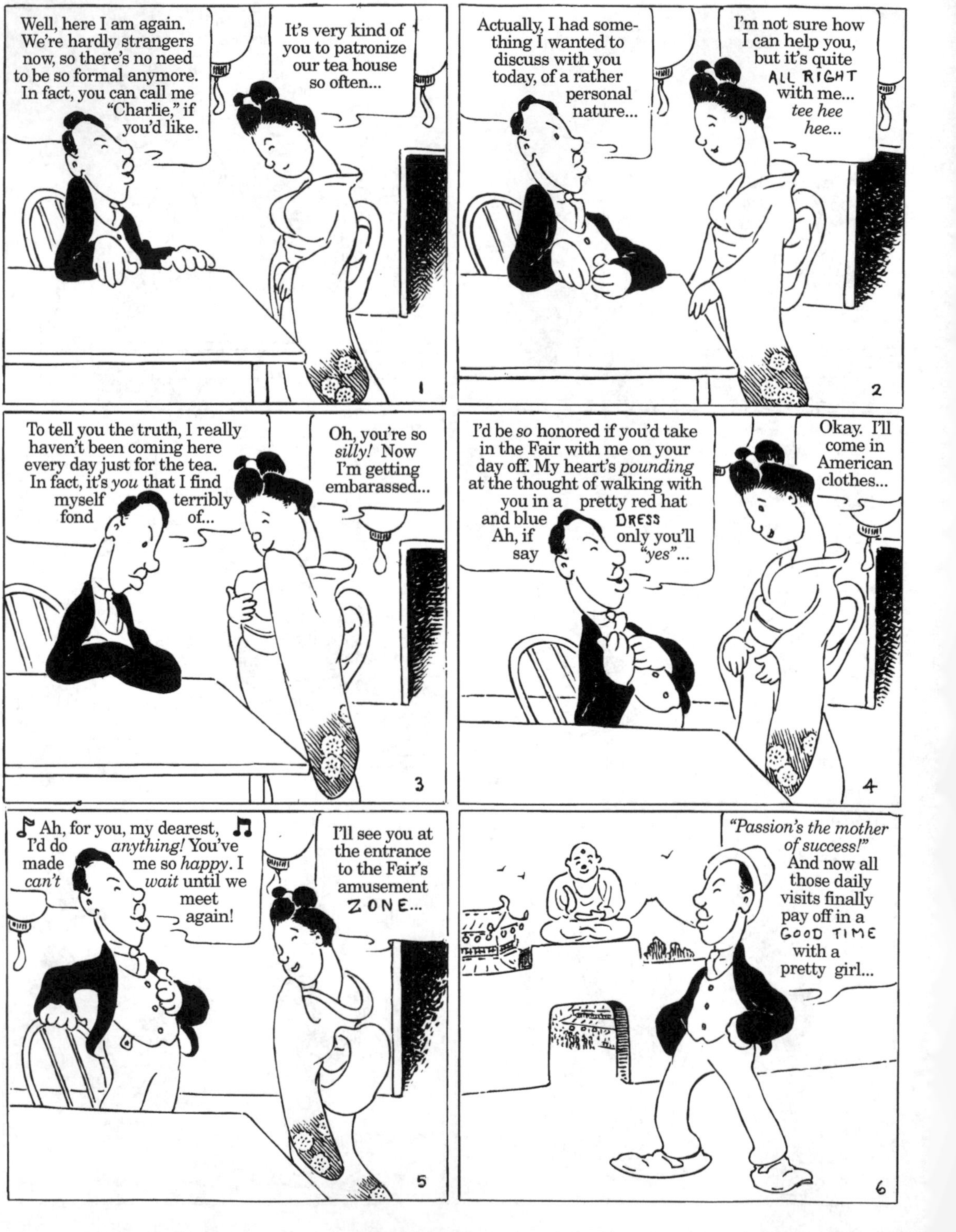
Well, here I am again. We're hardly strangers now, so there's no need to be so formal anymore. In fact, you can call me "Charlie," if you'd like.
It's very kind of you to patronize our tea house so often...
1
Actually, I had something I wanted to discuss with you today, of a rather personal nature...
I'm not sure how I can help you, but it's quite ALL RIGHT with me... *tee hee hee...*
2
To tell you the truth, I really haven't been coming here every day just for the tea. In fact, it's *you* that I find myself terribly fond of...
Oh, you're so *silly!* Now I'm getting embarassed...
3
I'd be *so* honored if you'd take in the Fair with me on your day off. My heart's *pounding* at the thought of walking with you in a pretty red hat and blue DRESS Ah, if only you'll say *"yes"*...
Okay. I'll come in American clothes...
4
Ah, for you, my dearest, I'd do *anything!* You've made me so *happy*. I *can't wait* until we meet again!
I'll see you at the entrance to the Fair's amusement ZONE...
5
"Passion's the mother of success!" And now all those daily visits finally pay off in a GOOD TIME with a pretty girl...
6

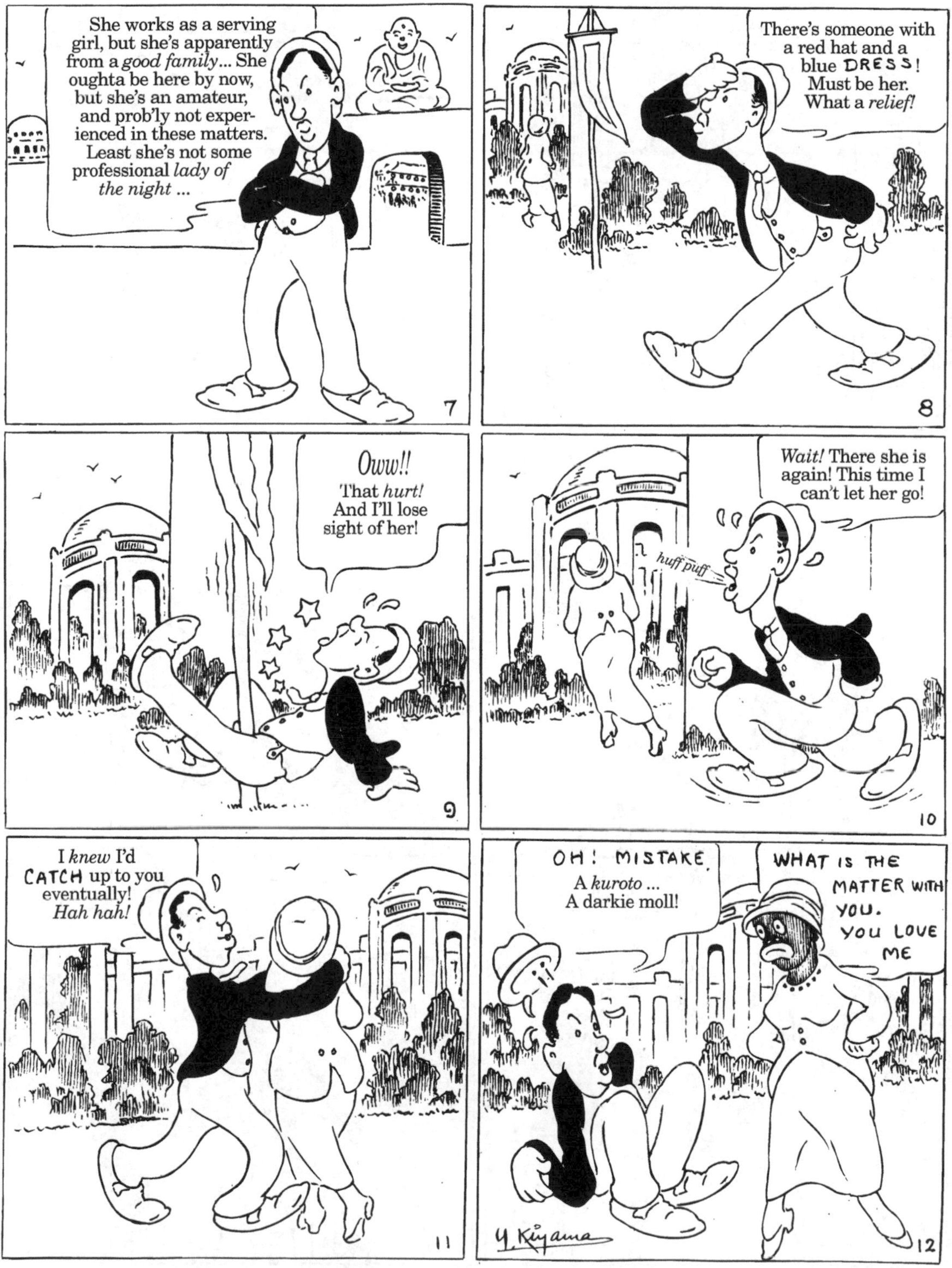

She works as a serving girl, but she's apparently from a *good family*... She oughta be here by now, but she's an amateur, and prob'ly not experienced in these matters. Least she's not some professional *lady of the night* ...
7
There's someone with a red hat and a blue DRESS! Must be her. What a *relief!*
8
Oww!! That *hurt!* And I'll lose sight of her!
9
Wait! There she is again! This time I can't let her go!
huff puff
10
I *knew* I'd CATCH up to you eventually! *Hah hah!*
11
OH! MISTAKE. A *kuroto* ... A darkie moll!
WHAT IS THE MATTER WITH YOU. YOU LOVE ME
Y. Kiyama
12

The Panama Pacific International Exposition

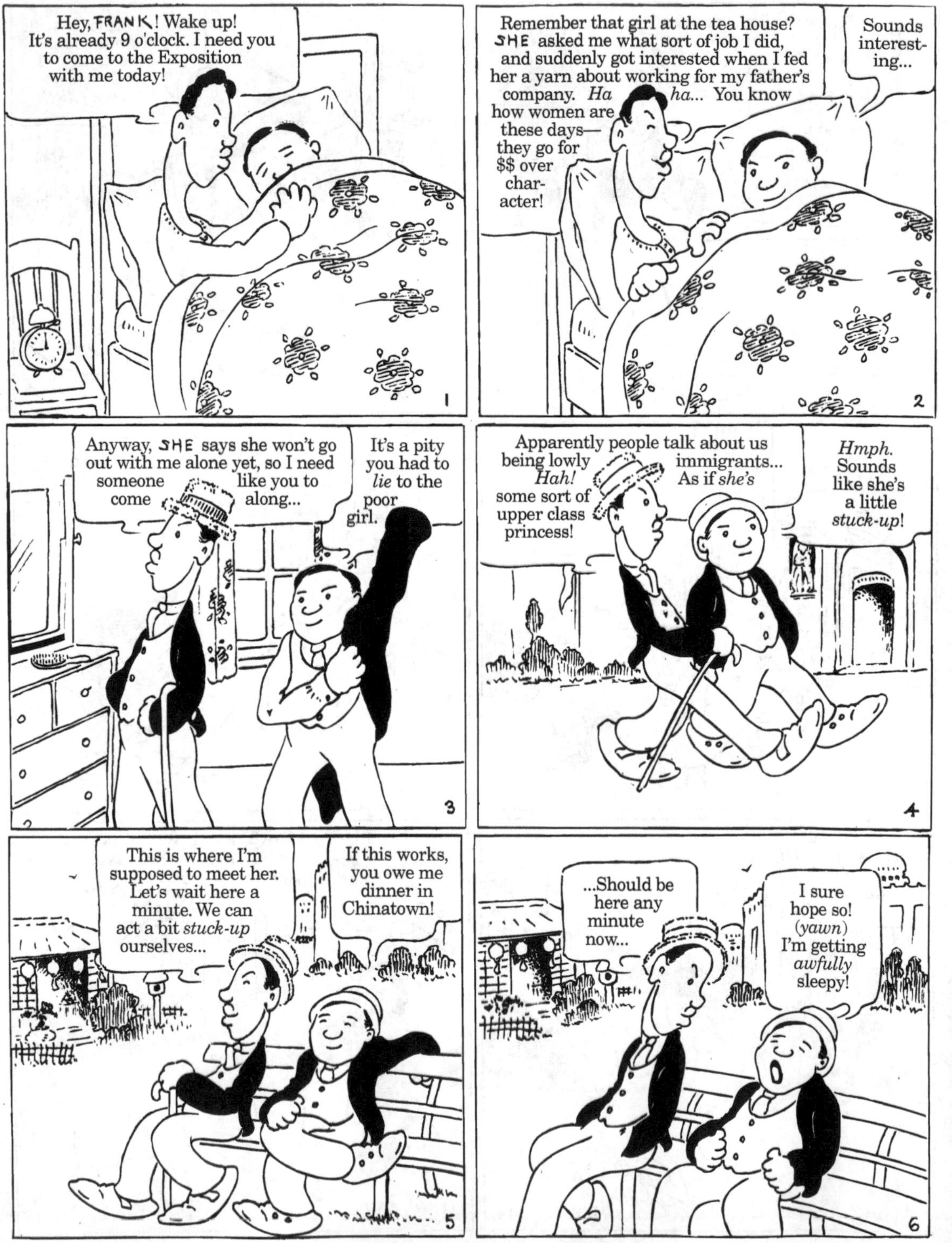
Hey, FRANK! Wake up! It's already 9 o'clock. I need you to come to the Exposition with me today!
1
Remember that girl at the tea house? SHE asked me what sort of job I did, and suddenly got interested when I fed her a yarn about working for my father's company. *Ha ha...* You know how women are these days— they go for $$ over char-acter!
Sounds interest-ing...
2
Anyway, SHE says she won't go out with me alone yet, so I need someone like you to come along...
It's a pity you had to *lie* to the poor girl.
3
Apparently people talk about us being lowly immigrants... *Hah!* As if *she's* some sort of upper class princess!
Hmph. Sounds like she's a little *stuck-up*!
4
This is where I'm supposed to meet her. Let's wait here a minute. We can act a bit *stuck-up* ourselves...
If this works, you owe me dinner in Chinatown!
5
...Should be here any minute now...
I sure hope so! (*yawn*) I'm getting *awfully* sleepy!
6

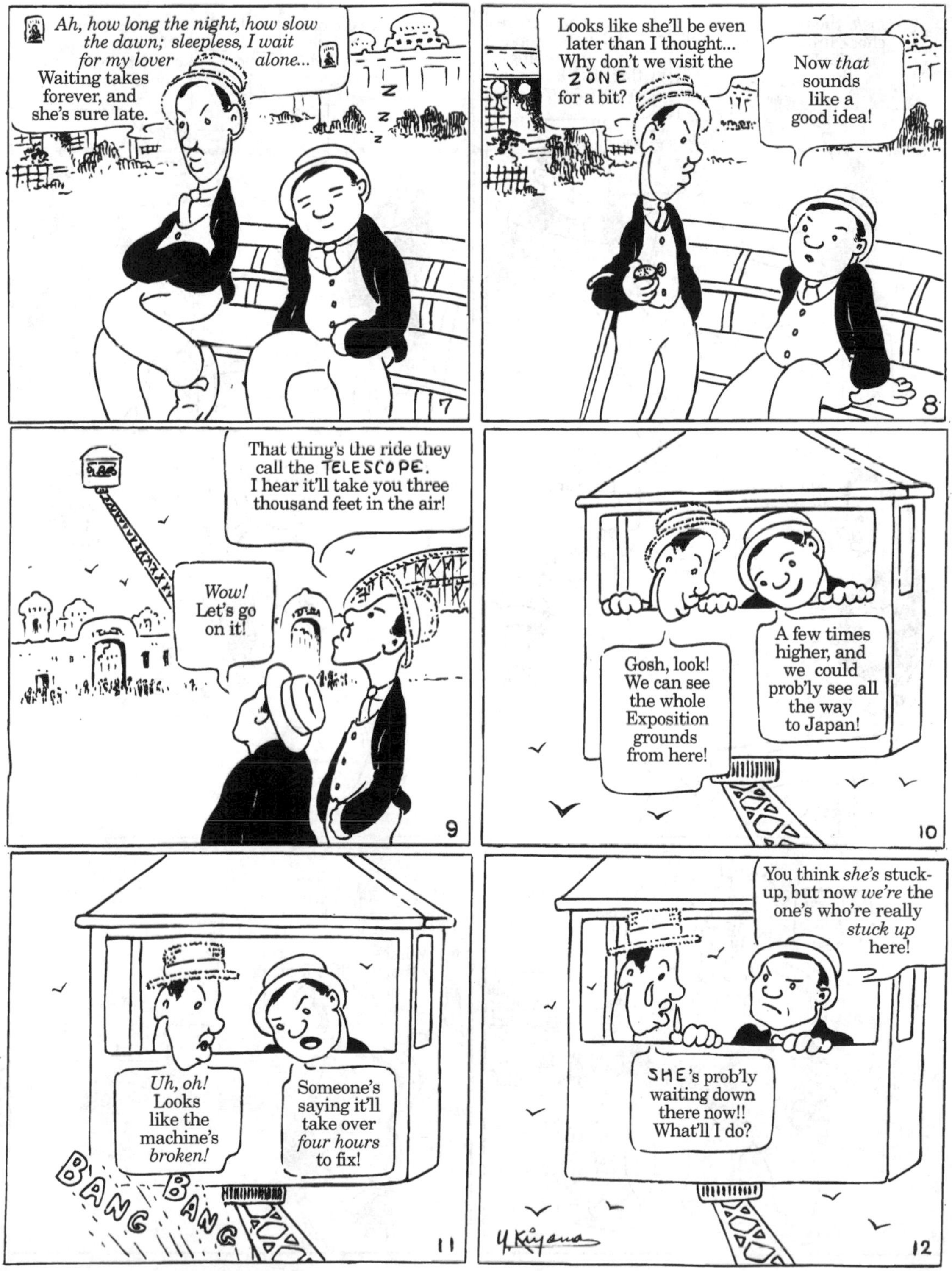
Ah, how long the night, how slow the dawn; sleepless, I wait for my lover alone...
Waiting takes forever, and she's sure late.
7
Looks like she'll be even later than I thought... Why don't we visit the ZONE for a bit?
Now that sounds like a good idea!
8
That thing's the ride they call the TELESCOPE. I hear it'll take you three thousand feet in the air!
Wow! Let's go on it!
9
Gosh, look! We can see the whole Exposition grounds from here!
A few times higher, and we could prob'ly see all the way to Japan!
10
Uh, oh! Looks like the machine's broken!
Someone's saying it'll take over four hours to fix!
BANG BANG
11
SHE's prob'ly waiting down there now!! What'll I do?
You think she's stuck-up, but now we're the one's who're really stuck up here!
Y. Kiyama
12

EPISODE 35

The Panama Pacific International Exposition

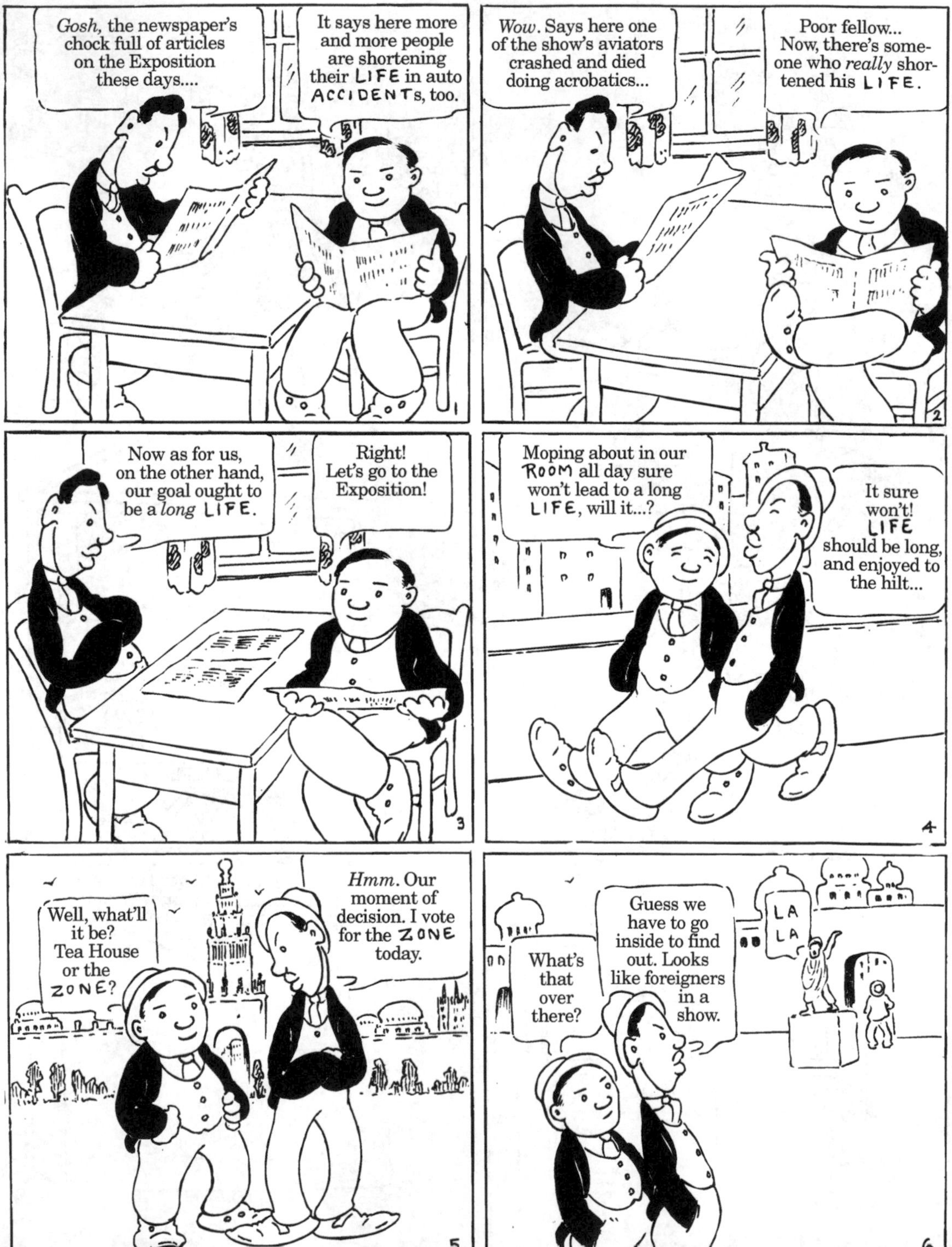

Gosh, the newspaper's chock full of articles on the Exposition these days....
It says here more and more people are shortening their LIFE in auto ACCIDENTs, too.
Wow. Says here one of the show's aviators crashed and died doing acrobatics...
Poor fellow... Now, there's someone who *really* shortened his LIFE.
Now as for us, on the other hand, our goal ought to be a *long* LIFE.
Right! Let's go to the Exposition!
Moping about in our ROOM all day sure won't lead to a long LIFE, will it...?
It sure won't! LIFE should be long, and enjoyed to the hilt...
Well, what'll it be? Tea House or the ZONE?
Hmm. Our moment of decision. I vote for the ZONE today.
What's that over there?
Guess we have to go inside to find out. Looks like foreigners in a show.
LA LA

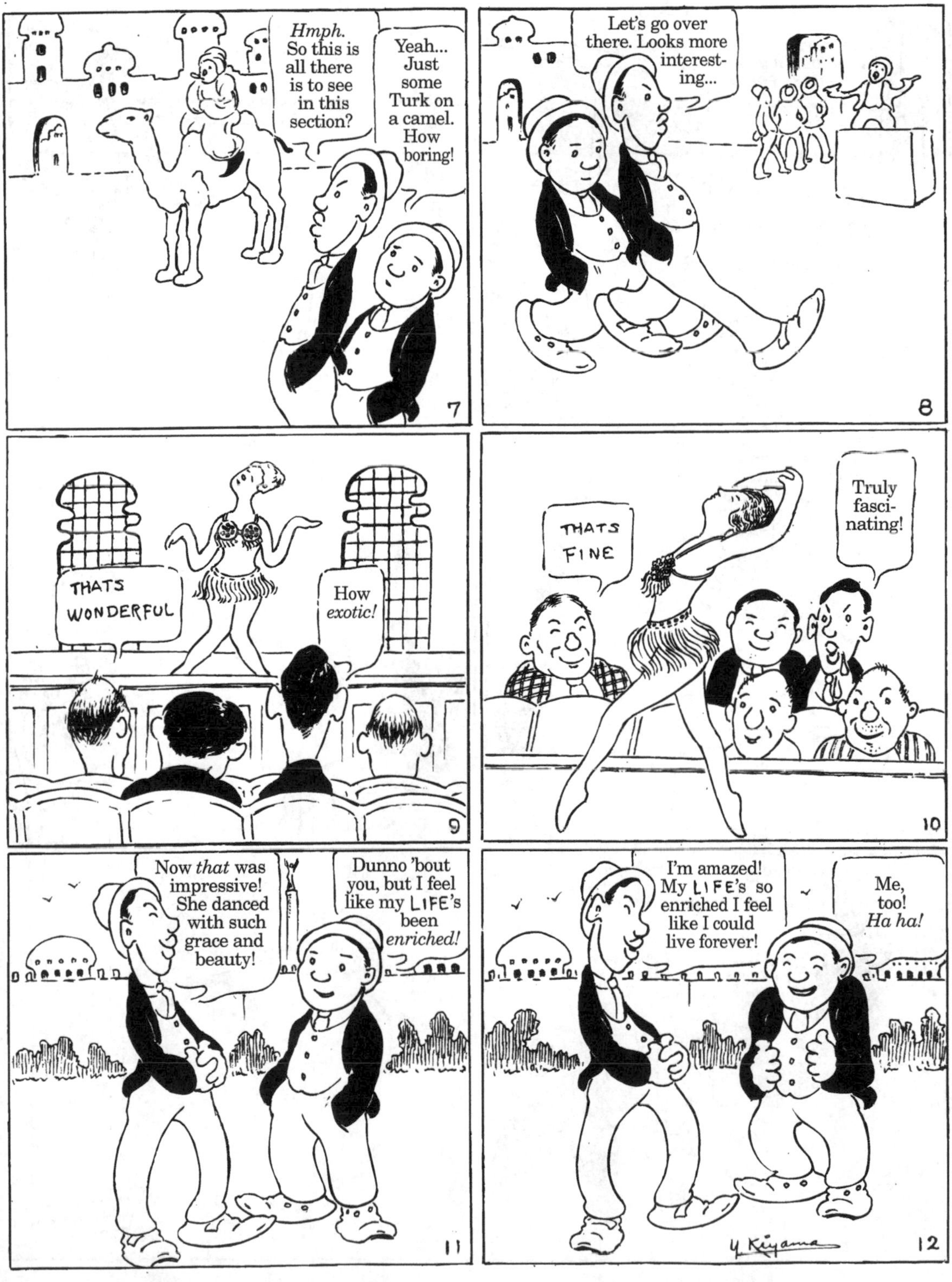
Hmph. So this is all there is to see in this section?
Yeah... Just some Turk on a camel. How boring!
7
Let's go over there. Looks more interesting...
8
THATS WONDERFUL
How *exotic!*
9
THATS FINE
Truly fascinating!
10
Now *that* was impressive! She danced with such grace and beauty!
Dunno 'bout you, but I feel like my LIFE's been *enriched!*
11
I'm amazed! My LIFE's so enriched I feel like I could live forever!
Me, too! *Ha ha!*
Y. Kiyama
12

EPISODE 36

The Rice of Colusa

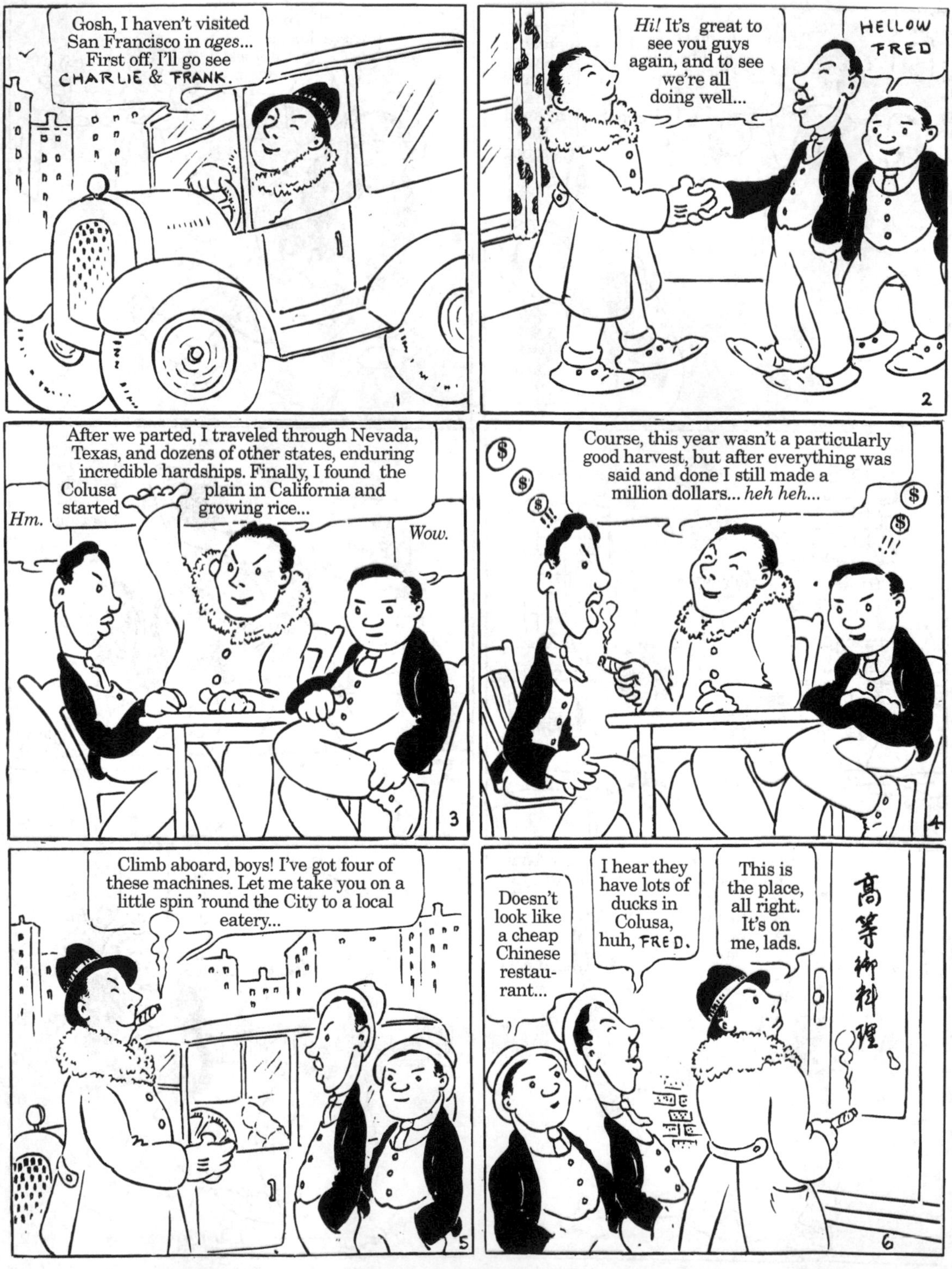
Gosh, I haven't visited San Francisco in *ages*... First off, I'll go see CHARLIE & FRANK.
1
Hi! It's great to see you guys again, and to see we're all doing well...
HELLOW FRED
2
Hm.
After we parted, I traveled through Nevada, Texas, and dozens of other states, enduring incredible hardships. Finally, I found the Colusa plain in California and started growing rice...
Wow.
3
Course, this year wasn't a particularly good harvest, but after everything was said and done I still made a million dollars... *heh heh*...
!!!
!!!
4
Climb aboard, boys! I've got four of these machines. Let me take you on a little spin 'round the City to a local eatery...
5
Doesn't look like a cheap Chinese restaurant...
I hear they have lots of ducks in Colusa, huh, FRED.
This is the place, all right. It's on me, lads.
高等御料理
6

Sign: *High Class Japanese Restaurant*

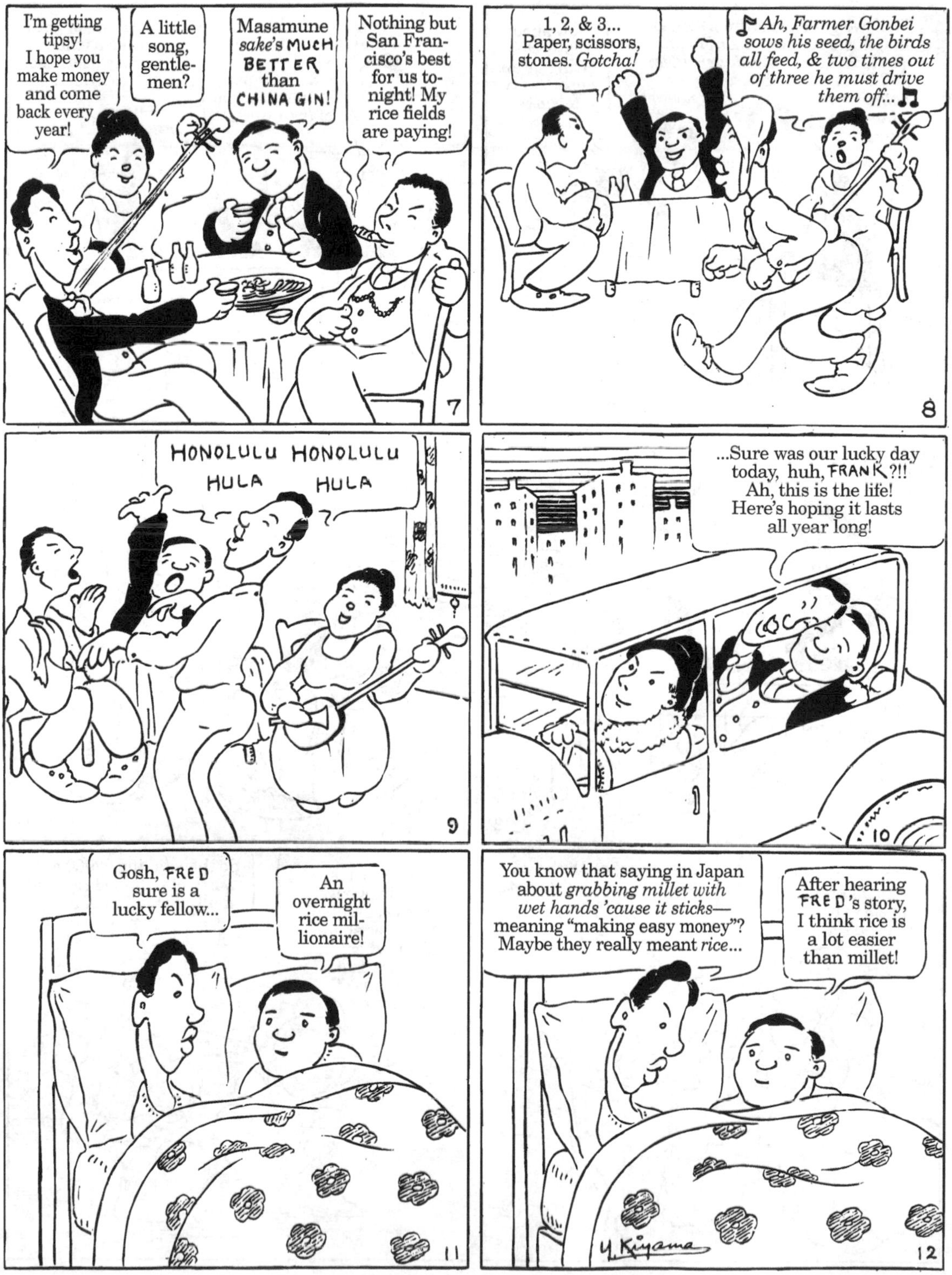
I'm getting tipsy! I hope you make money and come back every year!
A little song, gentlemen?
Masamune *sake*'s MUCH BETTER than CHINA GIN!
Nothing but San Francisco's best for us tonight! My rice fields are paying!
7
1, 2, & 3... Paper, scissors, stones. *Gotcha!*
♪ *Ah, Farmer Gonbei sows his seed, the birds all feed, & two times out of three he must drive them off...* ♫
8
HONOLULU HONOLULU HULA HULA
9
...Sure was our lucky day today, huh, FRANK?!! Ah, this is the life! Here's hoping it lasts all year long!
10
Gosh, FRED sure is a lucky fellow...
An overnight rice millionaire!
11
You know that saying in Japan about *grabbing millet with wet hands 'cause it sticks*—meaning "making easy money"? Maybe they really meant *rice*...
After hearing FRED's story, I think rice is a lot easier than millet!
Y. Kiyama
12

The Rice of Colusa

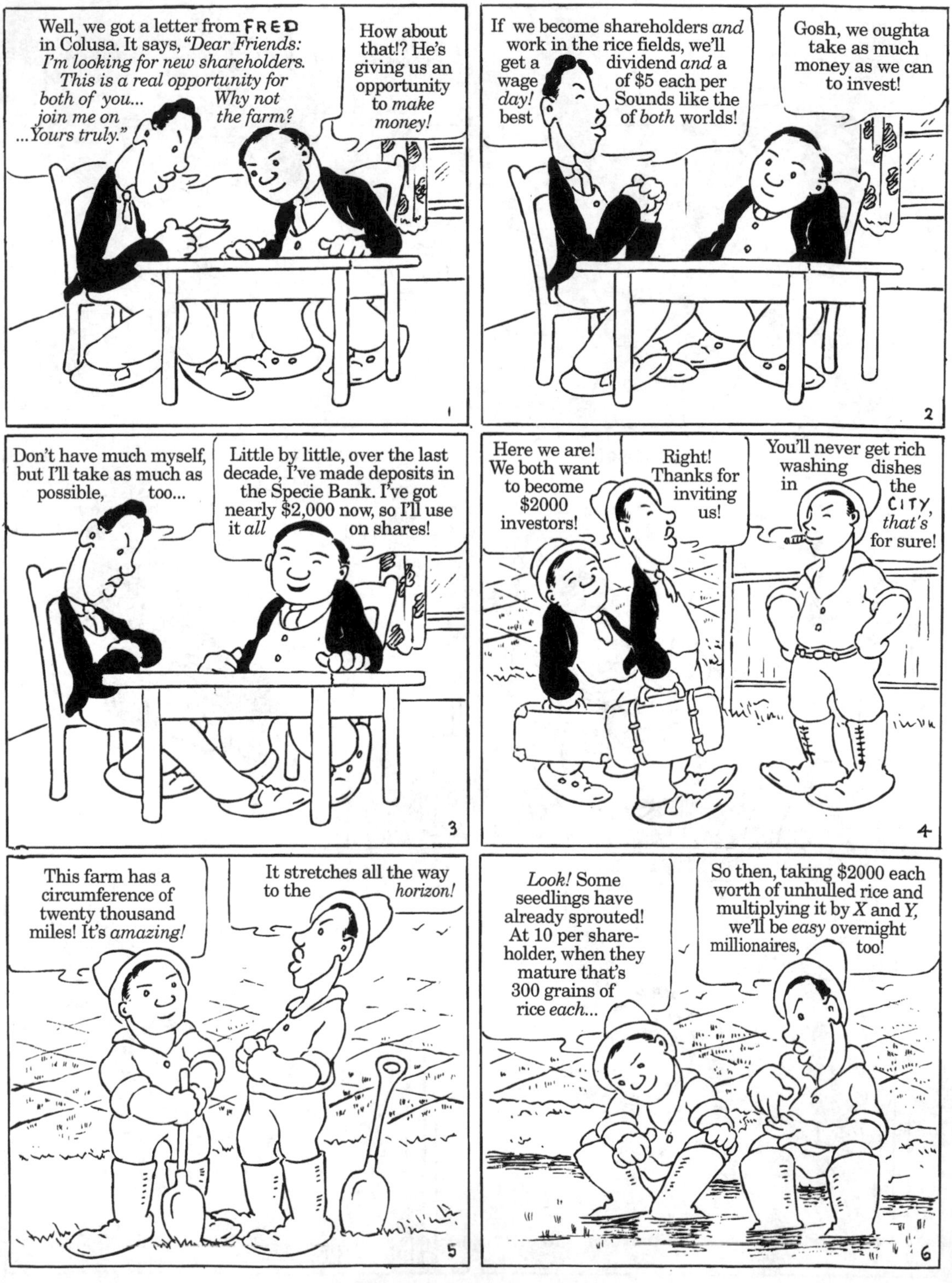
Well, we got a letter from FRED in Colusa. It says, "*Dear Friends: I'm looking for new shareholders. This is a real opportunity for both of you... Why not join me on the farm? ...Yours truly.*"
How about that!? He's giving us an opportunity to *make money!*
If we become shareholders *and* work in the rice fields, we'll get a dividend *and* a wage of $5 each per *day!* Sounds like the best of *both* worlds!
Gosh, we oughta take as much money as we can to invest!
Don't have much myself, but I'll take as much as possible, too...
Little by little, over the last decade, I've made deposits in the Specie Bank. I've got nearly $2,000 now, so I'll use it *all* on shares!
Here we are! We both want to become $2000 investors!
Right! Thanks for inviting us!
You'll never get rich washing dishes in the CITY, *that's* for sure!
This farm has a circumference of twenty thousand miles! It's *amazing!*
It stretches all the way to the *horizon!*
Look! Some seedlings have already sprouted! At 10 per shareholder, when they mature that's 300 grains of rice *each...*
So then, taking $2000 each worth of unhulled rice and multiplying it by *X* and *Y,* we'll be *easy* overnight millionaires, too!

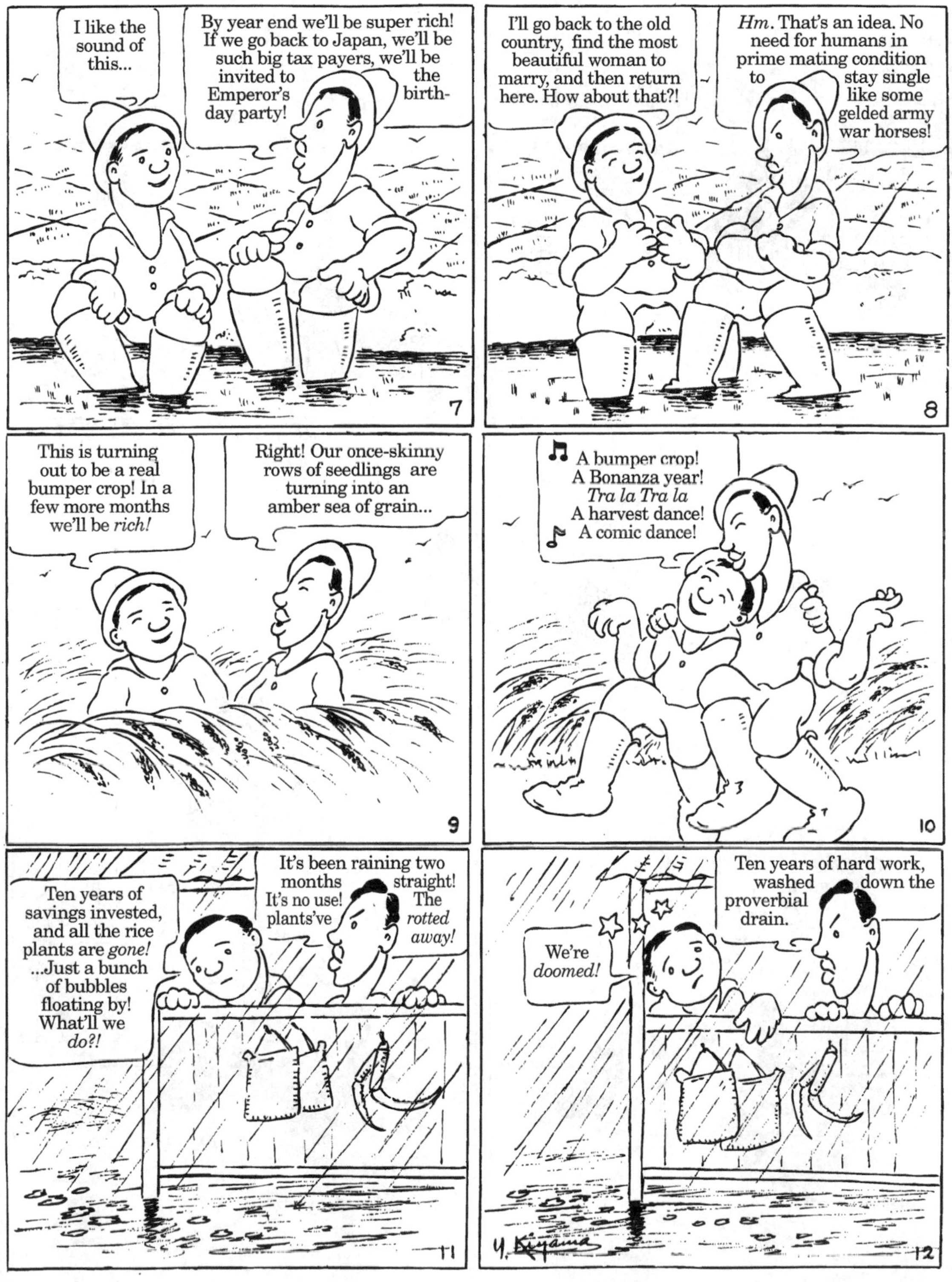
I like the sound of this...
By year end we'll be super rich! If we go back to Japan, we'll be such big tax payers, we'll be invited to the Emperor's birthday party!
7
I'll go back to the old country, find the most beautiful woman to marry, and then return here. How about that?!
Hm. That's an idea. No need for humans in prime mating condition to stay single like some gelded army war horses!
8
This is turning out to be a real bumper crop! In a few more months we'll be *rich!*
Right! Our once-skinny rows of seedlings are turning into an amber sea of grain...
9
A bumper crop! A Bonanza year! *Tra la Tra la* A harvest dance! A comic dance!
10
Ten years of savings invested, and all the rice plants are *gone!* ...Just a bunch of bubbles floating by! What'll we *do?!*
It's been raining two months straight! It's no use! The plants've *rotted away!*
11
We're *doomed!*
Ten years of hard work, washed down the proverbial drain.
Y. Kiyama
12

EPISODE 38

The Rice of Colusa

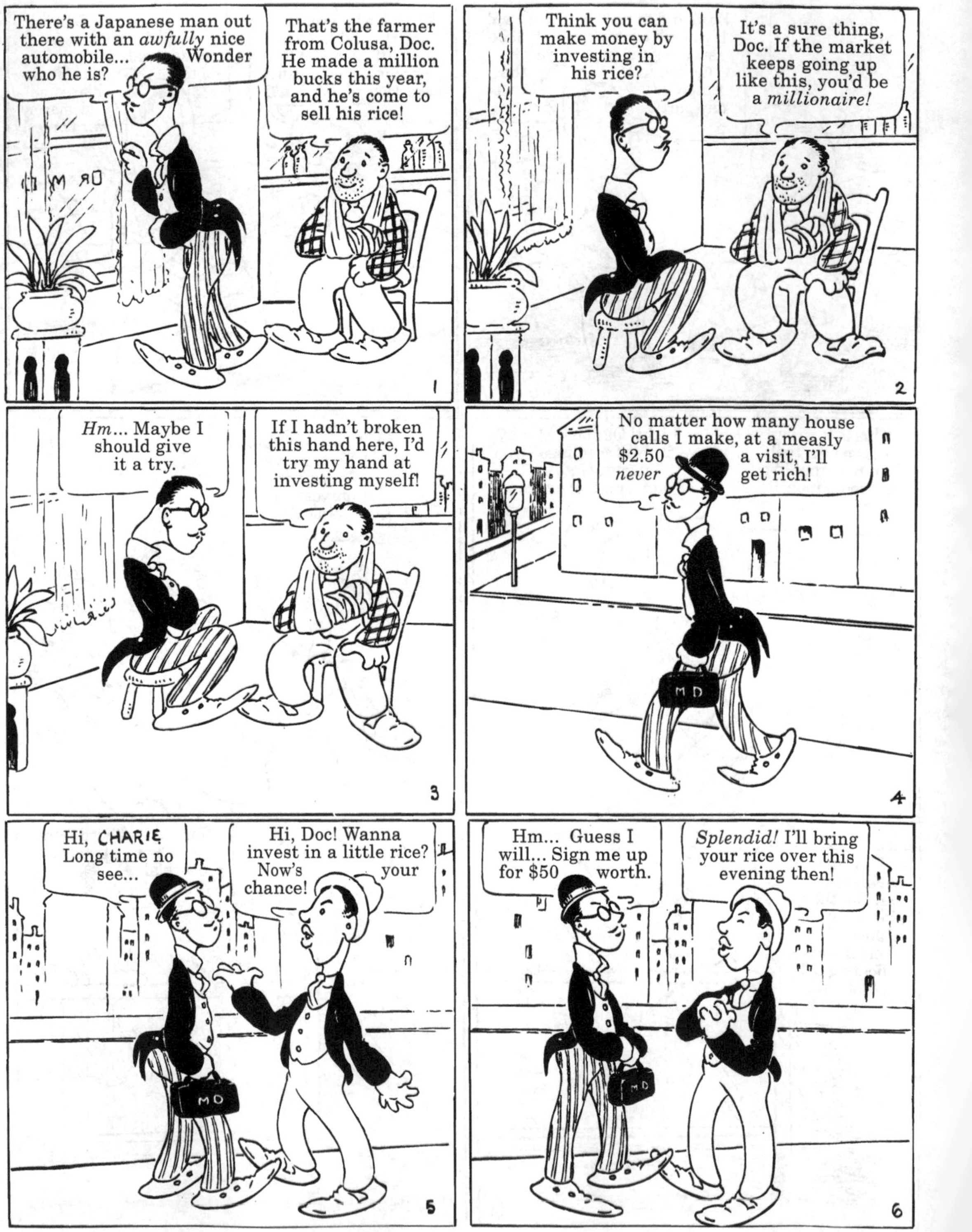

There's a Japanese man out there with an *awfully* nice automobile... Wonder who he is?
That's the farmer from Colusa, Doc. He made a million bucks this year, and he's come to sell his rice!
DR M
1
Think you can make money by investing in his rice?
It's a sure thing, Doc. If the market keeps going up like this, you'd be a *millionaire!*
2
Hm... Maybe I should give it a try.
If I hadn't broken this hand here, I'd try my hand at investing myself!
3
No matter how many house calls I make, at a measly $2.50 a visit, I'll *never* get rich!
MD
4
Hi, CHARIE Long time no see...
Hi, Doc! Wanna invest in a little rice? Now's your chance!
MD
5
Hm... Guess I will... Sign me up for $50 worth.
Splendid! I'll bring your rice over this evening then!
MD
6

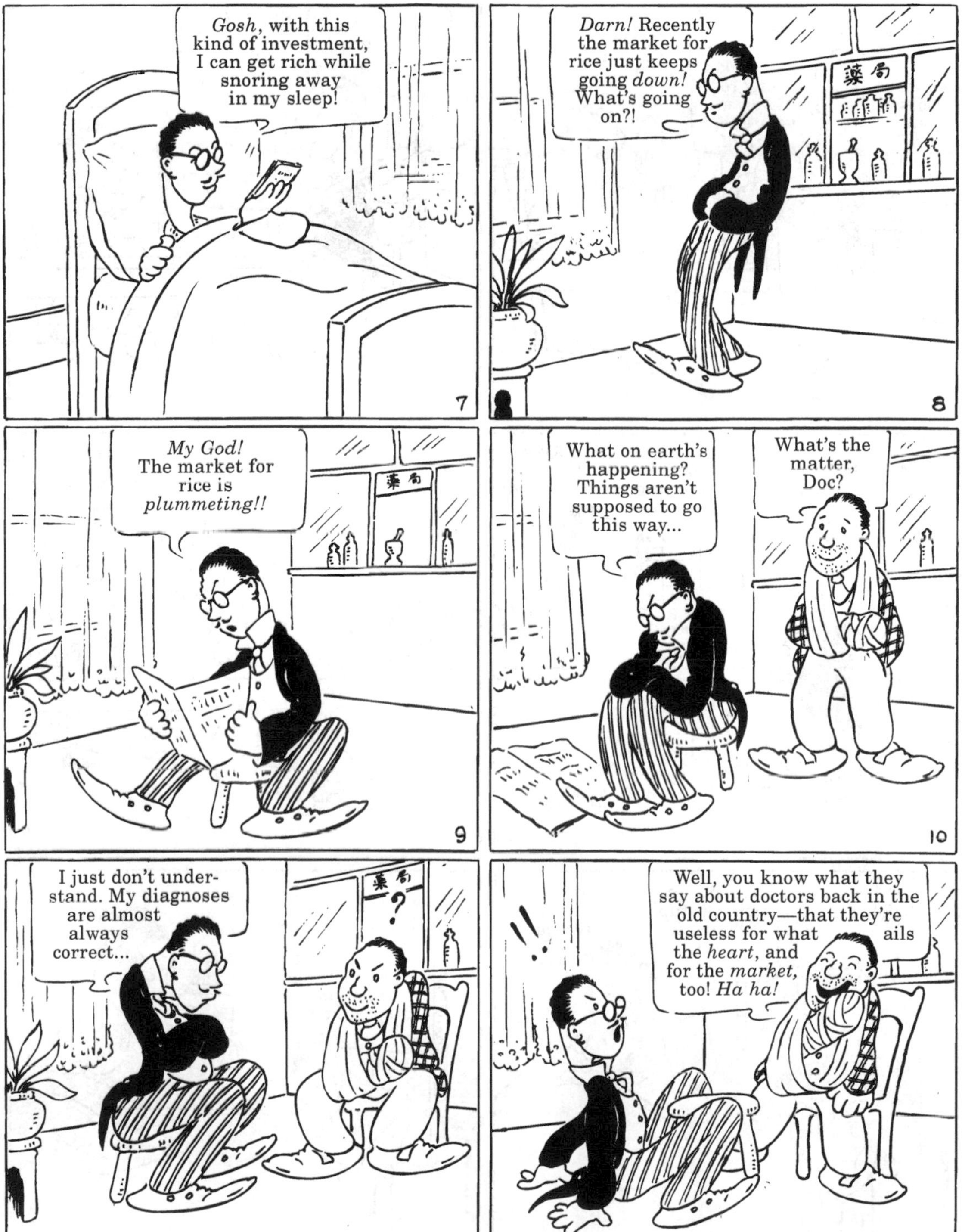
Gosh, with this kind of investment, I can get rich while snoring away in my sleep!
7
Darn! Recently the market for rice just keeps going *down!* What's going on?!
藥局
8
My God! The market for rice is *plummeting!!*
藥局
9
What on earth's happening? Things aren't supposed to go this way...
What's the matter, Doc?
10
I just don't understand. My diagnoses are almost always correct...
藥局
?
11
!!
Well, you know what they say about doctors back in the old country—that they're useless for what ails the *heart*, and for the *market*, too! *Ha ha!*
Y. Kiyama
12

Sign on wall window: *Pharmacy*

EPISODE 39

The Rice of Colusa

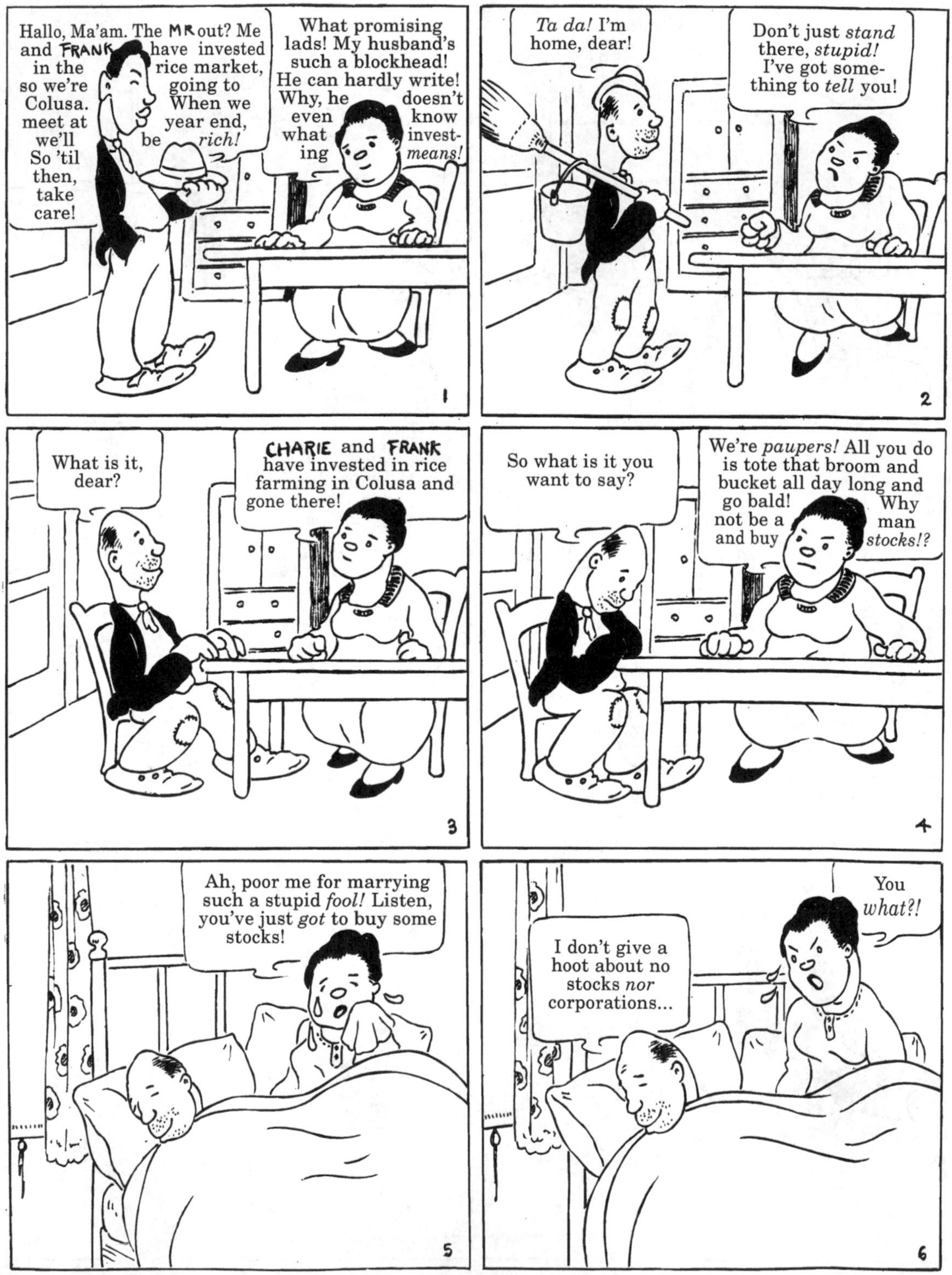
Hallo, Ma'am. The MR out? Me and FRANK have invested in the rice market, so we're going to Colusa. When we meet at year end, we'll be *rich!* So 'til then, take care!
What promising lads! My husband's such a blockhead! He can hardly write! Why, he doesn't even know what investing *means!*
Ta da! I'm home, dear!
Don't just *stand* there, *stupid!* I've got something to *tell* you!
What is it, dear?
CHARIE and FRANK have invested in rice farming in Colusa and gone there!
So what is it you want to say?
We're *paupers!* All you do is tote that broom and bucket all day long and go bald! Why not be a man and buy *stocks!?*
Ah, poor me for marrying such a stupid *fool!* Listen, you've just *got* to buy some stocks!
I don't give a hoot about no stocks *nor* corporations...
You *what?!*

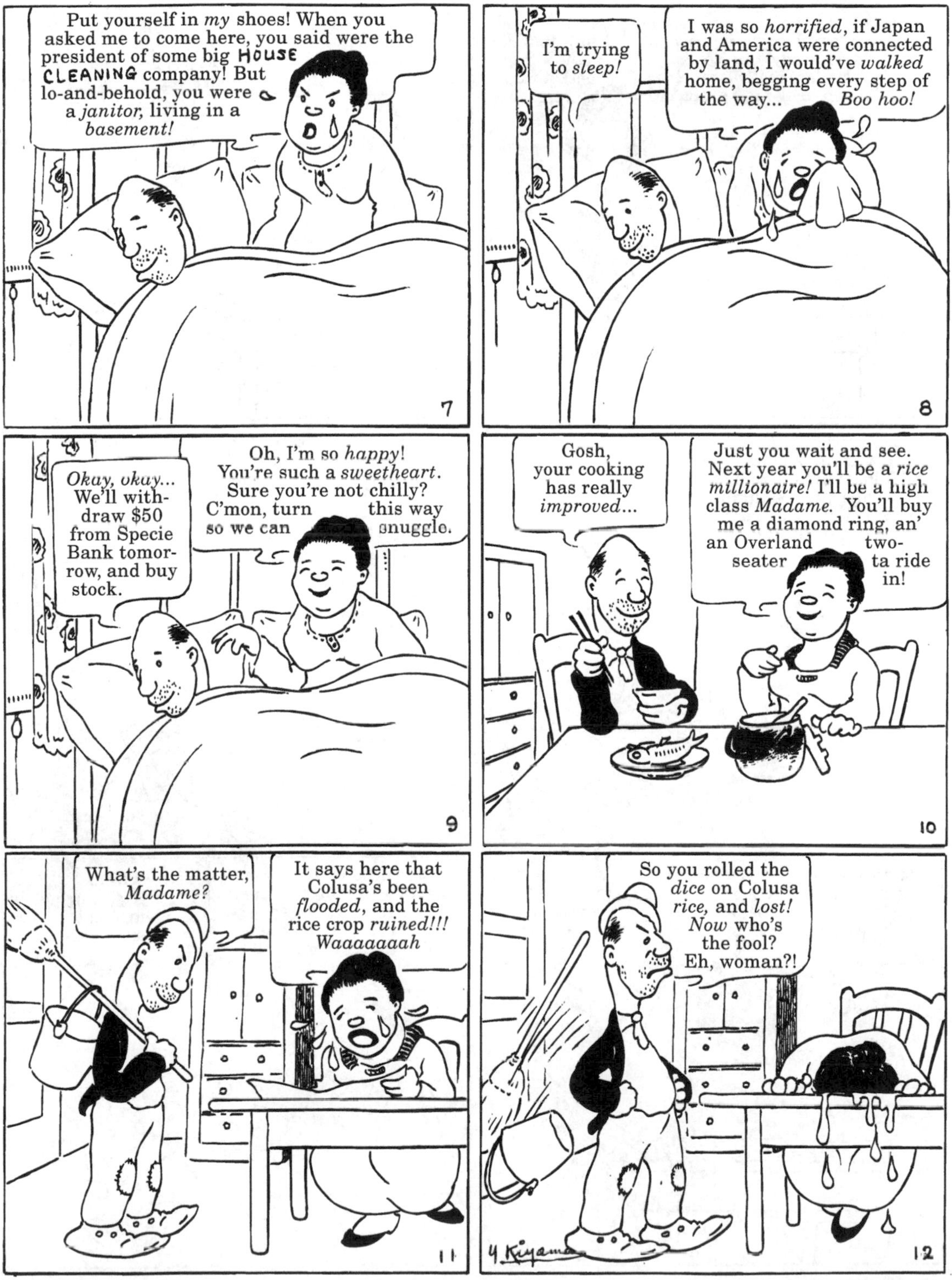
Put yourself in *my* shoes! When you asked me to come here, you said were the president of some big HOUSE CLEANING company! But lo-and-behold, you were a *janitor,* living in a *basement!*
7
I'm trying to *sleep!*
I was so *horrified*, if Japan and America were connected by land, I would've *walked* home, begging every step of the way... *Boo hoo!*
8
Okay, okay... We'll with-draw $50 from Specie Bank tomor-row, and buy stock.
Oh, I'm so *happy*! You're such a *sweetheart*. Sure you're not chilly? C'mon, turn this way so we can snuggle.
9
Gosh, your cooking has really *improved...*
Just you wait and see. Next year you'll be a *rice millionaire!* I'll be a high class *Madame.* You'll buy me a diamond ring, an' an Overland two-seater ta ride in!
10
What's the matter, *Madame?*
It says here that Colusa's been *flooded*, and the rice crop *ruined!!!* *Waaaaaaah*
11
So you rolled the *dice* on Colusa *rice,* and *lost!* *Now* who's the fool? Eh, woman?!
Y. Kiyama
12

EPISODE 40

Picture Brides

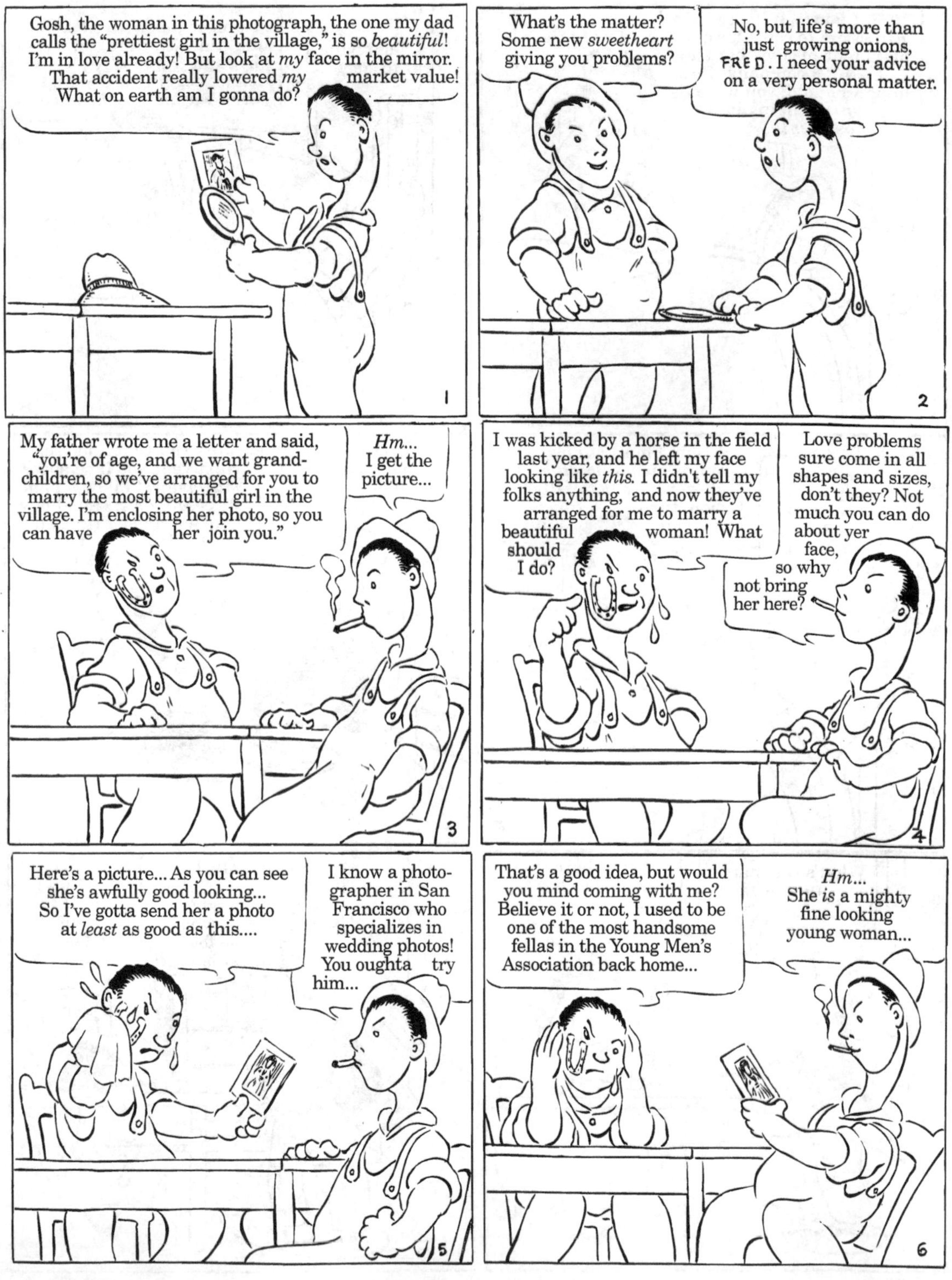
Gosh, the woman in this photograph, the one my dad calls the "prettiest girl in the village," is so *beautiful*! I'm in love already! But look at *my* face in the mirror. That accident really lowered *my* market value! What on earth am I gonna do?
1
What's the matter? Some new *sweetheart* giving you problems?
No, but life's more than just growing onions, FRED. I need your advice on a very personal matter.
2
My father wrote me a letter and said, "you're of age, and we want grand-children, so we've arranged for you to marry the most beautiful girl in the village. I'm enclosing her photo, so you can have her join you."
Hm... I get the picture...
3
I was kicked by a horse in the field last year, and he left my face looking like *this.* I didn't tell my folks anything, and now they've arranged for me to marry a beautiful woman! What should I do?
Love problems sure come in all shapes and sizes, don't they? Not much you can do about yer face, so why not bring her here?
4
Here's a picture... As you can see she's awfully good looking... So I've gotta send her a photo at *least* as good as this....
I know a photo-grapher in San Francisco who specializes in wedding photos! You oughta try him...
5
That's a good idea, but would you mind coming with me? Believe it or not, I used to be one of the most handsome fellas in the Young Men's Association back home...
Hm... She *is* a mighty fine looking young woman...
6

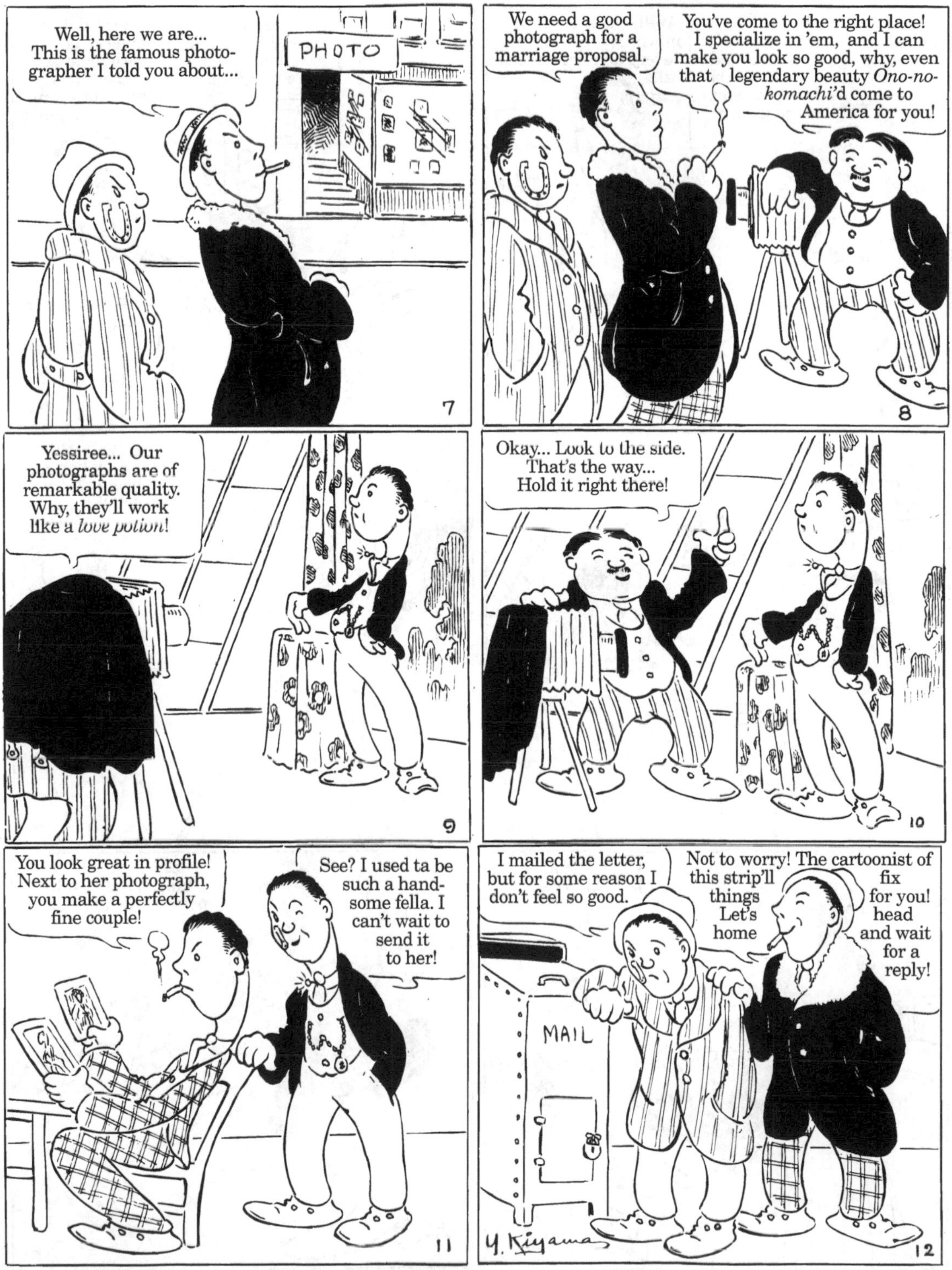
Well, here we are... This is the famous photographer I told you about...
PHOTO
7
We need a good photograph for a marriage proposal.
You've come to the right place! I specialize in 'em, and I can make you look so good, why, even that legendary beauty *Ono-no-komachi*'d come to America for you!
8
Yessiree... Our photographs are of remarkable quality. Why, they'll work like a *love potion*!
9
Okay... Look to the side. That's the way... Hold it right there!
10
You look great in profile! Next to her photograph, you make a perfectly fine couple!
See? I used ta be such a handsome fella. I can't wait to send it to her!
11
I mailed the letter, but for some reason I don't feel so good.
Not to worry! The cartoonist of this strip'll fix things for you! Let's head home and wait for a reply!
MAIL
Y. Kiyama
12

Picture Brides

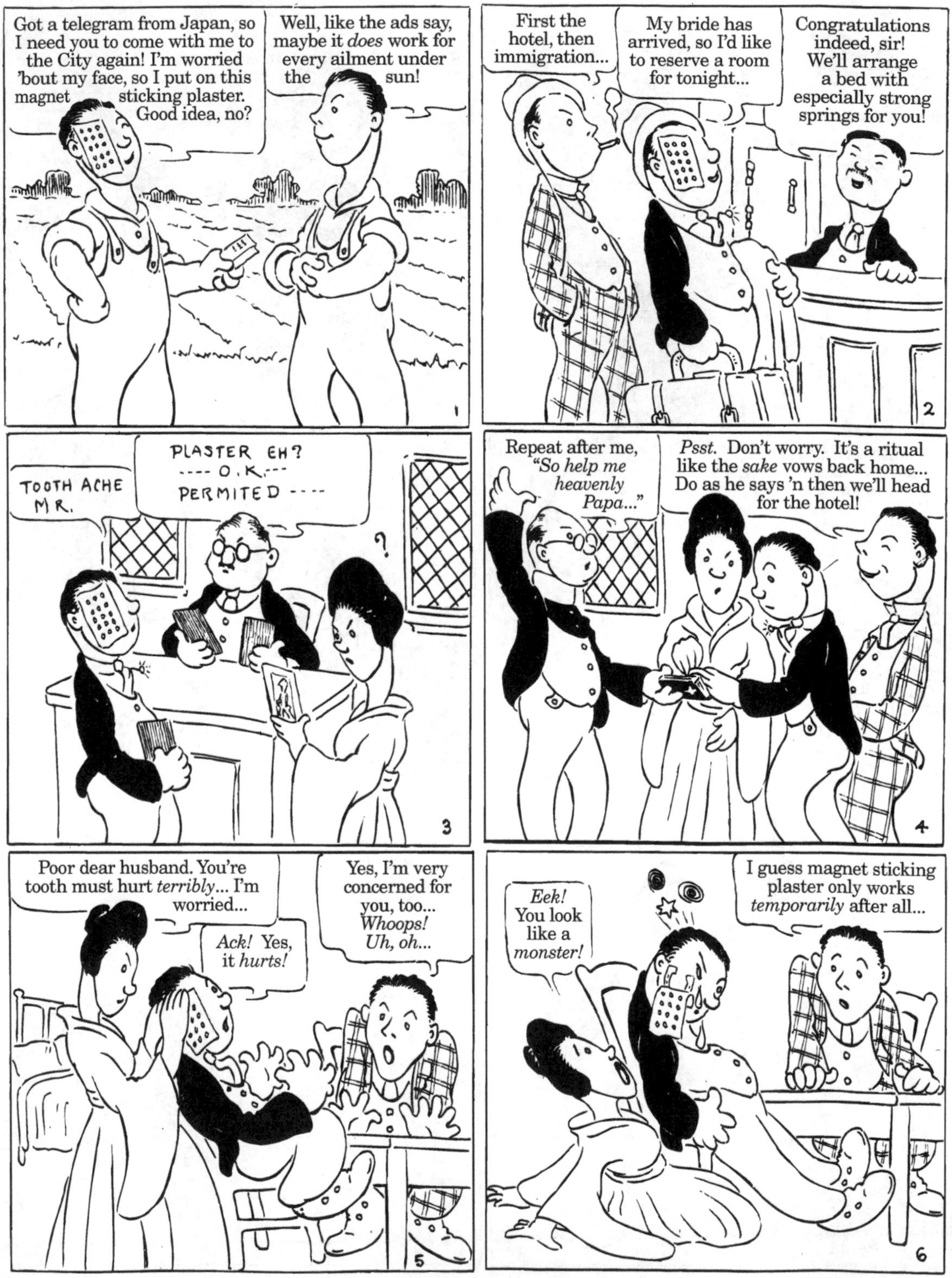
Got a telegram from Japan, so I need you to come with me to the City again! I'm worried 'bout my face, so I put on this magnet sticking plaster. Good idea, no?
Well, like the ads say, maybe it *does* work for every ailment under the sun!
1
First the hotel, then immigration...
My bride has arrived, so I'd like to reserve a room for tonight...
Congratulations indeed, sir! We'll arrange a bed with especially strong springs for you!
2
TOOTH ACHE MR.
PLASTER EH? ---- O.K.--- PERMITED ----
?
3
Repeat after me, "*So help me heavenly Papa...*"
Psst. Don't worry. It's a ritual like the *sake* vows back home... Do as he says 'n then we'll head for the hotel!
4
Poor dear husband. You're tooth must hurt *terribly*... I'm worried...
Ack! Yes, it *hurts!*
Yes, I'm very concerned for you, too... *Whoops! Uh, oh...*
5
Eek! You look like a *monster!*
I guess magnet sticking plaster only works *temporarily* after all...
6

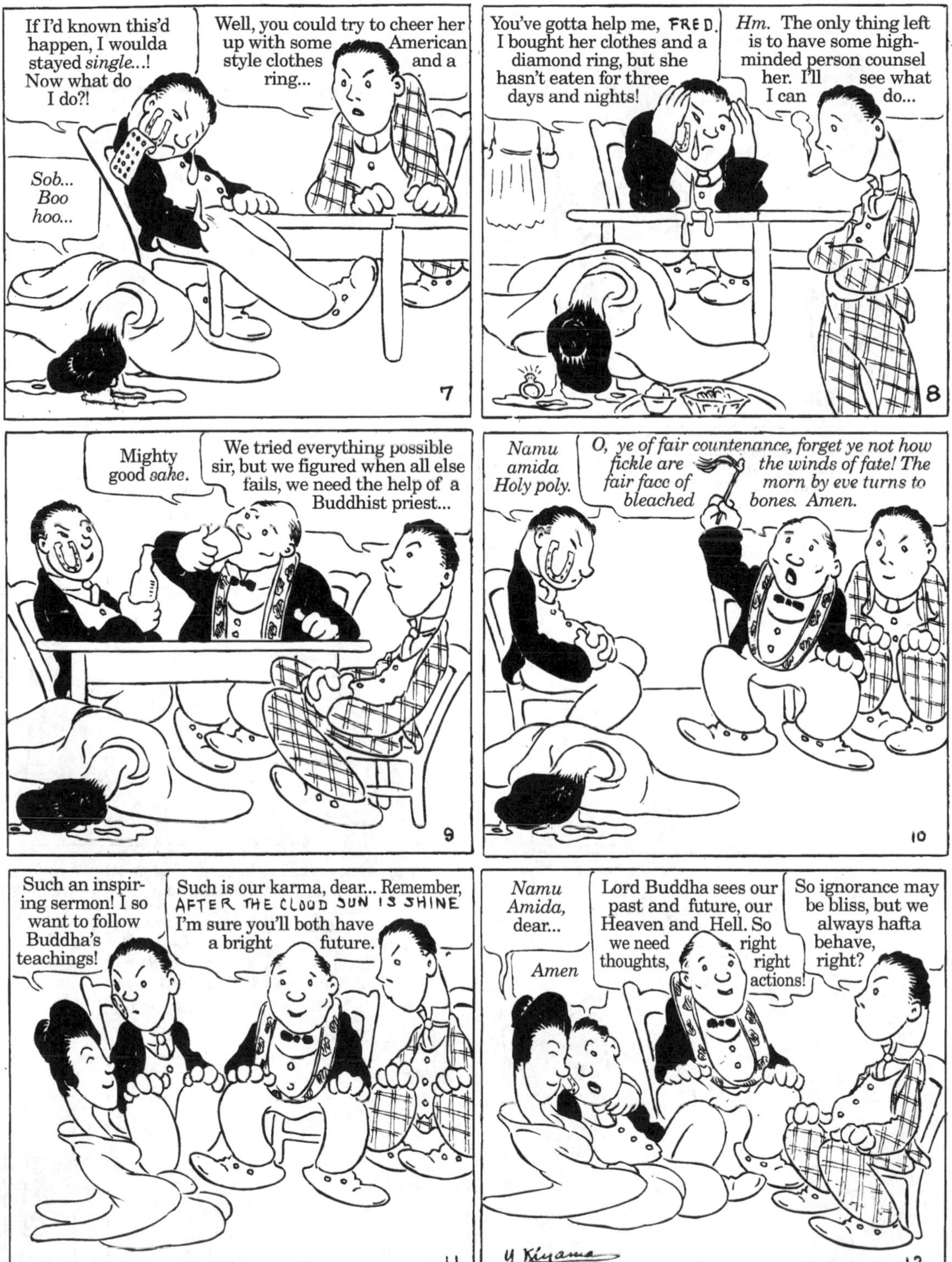

If I'd known this'd happen, I woulda stayed *single*...! Now what do I do?!
Well, you could try to cheer her up with some American style clothes and a ring...
Sob... Boo hoo...
7
You've gotta help me, FRED. I bought her clothes and a diamond ring, but she hasn't eaten for three days and nights!
Hm. The only thing left is to have some high-minded person counsel her. I'll see what I can do...
8
Mighty good *sake*.
We tried everything possible sir, but we figured when all else fails, we need the help of a Buddhist priest...
9
Namu amida Holy poly.
O, ye of fair countenance, forget ye not how fickle are the winds of fate! The fair face of morn by eve turns to bleached bones. Amen.
10
Such an inspiring sermon! I so want to follow Buddha's teachings!
Such is our karma, dear... Remember, AFTER THE CLOUD SUN IS SHINE I'm sure you'll both have a bright future.
11
Namu Amida, dear...
Amen
Lord Buddha sees our past and future, our Heaven and Hell. So we need right thoughts, right actions!
So ignorance may be bliss, but we always hafta behave, right?
Y. Kiyama
12

Picture Brides

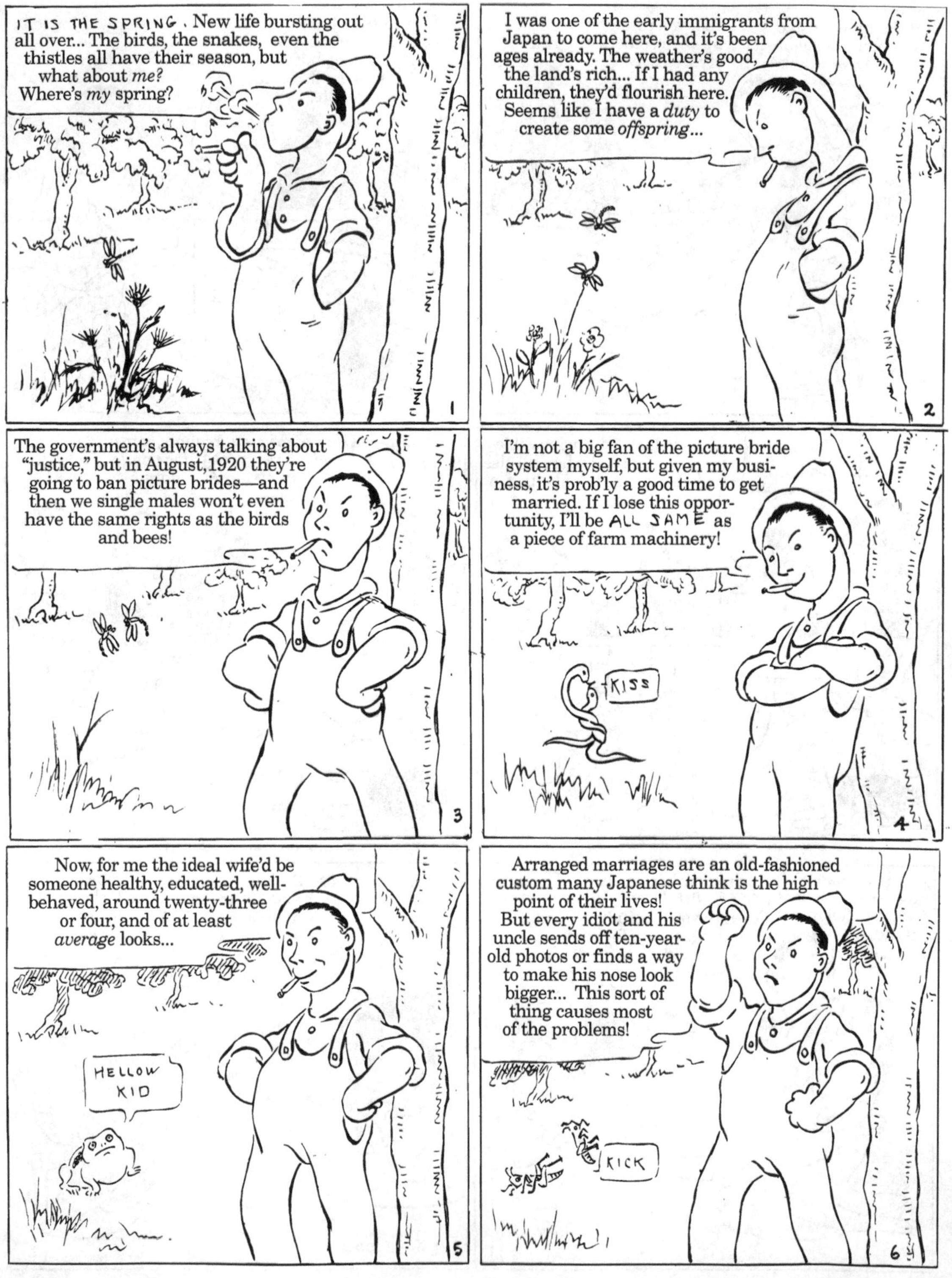
IT IS THE SPRING. New life bursting out all over... The birds, the snakes, even the thistles all have their season, but what about *me?* Where's *my* spring?
I was one of the early immigrants from Japan to come here, and it's been ages already. The weather's good, the land's rich... If I had any children, they'd flourish here. Seems like I have a *duty* to create some *offspring*...
The government's always talking about "justice," but in August, 1920 they're going to ban picture brides—and then we single males won't even have the same rights as the birds and bees!
I'm not a big fan of the picture bride system myself, but given my business, it's prob'ly a good time to get married. If I lose this opportunity, I'll be ALL SAME as a piece of farm machinery!
KISS
Now, for me the ideal wife'd be someone healthy, educated, well-behaved, around twenty-three or four, and of at least *average* looks...
HELLOW KID
Arranged marriages are an old-fashioned custom many Japanese think is the high point of their lives! But every idiot and his uncle sends off ten-year-old photos or finds a way to make his nose look bigger... This sort of thing causes most of the problems!
KICK

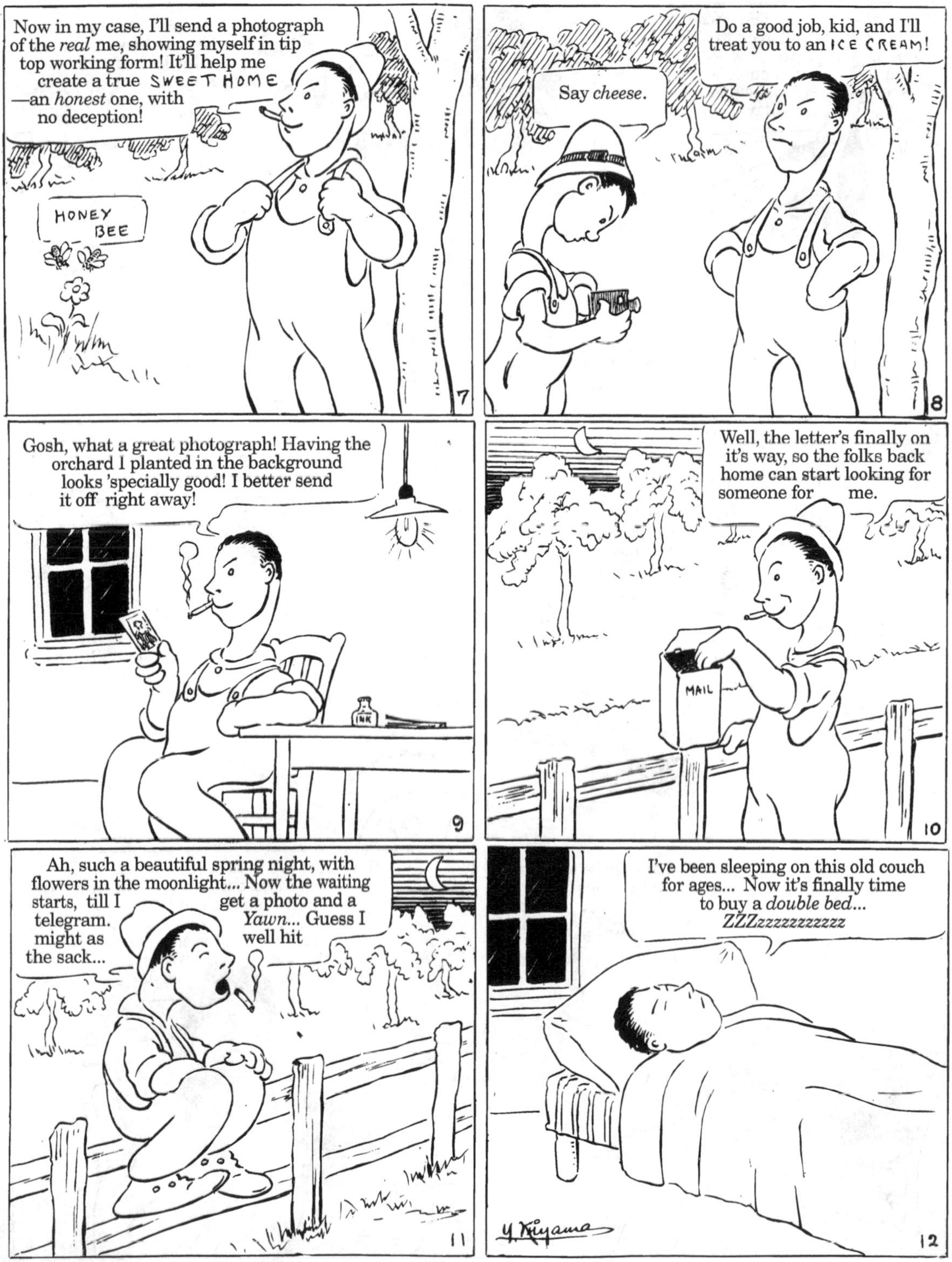
Now in my case, I'll send a photograph of the *real* me, showing myself in tip top working form! It'll help me create a true SWEET HOME—an *honest* one, with no deception!
HONEY BEE
7
Do a good job, kid, and I'll treat you to an ICE CREAM!
Say *cheese*.
8
Gosh, what a great photograph! Having the orchard I planted in the background looks 'specially good! I better send it off right away!
INK
9
Well, the letter's finally on it's way, so the folks back home can start looking for someone for me.
MAIL
10
Ah, such a beautiful spring night, with flowers in the moonlight... Now the waiting starts, till I get a photo and a telegram. *Yawn*... Guess I might as well hit the sack...
11
I've been sleeping on this old couch for ages... Now it's finally time to buy a *double bed*... ZZZzzzzzzzzzzz
Y. Kiyama
12

Picture Brides

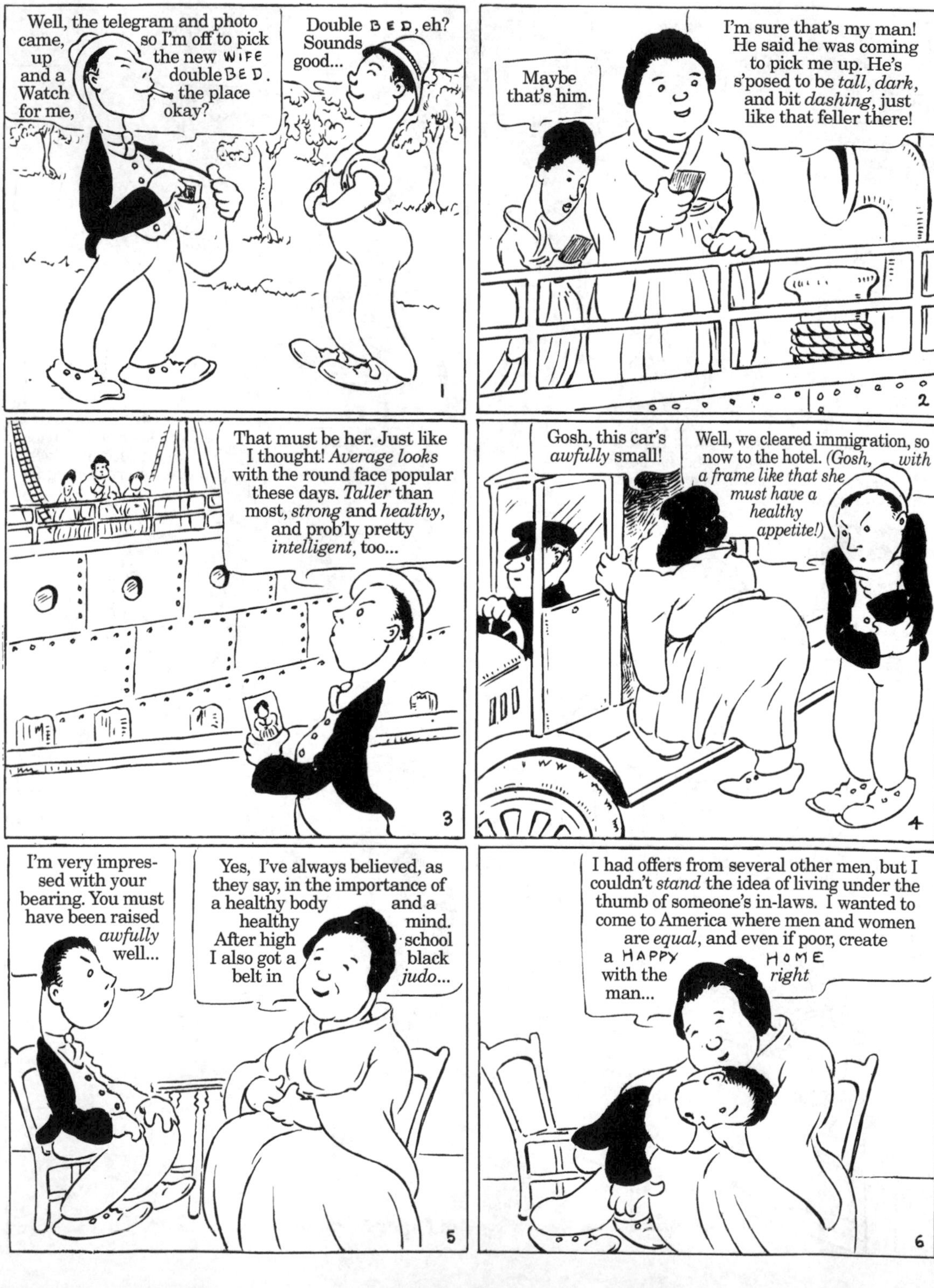
Well, the telegram and photo came, so I'm off to pick up the new WIFE and a double BED. Watch the place for me, okay?
Double BED, eh? Sounds good...
1
Maybe that's him.
I'm sure that's my man! He said he was coming to pick me up. He's s'posed to be *tall*, *dark*, and bit *dashing*, just like that feller there!
2
That must be her. Just like I thought! *Average looks* with the round face popular these days. *Taller* than most, *strong* and *healthy*, and prob'ly pretty *intelligent*, too...
3
Gosh, this car's *awfully* small!
Well, we cleared immigration, so now to the hotel. *(Gosh, with a frame like that she must have a healthy appetite!)*
4
I'm very impressed with your bearing. You must have been raised *awfully* well...
Yes, I've always believed, as they say, in the importance of a healthy body and a healthy mind. After high school I also got a black belt in *judo*...
5
I had offers from several other men, but I couldn't *stand* the idea of living under the thumb of someone's in-laws. I wanted to come to America where men and women are *equal*, and even if poor, create a HAPPY HOME with the *right* man...
6

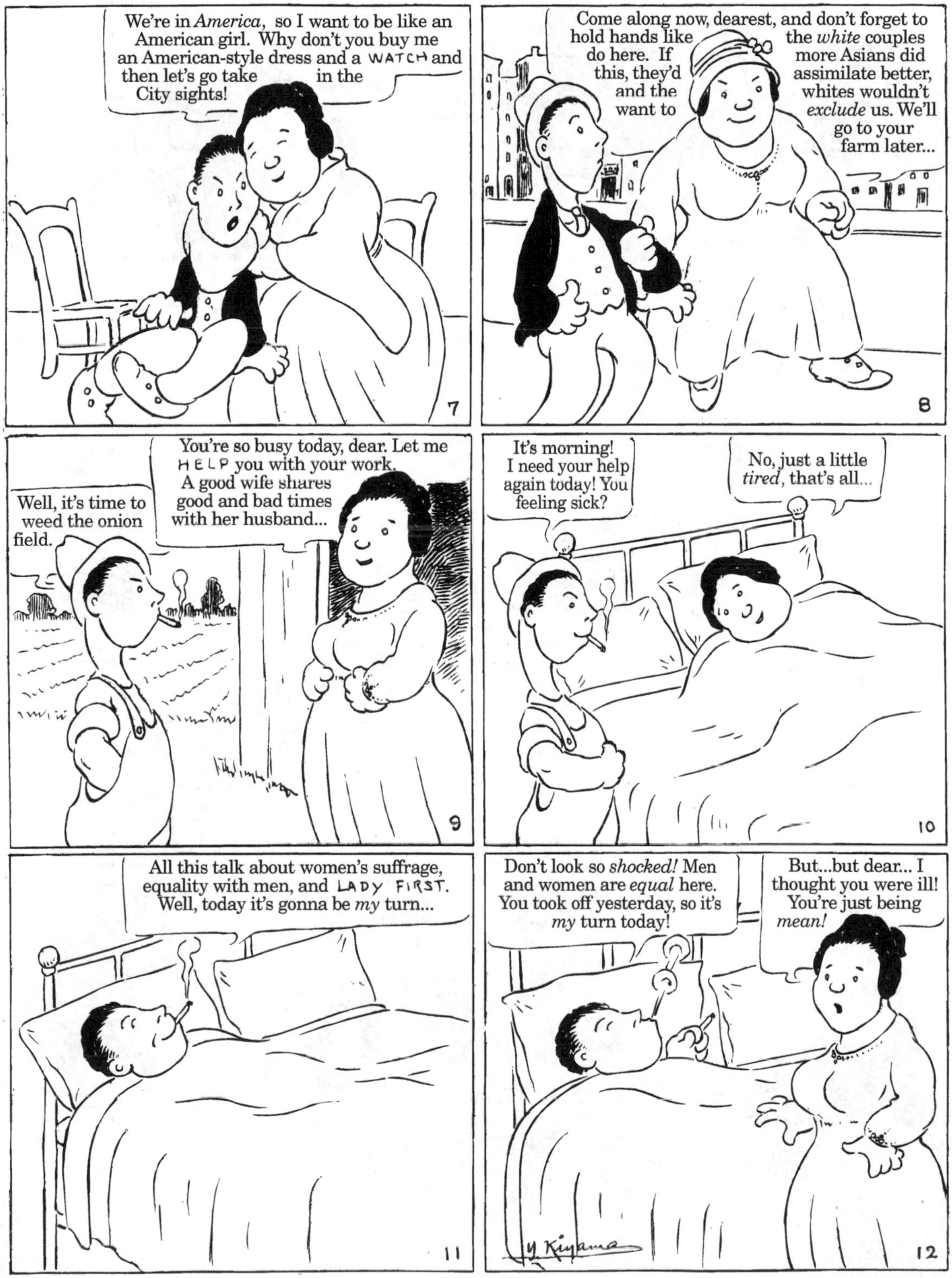
We're in *America*, so I want to be like an American girl. Why don't you buy me an American-style dress and a WATCH and then let's go take in the City sights!
Come along now, dearest, and don't forget to hold hands like the *white* couples do here. If more Asians did this, they'd assimilate better, and the whites wouldn't want to *exclude* us. We'll go to your farm later...
Well, it's time to weed the onion field.
You're so busy today, dear. Let me HELP you with your work. A good wife shares good and bad times with her husband...
It's morning! I need your help again today! You feeling sick?
No, just a little *tired*, that's all...
All this talk about women's suffrage, equality with men, and LADY FIRST. Well, today it's gonna be *my* turn...
Don't look so *shocked!* Men and women are *equal* here. You took off yesterday, so it's *my* turn today!
But...but dear... I thought you were ill! You're just being *mean!*
Y. Kiyama

EPISODE 44

The Great War in Europe

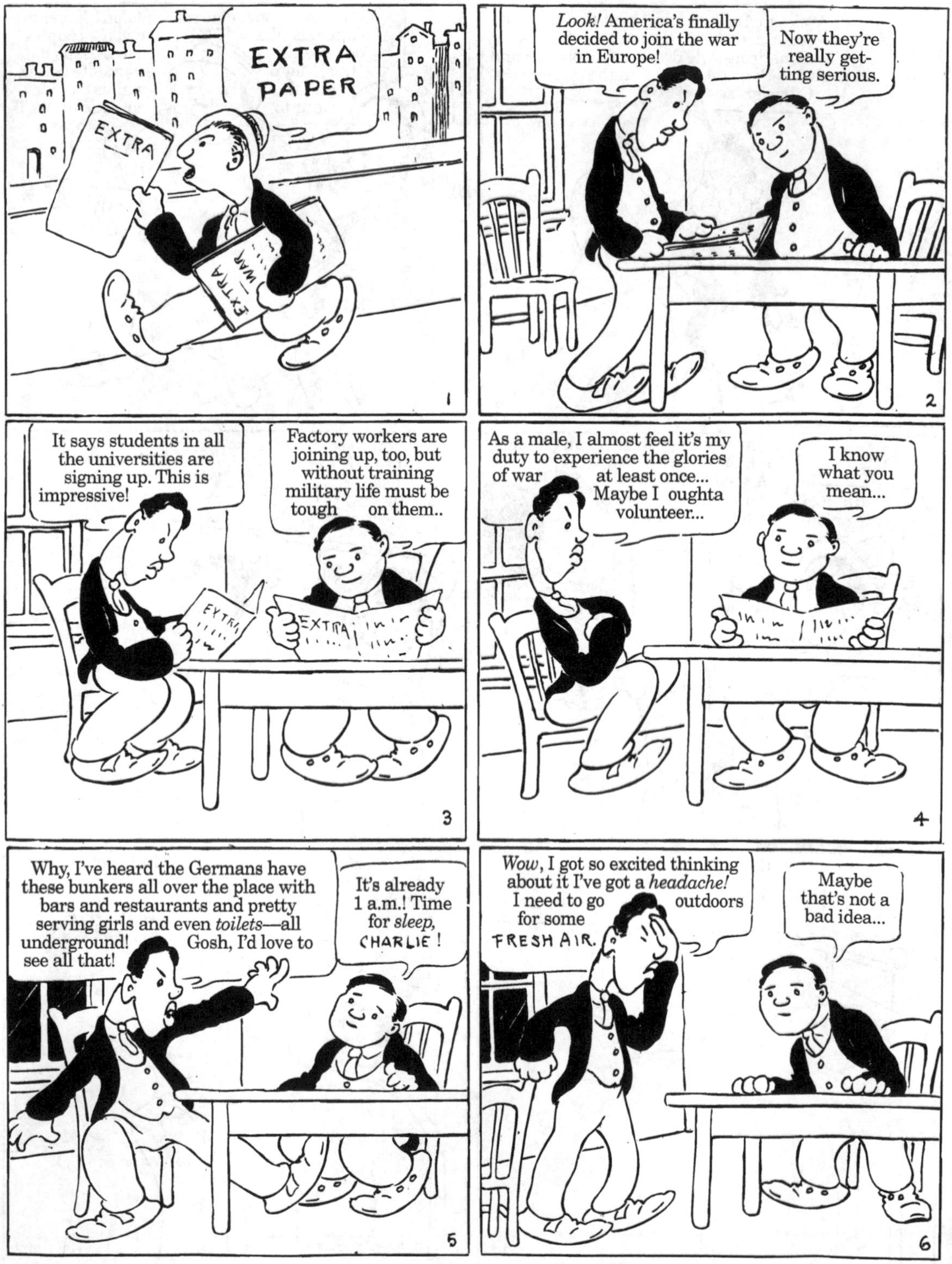
EXTRA PAPER
EXTRA
EXTRA WAR
1
Look! America's finally decided to join the war in Europe!
Now they're really get- ting serious.
2
It says students in all the universities are signing up. This is impressive!
Factory workers are joining up, too, but without training military life must be tough on them..
EXTRA
EXTRA
3
As a male, I almost feel it's my duty to experience the glories of war at least once... Maybe I oughta volunteer...
I know what you mean...
4
Why, I've heard the Germans have these bunkers all over the place with bars and restaurants and pretty serving girls and even toilets—all underground! Gosh, I'd love to see all that!
It's already 1 a.m.! Time for sleep, CHARLIE!
5
Wow, I got so excited thinking about it I've got a headache! I need to go outdoors for some FRESH AIR.
Maybe that's not a bad idea...
6

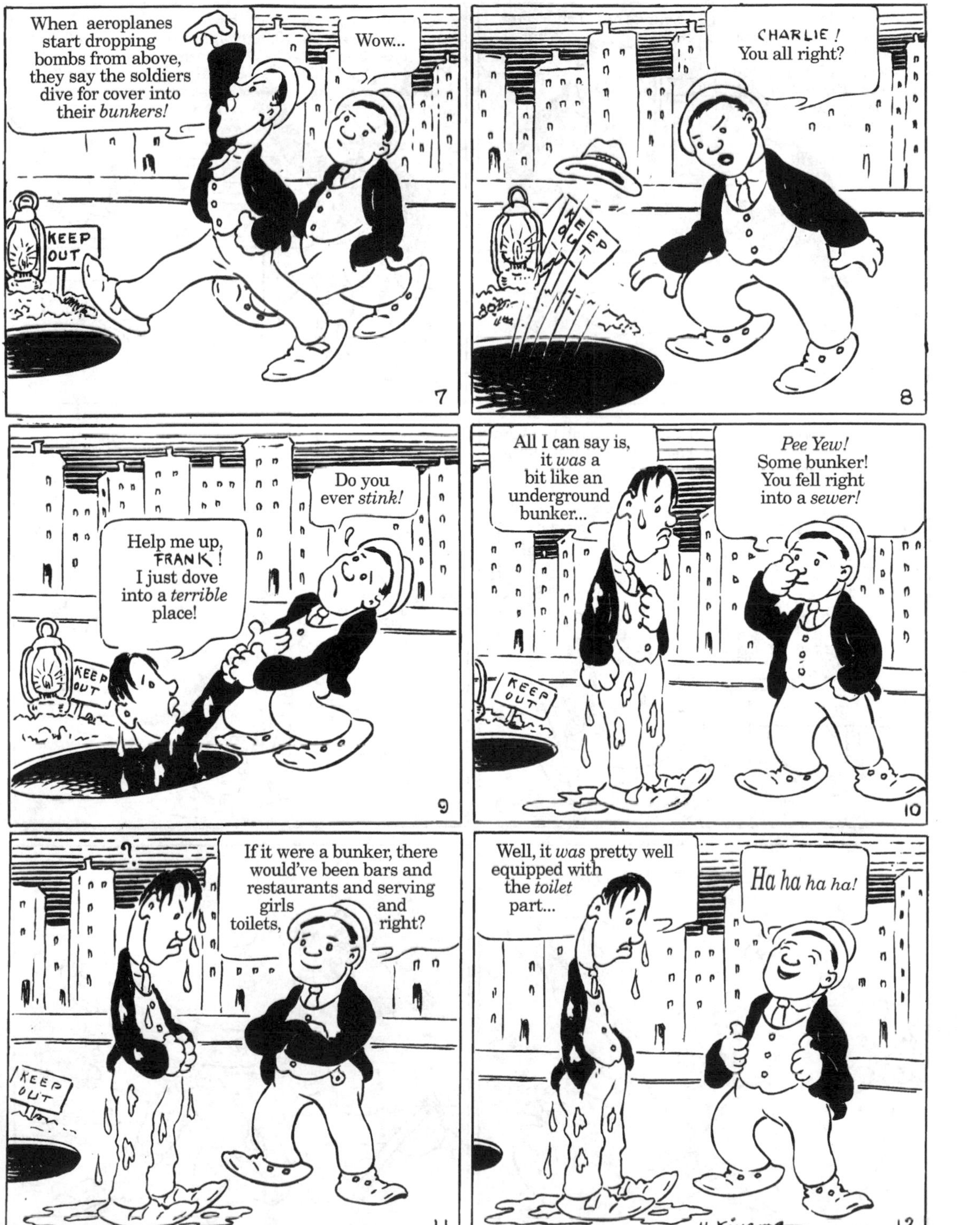
When aeroplanes start dropping bombs from above, they say the soldiers dive for cover into their *bunkers!*
Wow...
KEEP OUT
7
CHARLIE! You all right?
KEEP OUT
8
Help me up, FRANK! I just dove into a *terrible* place!
Do you ever *stink!*
KEEP OUT
9
All I can say is, it *was* a bit like an underground bunker...
Pee Yew! Some bunker! You fell right into a *sewer!*
KEEP OUT
10
If it were a bunker, there would've been bars and restaurants and serving girls and toilets, right?
KEEP OUT
11
Well, it *was* pretty well equipped with the *toilet* part...
Ha ha ha ha!
Y. Kiyama
12

The Great War in Europe

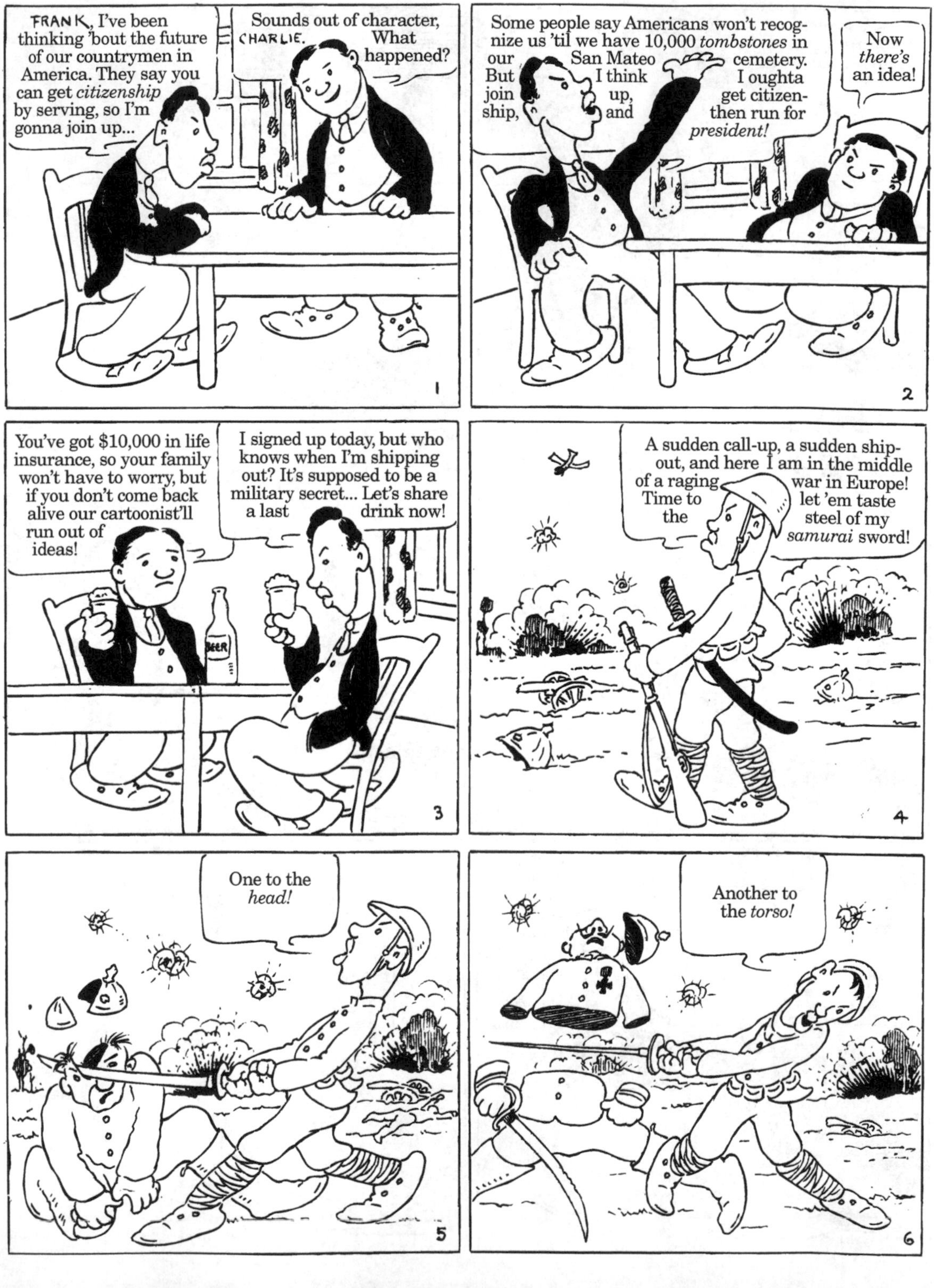
FRANK, I've been thinking 'bout the future of our countrymen in America. They say you can get *citizenship* by serving, so I'm gonna join up...
Sounds out of character, CHARLIE. What happened?
1
Some people say Americans won't recognize us 'til we have 10,000 *tombstones* in our San Mateo cemetery. But I think I oughta join up, get citizenship, and then run for *president!*
Now *there's* an idea!
2
You've got $10,000 in life insurance, so your family won't have to worry, but if you don't come back alive our cartoonist'll run out of ideas!
I signed up today, but who knows when I'm shipping out? It's supposed to be a military secret... Let's share a last drink now!
BEER
3
A sudden call-up, a sudden ship-out, and here I am in the middle of a raging war in Europe! Time to let 'em taste the steel of my *samurai* sword!
4
One to the *head!*
5
Another to the *torso!*
6

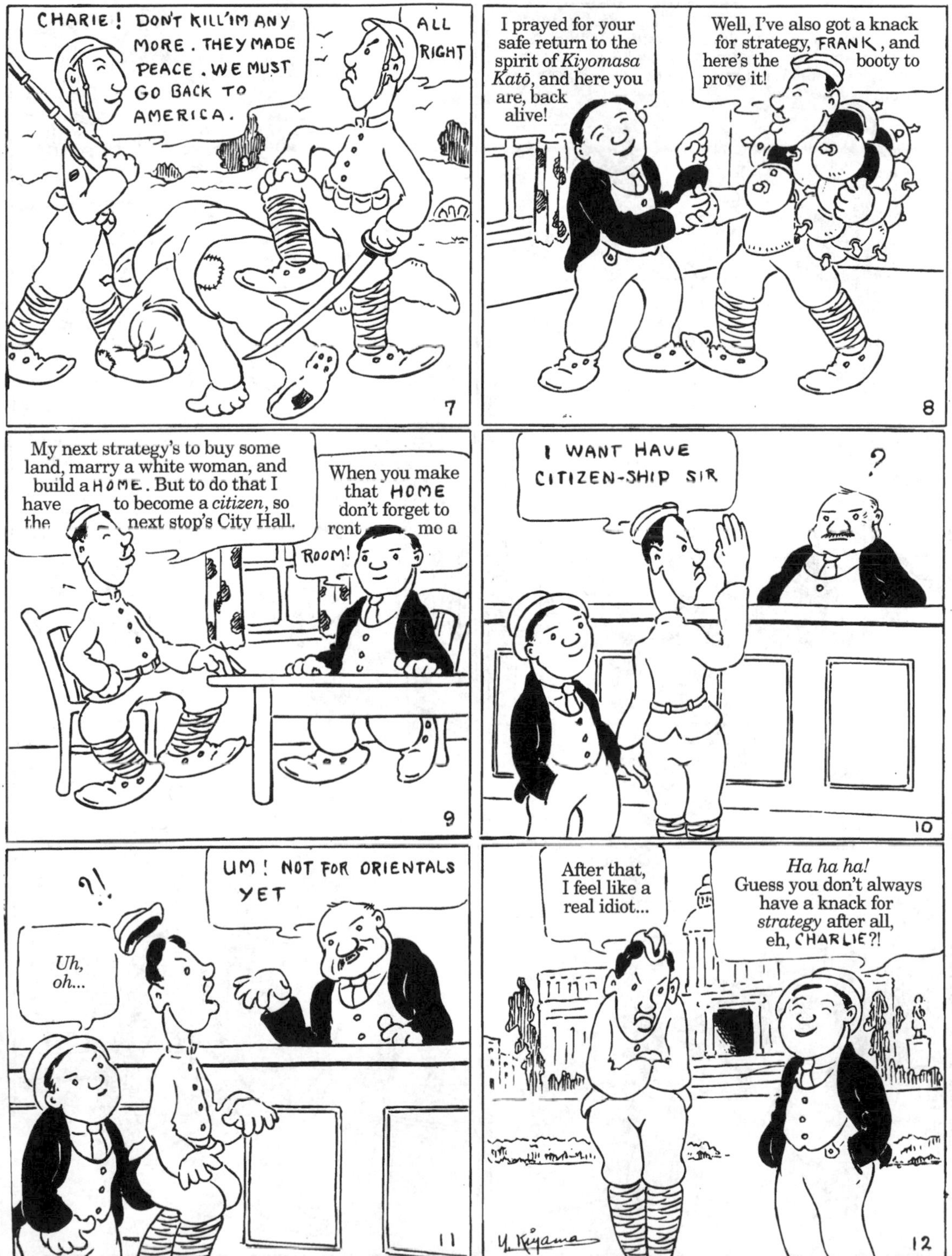
CHARIE! DON'T KILL'IM ANY MORE. THEY MADE PEACE. WE MUST GO BACK TO AMERICA.
ALL RIGHT
7
I prayed for your safe return to the spirit of *Kiyomasa Katō*, and here you are, back alive!
Well, I've also got a knack for strategy, FRANK, and here's the booty to prove it!
8
My next strategy's to buy some land, marry a white woman, and build a HOME. But to do that I have to become a *citizen*, so the next stop's City Hall.
When you make that HOME don't forget to rent me a ROOM!
9
I WANT HAVE CITIZEN-SHIP SIR
?
10
?!
UM! NOT FOR ORIENTALS YET
Uh, oh...
11
After that, I feel like a real idiot...
Ha ha ha! Guess you don't always have a knack for *strategy* after all, eh, CHARLIE?!
Y. Kiyama
12

Influenza

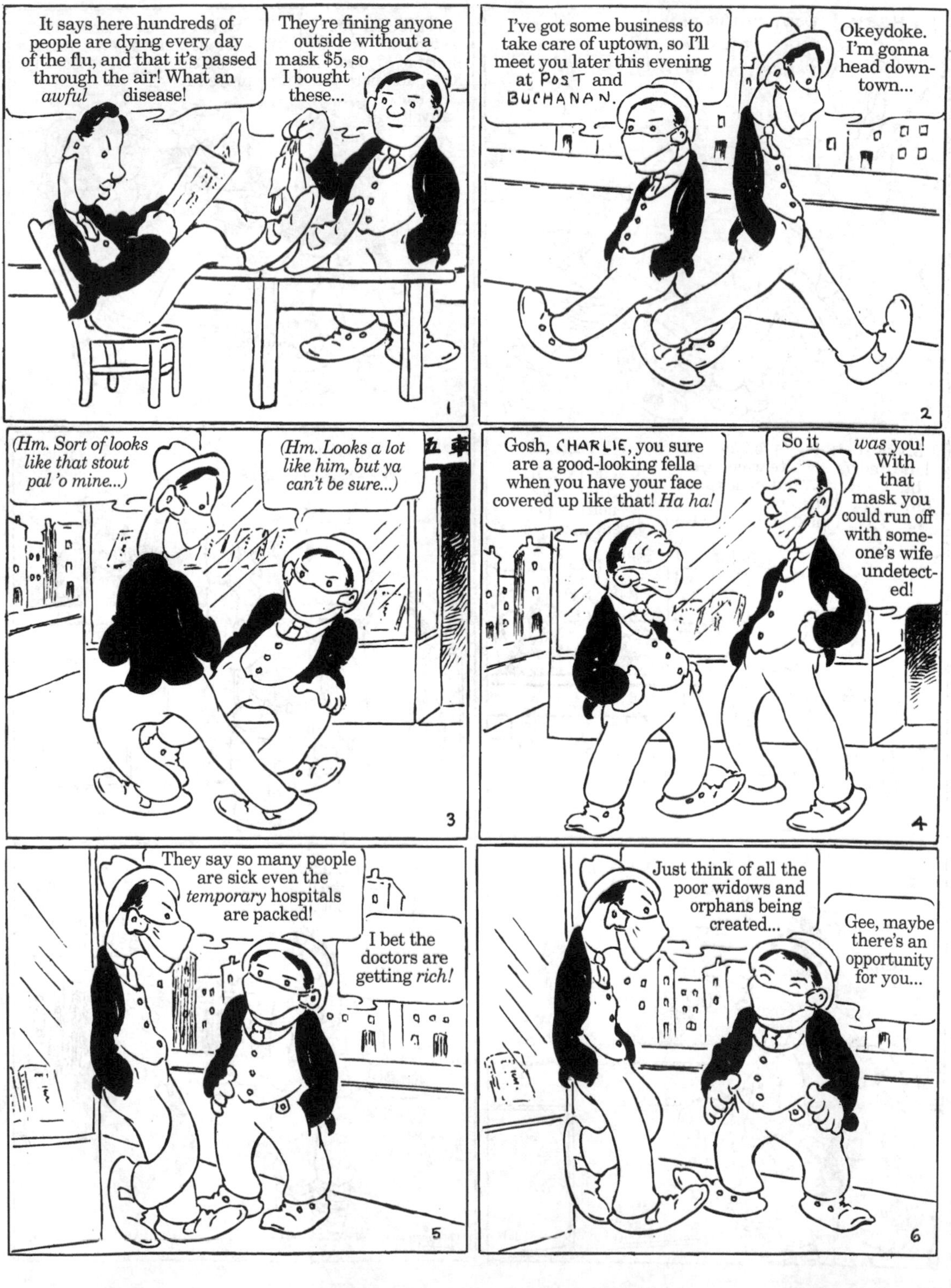
It says here hundreds of people are dying every day of the flu, and that it's passed through the air! What an *awful* disease!
They're fining anyone outside without a mask $5, so I bought these...
1
I've got some business to take care of uptown, so I'll meet you later this evening at POST and BUCHANAN.
Okeydoke. I'm gonna head down-town...
2
(Hm. Sort of looks like that stout pal 'o mine...)
(Hm. Looks a lot like him, but ya can't be sure...)
3
Gosh, CHARLIE, you sure are a good-looking fella when you have your face covered up like that! *Ha ha!*
So it *was* you! With that mask you could run off with some-one's wife undetect-ed!
4
They say so many people are sick even the *temporary* hospitals are packed!
I bet the doctors are getting *rich!*
5
Just think of all the poor widows and orphans being created...
Gee, maybe there's an opportunity for you...
6

Sign: *Gosha Bookstore*

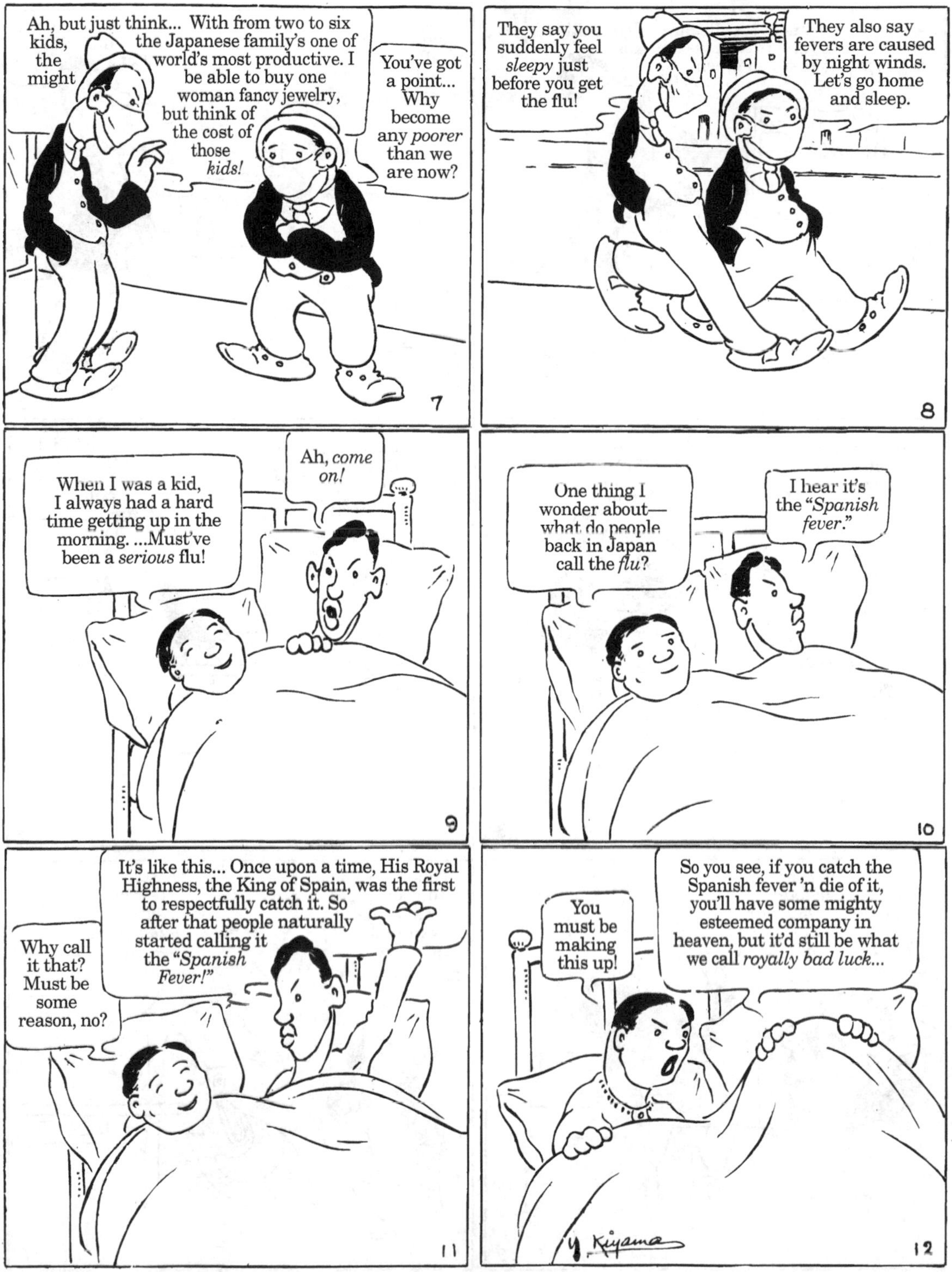
Ah, but just think... With from two to six kids, the Japanese family's one of the world's most productive. I might be able to buy one woman fancy jewelry, but think of the cost of those *kids!*
You've got a point... Why become any *poorer* than we are now?
7
They say you suddenly feel *sleepy* just before you get the flu!
They also say fevers are caused by night winds. Let's go home and sleep.
8
When I was a kid, I always had a hard time getting up in the morning. ...Must've been a *serious* flu!
Ah, *come on!*
9
One thing I wonder about—what do people back in Japan call the *flu*?
I hear it's the "*Spanish fever.*"
10
Why call it that? Must be some reason, no?
It's like this... Once upon a time, His Royal Highness, the King of Spain, was the first to respectfully catch it. So after that people naturally started calling it the "*Spanish Fever!*"
11
You must be making this up!
So you see, if you catch the Spanish fever 'n die of it, you'll have some mighty esteemed company in heaven, but it'd still be what we call *royally bad luck...*
Y. Kiyama
12

EPISODE 47

Prohibition

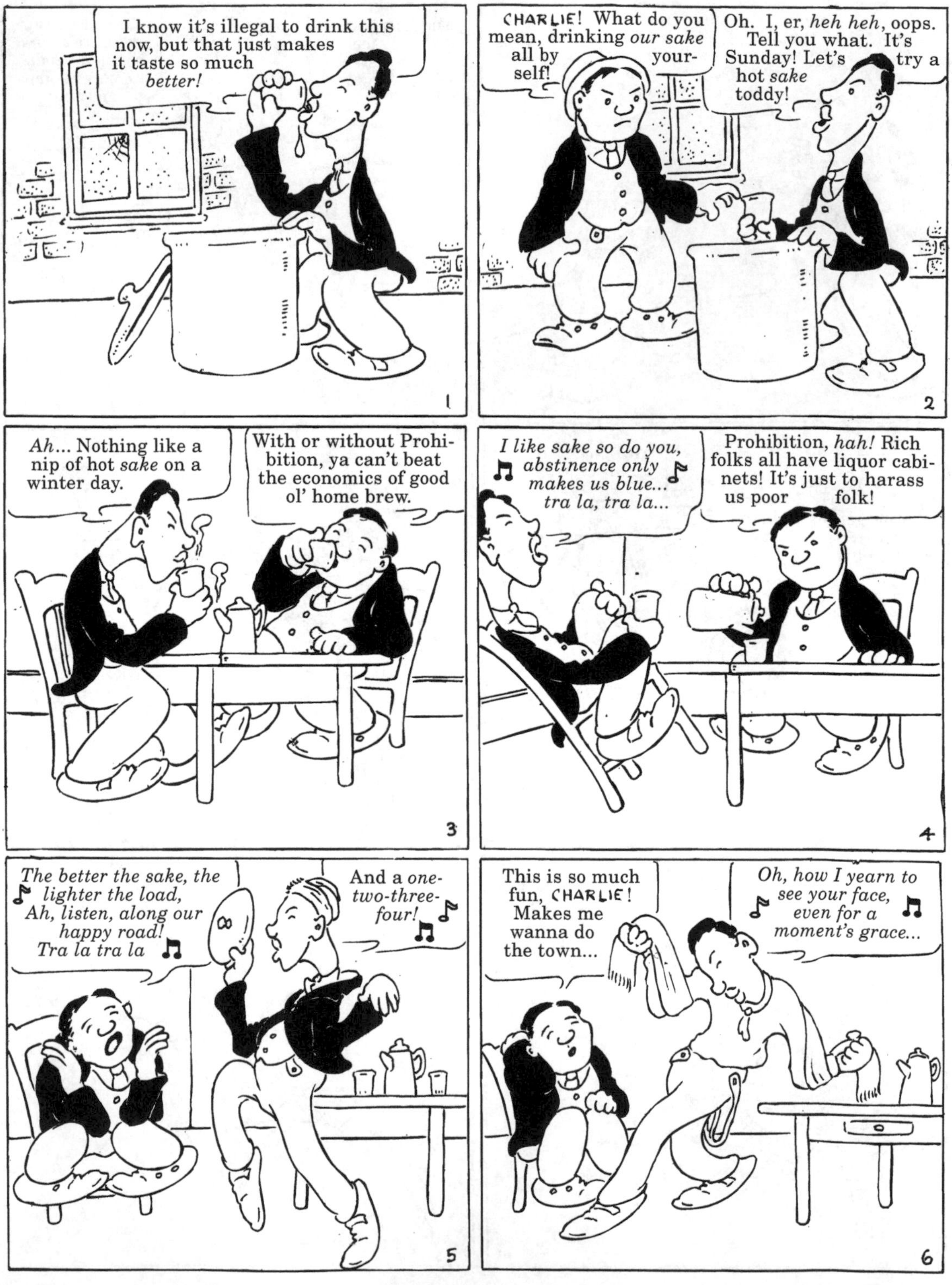

I know it's illegal to drink this now, but that just makes it taste so much *better!*
1
CHARLIE! What do you mean, drinking *our sake* all by yourself!
Oh. I, er, *heh heh*, oops. Tell you what. It's Sunday! Let's try a hot *sake* toddy!
2
Ah... Nothing like a nip of hot *sake* on a winter day.
With or without Prohibition, ya can't beat the economics of good ol' home brew.
3
I like sake so do you, abstinence only makes us blue... tra la, tra la...
Prohibition, *hah!* Rich folks all have liquor cabinets! It's just to harass us poor folk!
4
The better the sake, the lighter the load, Ah, listen, along our happy road! Tra la tra la
And a *one-two-three-four!*
5
This is so much fun, CHARLIE! Makes me wanna do the town...
Oh, how I yearn to see your face, even for a moment's grace...
6

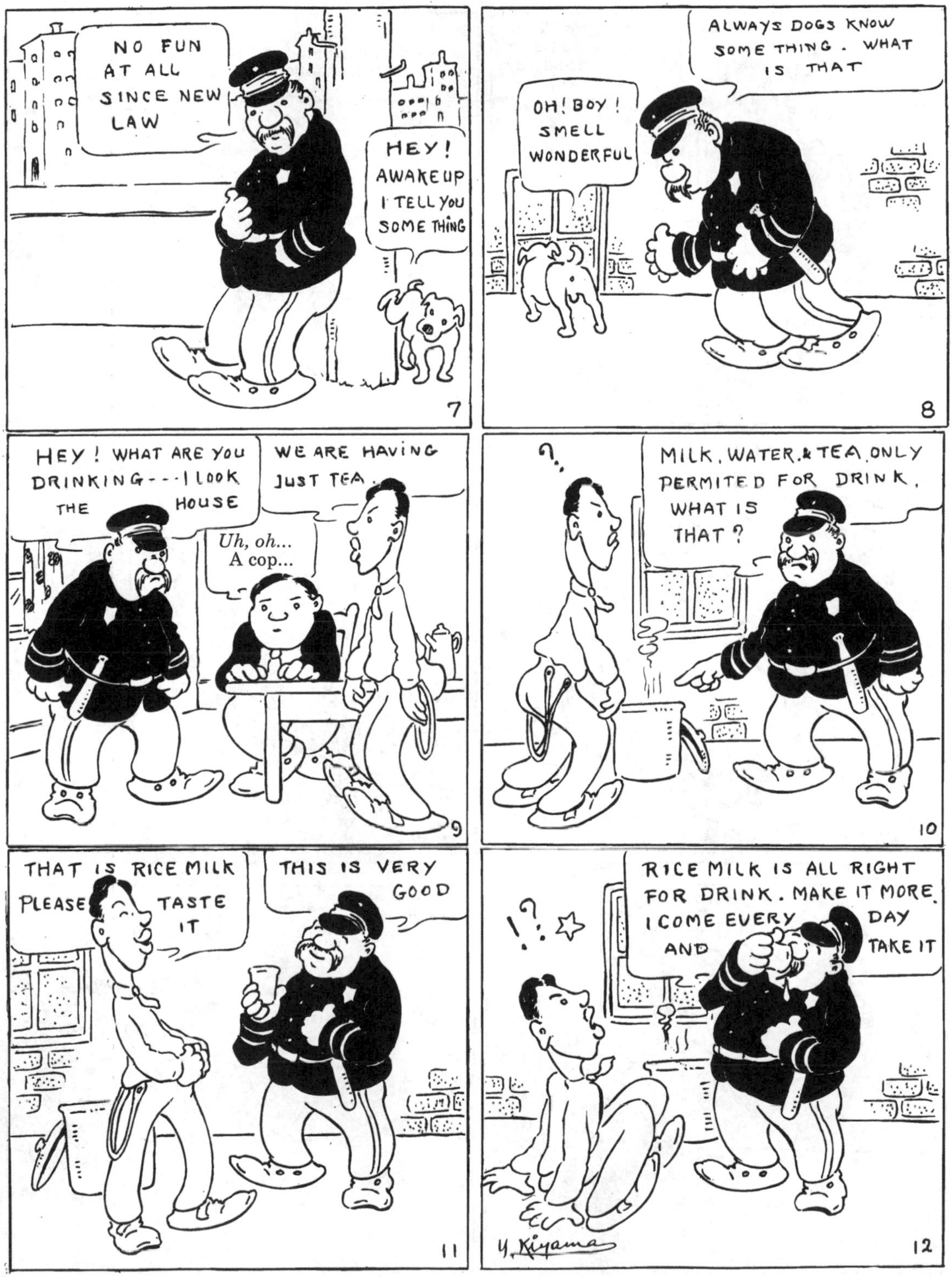
NO FUN AT ALL SINCE NEW LAW
HEY! AWAKE UP I TELL YOU SOME THING
7
ALWAYS DOGS KNOW SOME THING. WHAT IS THAT
OH! BOY! SMELL WONDERFUL
8
HEY! WHAT ARE YOU DRINKING---I LOOK THE HOUSE
WE ARE HAVING JUST TEA.
Uh, oh... A cop...
9
?..
MILK, WATER & TEA ONLY PERMITED FOR DRINK. WHAT IS THAT?
10
THAT IS RICE MILK PLEASE TASTE IT
THIS IS VERY GOOD
11
!?.. ☆
RICE MILK IS ALL RIGHT FOR DRINK. MAKE IT MORE. I COME EVERY DAY AND TAKE IT
Y. Kiyama
12

The Turlock Incident

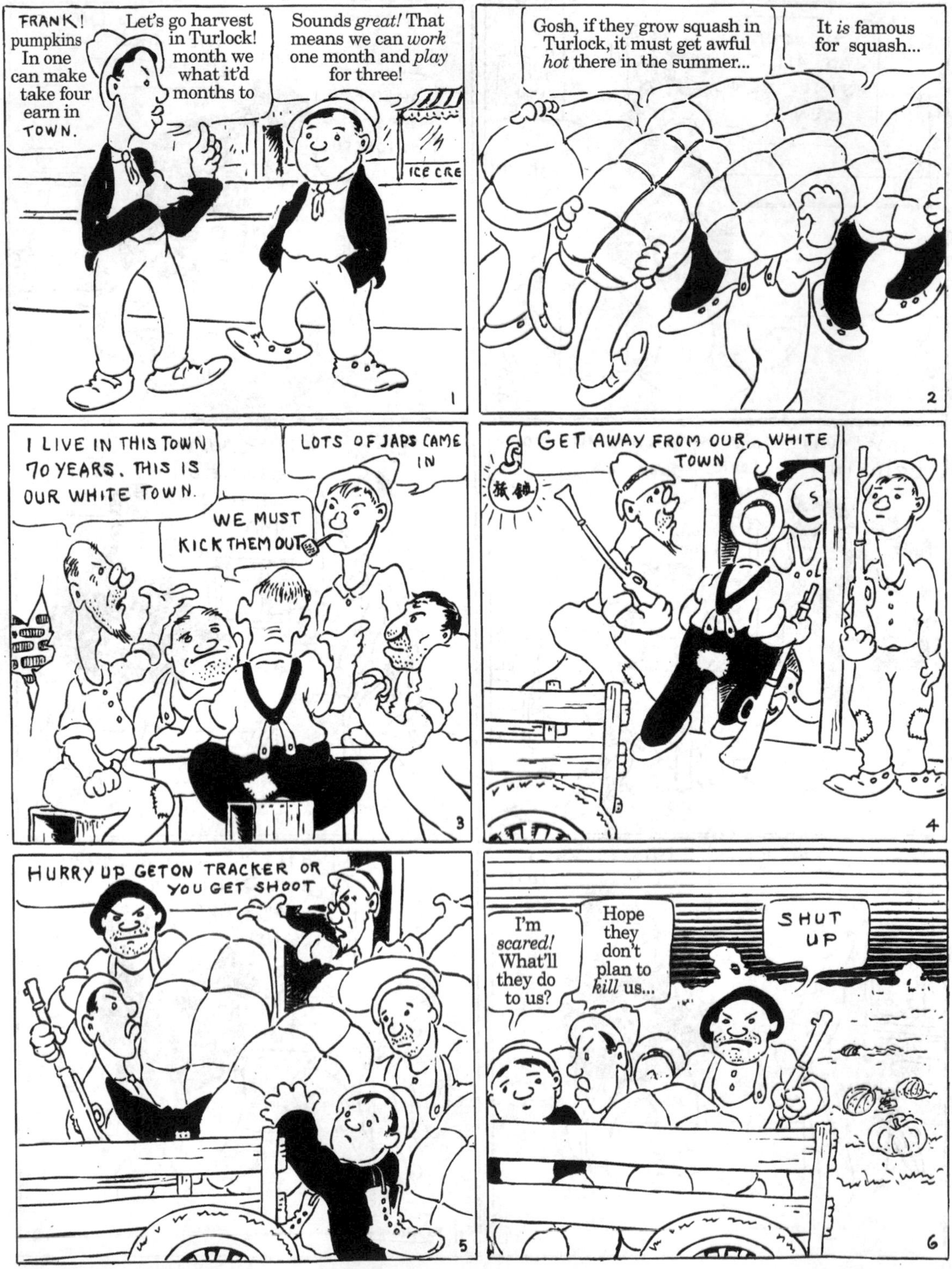
FRANK! Let's go harvest pumpkins in Turlock! In one month we can make what it'd take four months to earn in TOWN.
Sounds *great!* That means we can *work* one month and *play* for three!
ICE CRE
1
Gosh, if they grow squash in Turlock, it must get awful *hot* there in the summer...
It *is* famous for squash...
2
I LIVE IN THIS TOWN 70 YEARS. THIS IS OUR WHITE TOWN.
LOTS OF JAPS CAME IN
WE MUST KICK THEM OUT
3
GET AWAY FROM OUR WHITE TOWN
旅舘
4
HURRY UP GET ON TRACKER OR YOU GET SHOOT
5
I'm *scared!* What'll they do to us?
Hope they don't plan to *kill* us...
SHUT UP
6

Sign on hanging lamp: *Japanese Inn*

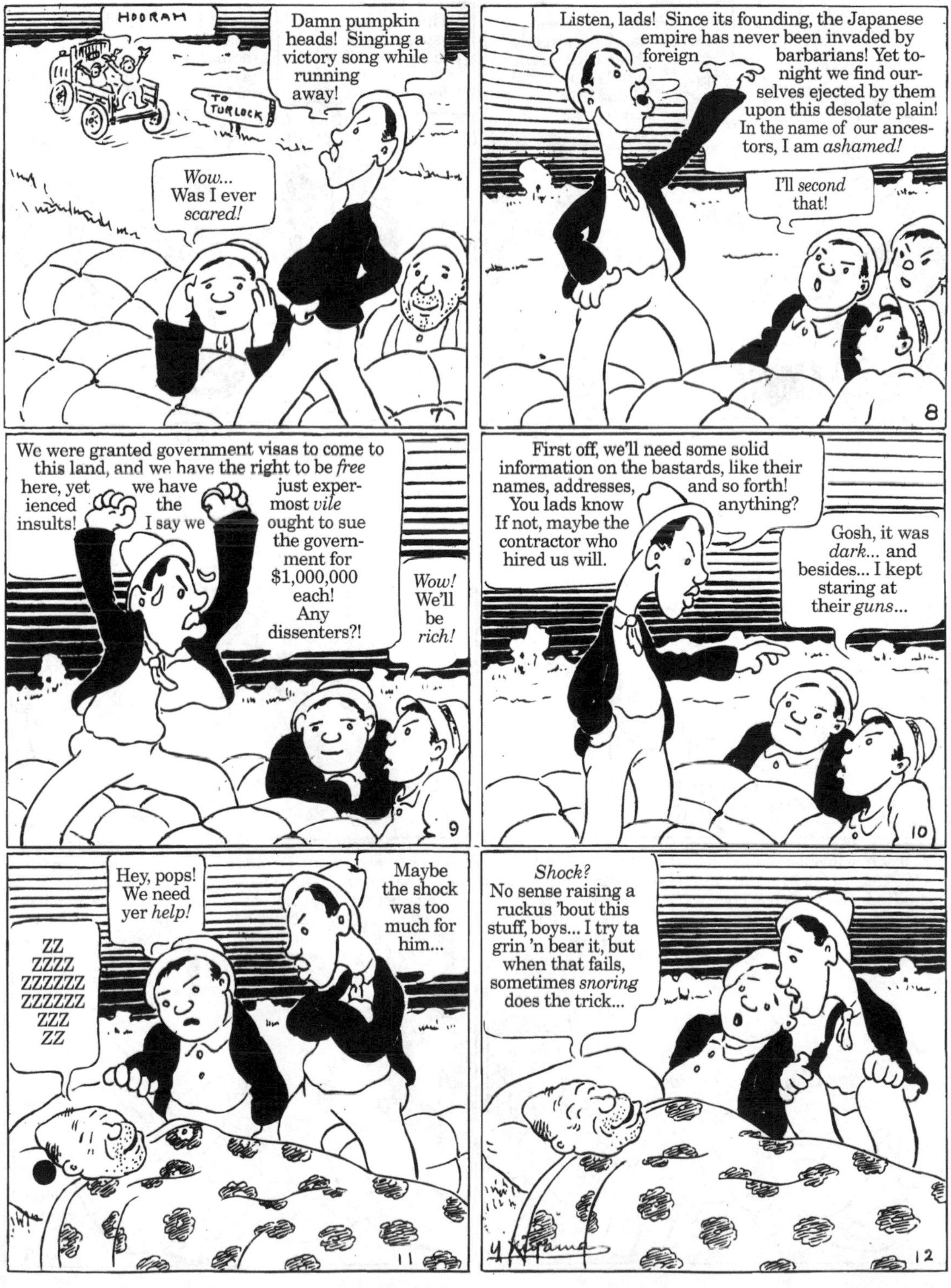

HOORAH
TO TURLOCK
Damn pumpkin heads! Singing a victory song while running away!
Wow... Was I ever *scared!*
Listen, lads! Since its founding, the Japanese empire has never been invaded by foreign barbarians! Yet tonight we find ourselves ejected by them upon this desolate plain! In the name of our ancestors, I am *ashamed!*
I'll *second* that!
We were granted government visas to come to this land, and we have the right to be *free* here, yet we have just experienced the most *vile* insults! I say we ought to sue the government for $1,000,000 each! Any dissenters?!
Wow! We'll be *rich!*
First off, we'll need some solid information on the bastards, like their names, addresses, and so forth! You lads know anything? If not, maybe the contractor who hired us will.
Gosh, it was *dark...* and besides... I kept staring at their *guns...*
Hey, pops! We need yer *help!*
Maybe the shock was too much for him...
ZZ ZZZZ ZZZZZZ ZZZZZZ ZZZ ZZ
Shock? No sense raising a ruckus 'bout this stuff, boys... I try ta grin 'n bear it, but when that fails, sometimes *snoring* does the trick...

EPISODE 49

The Alien Land Act

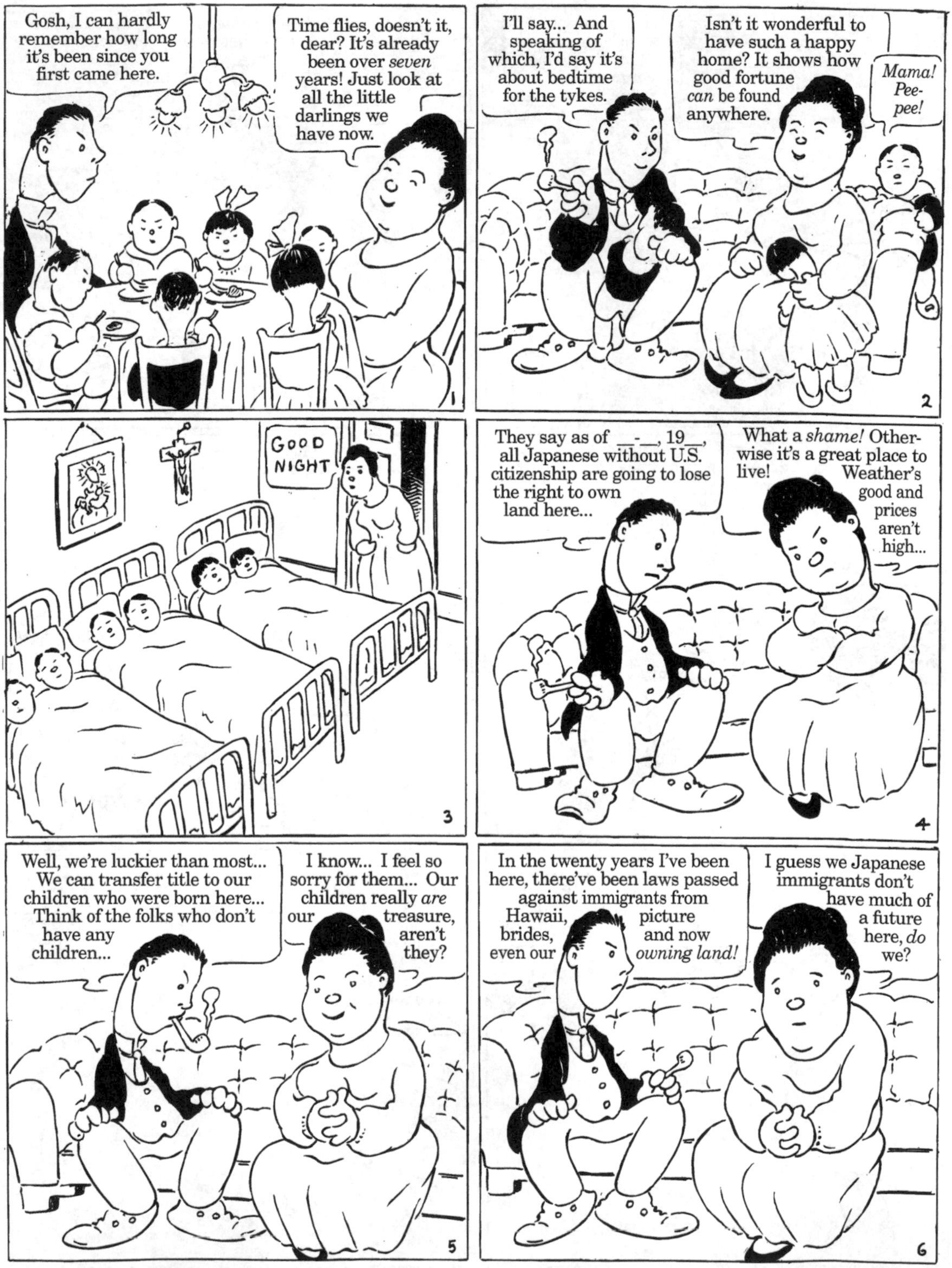
Gosh, I can hardly remember how long it's been since you first came here.
Time flies, doesn't it, dear? It's already been over *seven* years! Just look at all the little darlings we have now.
I'll say... And speaking of which, I'd say it's about bedtime for the tykes.
Isn't it wonderful to have such a happy home? It shows how good fortune *can* be found anywhere.
Mama! Pee-pee!
2
GOOD NIGHT
3
They say as of __-__, 19__, all Japanese without U.S. citizenship are going to lose the right to own land here...
What a *shame!* Otherwise it's a great place to live! Weather's good and prices aren't high...
4
Well, we're luckier than most... We can transfer title to our children who were born here... Think of the folks who don't have any children...
I know... I feel so sorry for them... Our children really *are* our treasure, aren't they?
5
In the twenty years I've been here, there've been laws passed against immigrants from Hawaii, picture brides, and now even our *owning land!*
I guess we Japanese immigrants don't have much of a future here, *do* we?
6

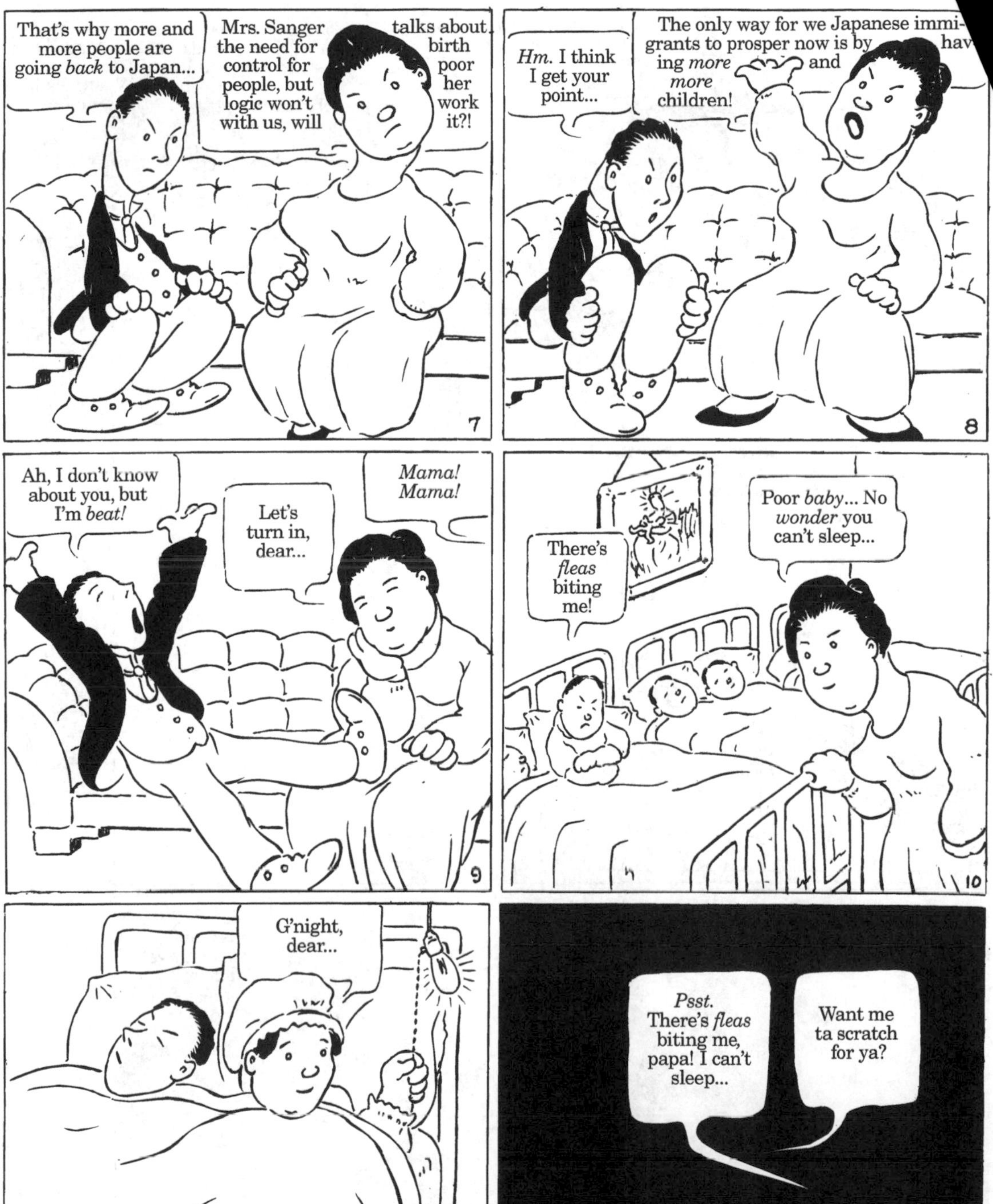

That's why more and more people are going *back* to Japan...
Mrs. Sanger talks about the need for birth control for poor people, but her logic won't work with us, will it?!
Hm. I think I get your point...
The only way for we Japanese immi-grants to prosper now is by having *more* and *more* children!
Ah, I don't know about you, but I'm *beat!*
Let's turn in, dear...
Mama! Mama!
There's *fleas* biting me!
Poor *baby*... No *wonder* you can't sleep...
G'night, dear...
Y. Kiyama
Psst. There's *fleas* biting me, papa! I can't sleep...
Want me ta scratch for ya?

EPISODE 50

Meant for Each Other

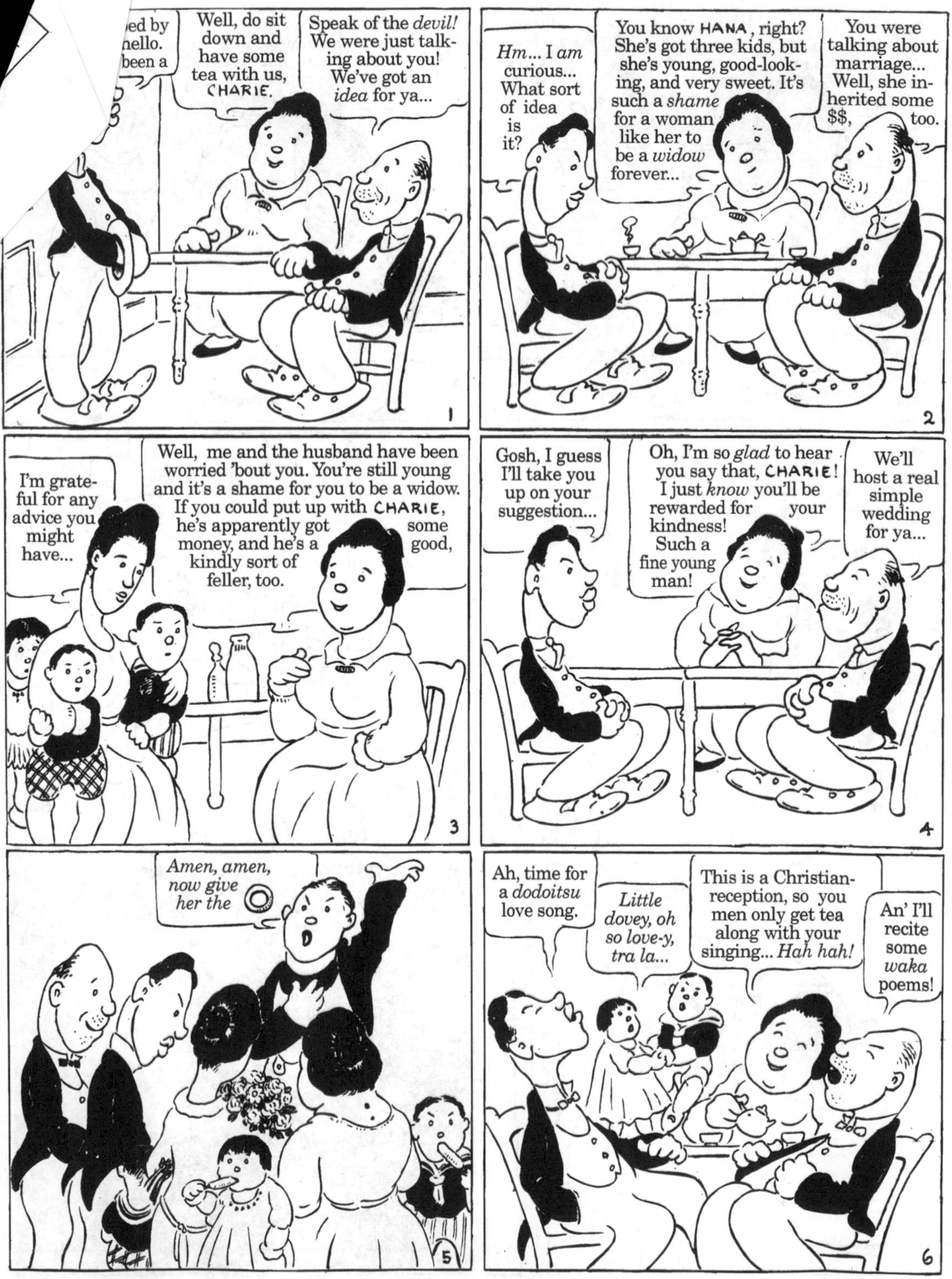

ed by hello. been a
Well, do sit down and have some tea with us, CHARIE.
Speak of the *devil!* We were just talking about you! We've got an *idea* for ya...
1
Hm... I *am* curious... What sort of idea is it?
You know HANA, right? She's got three kids, but she's young, good-looking, and very sweet. It's such a *shame* for a woman like her to be a *widow* forever...
You were talking about marriage... Well, she inherited some $$, too.
2
I'm grateful for any advice you might have...
Well, me and the husband have been worried 'bout you. You're still young and it's a shame for you to be a widow. If you could put up with CHARIE, he's apparently got some money, and he's a good, kindly sort of feller, too.
3
Gosh, I guess I'll take you up on your suggestion...
Oh, I'm so *glad* to hear you say that, CHARIE! I just *know* you'll be rewarded for your kindness! Such a fine young man!
We'll host a real simple wedding for ya...
4
Amen, amen, now give her the
5
Ah, time for a *dodoitsu* love song.
Little dovey, oh so love-y, tra la...
This is a Christian-reception, so you men only get tea along with your singing... *Hah hah!*
An' I'll recite some *waka* poems!
6

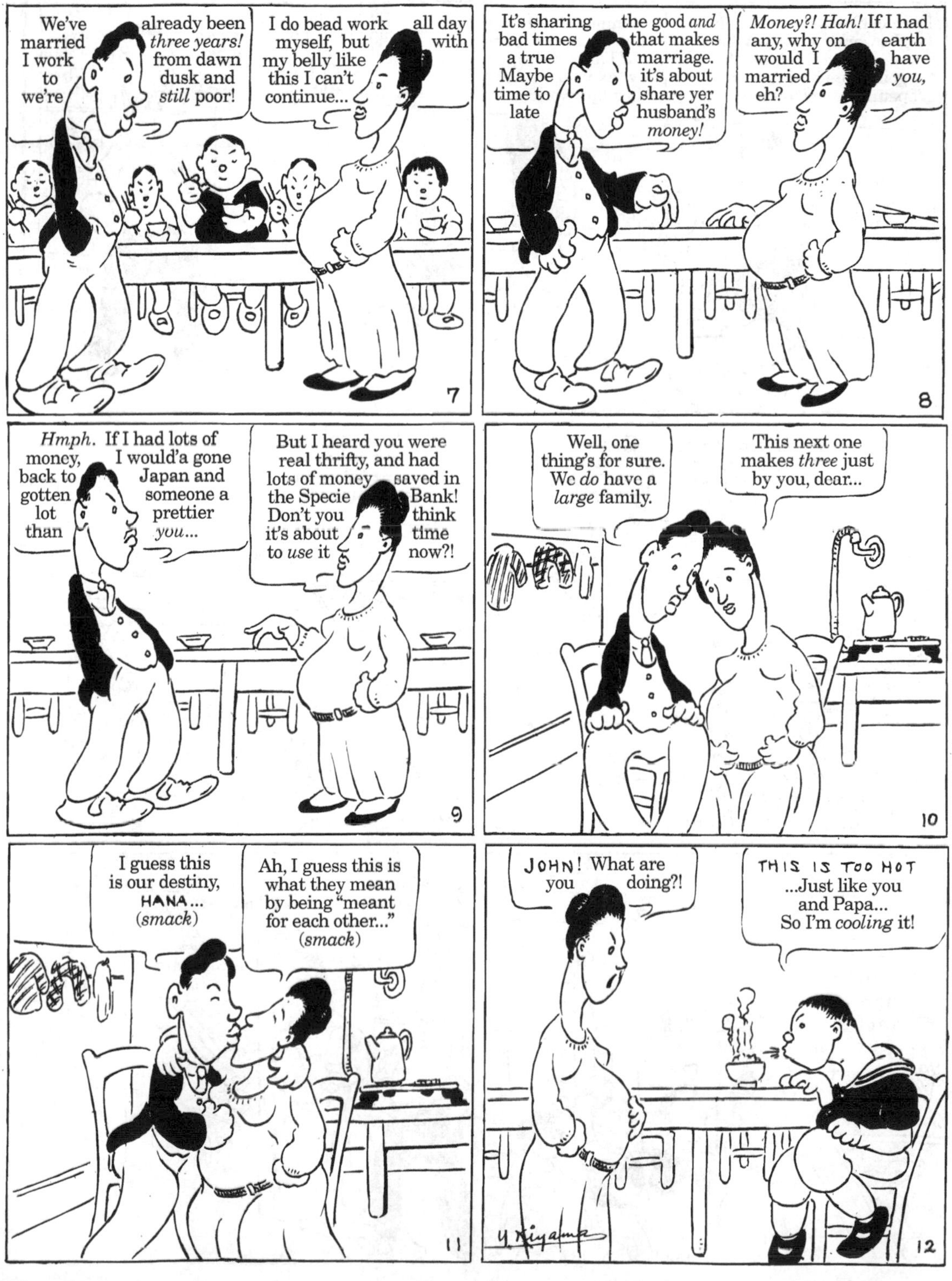
We've already been married *three years!* I work from dawn to dusk and we're *still* poor!
I do bead work all day myself, but with my belly like this I can't continue...
7
It's sharing the good *and* bad times that makes a true marriage. Maybe it's about time to share yer late husband's *money!*
Money?! Hah! If I had any, why on earth would I have married *you,* eh?
8
Hmph. If I had lots of money, I would'a gone back to Japan and gotten someone a lot prettier than *you...*
But I heard you were real thrifty, and had lots of money saved in the Specie Bank! Don't you think it's about time to *use* it now?!
9
Well, one thing's for sure. We *do* have a *large* family.
This next one makes *three* just by you, dear...
10
I guess this is our destiny, HANA... (*smack*)
Ah, I guess this is what they mean by being "meant for each other..." (*smack*)
11
JOHN! What are you doing?!
THIS IS TOO HOT ...Just like you and Papa... So I'm *cooling* it!
Y. Kiyama
12

EPISODE 51

Mutual Downfall

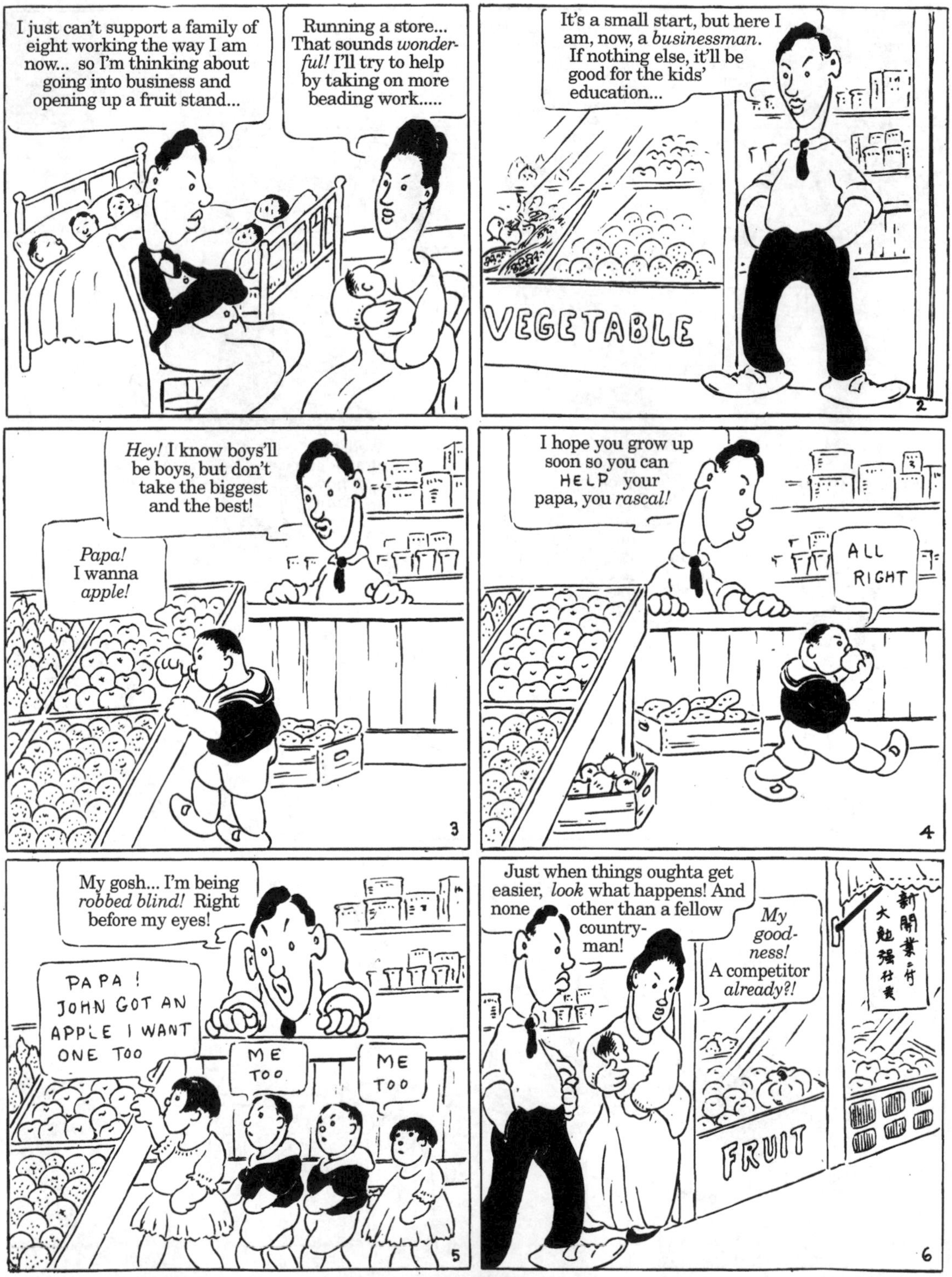
I just can't support a family of eight working the way I am now... so I'm thinking about going into business and opening up a fruit stand...
Running a store... That sounds *wonderful!* I'll try to help by taking on more beading work.....
It's a small start, but here I am, now, a *businessman*. If nothing else, it'll be good for the kids' education...
VEGETABLE
Hey! I know boys'll be boys, but don't take the biggest and the best!
Papa! I wanna *apple!*
I hope you grow up soon so you can HELP your papa, you *rascal!*
ALL RIGHT
My gosh... I'm being *robbed blind!* Right before my eyes!
PAPA! JOHN GOT AN APPLE I WANT ONE TOO
ME TOO
ME TOO
Just when things oughta get easier, *look* what happens! And none other than a fellow countryman!
My goodness! A competitor *already?!*
新開業ニ付
大勉強仕候
FRUIT

Sign: *New Opening! Bargains Galore!*

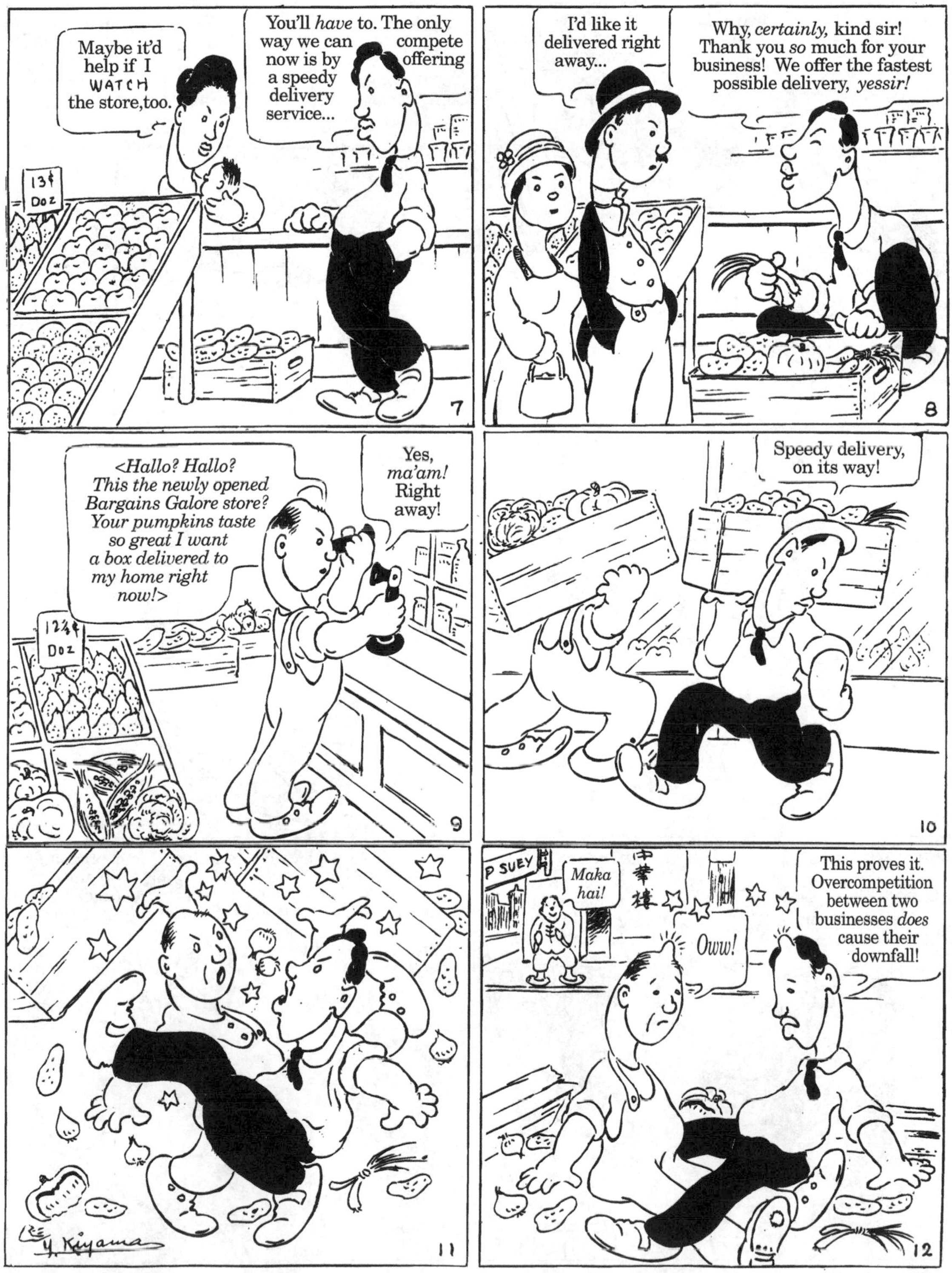
Maybe it'd help if I WATCH the store,too.
You'll *have* to. The only way we can compete now is by offering a speedy delivery service...
13¢ DOZ
7
I'd like it delivered right away...
Why, *certainly*, kind sir! Thank you *so* much for your business! We offer the fastest possible delivery, *yessir!*
8
<Hallo? Hallo? This the newly opened Bargains Galore store? Your pumpkins taste so great I want a box delivered to my home right now!>
Yes, *ma'am!* Right away!
12¾¢ DOZ
9
Speedy delivery, on its way!
10
Y. Kiyama
11
P SUEY
Maka hai!
Oww!
This proves it. Overcompetition between two businesses *does* cause their downfall!
12

Sign: *China Tower Restaurant*

Good Bye

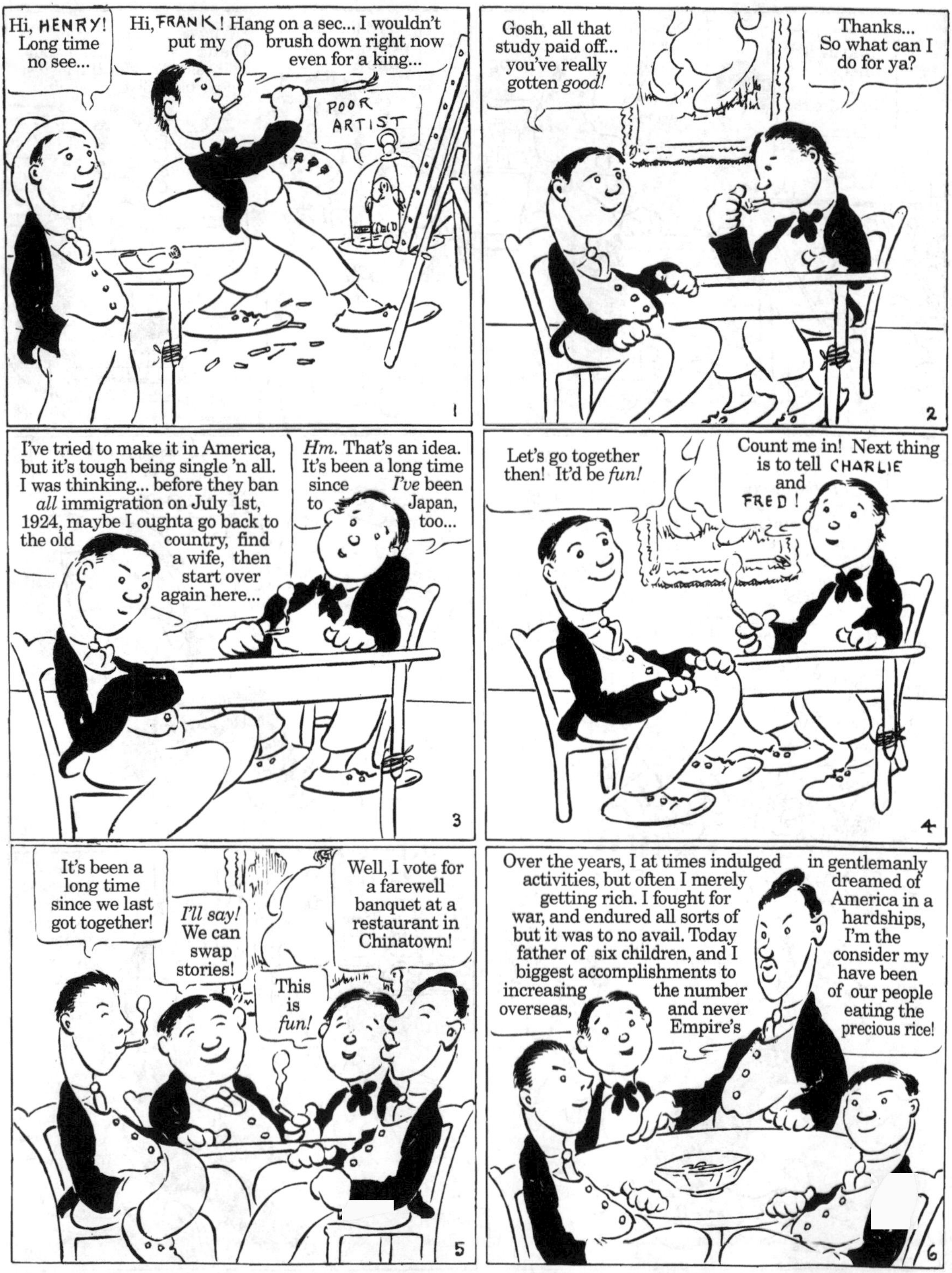
Hi, HENRY! Long time no see...
Hi, FRANK! Hang on a sec... I wouldn't put my brush down right now even for a king...
POOR ARTIST
Gosh, all that study paid off... you've really gotten *good!*
Thanks... So what can I do for ya?
I've tried to make it in America, but it's tough being single 'n all. I was thinking... before they ban *all* immigration on July 1st, 1924, maybe I oughta go back to the old country, find a wife, then start over again here...
Hm. That's an idea. It's been a long time since *I've* been to Japan, too...
Let's go together then! It'd be *fun!*
Count me in! Next thing is to tell CHARLIE and FRED!
It's been a long time since we last got together!
I'll say! We can swap stories!
This is *fun!*
Well, I vote for a farewell banquet at a restaurant in Chinatown!
Over the years, I at times indulged in gentlemanly activities, but often I merely dreamed of getting rich. I fought for America in a war, and endured all sorts of hardships, but it was to no avail. Today I'm the father of six children, and I consider my biggest accomplishments to have been increasing the number of our people overseas, and never eating the Empire's precious rice!

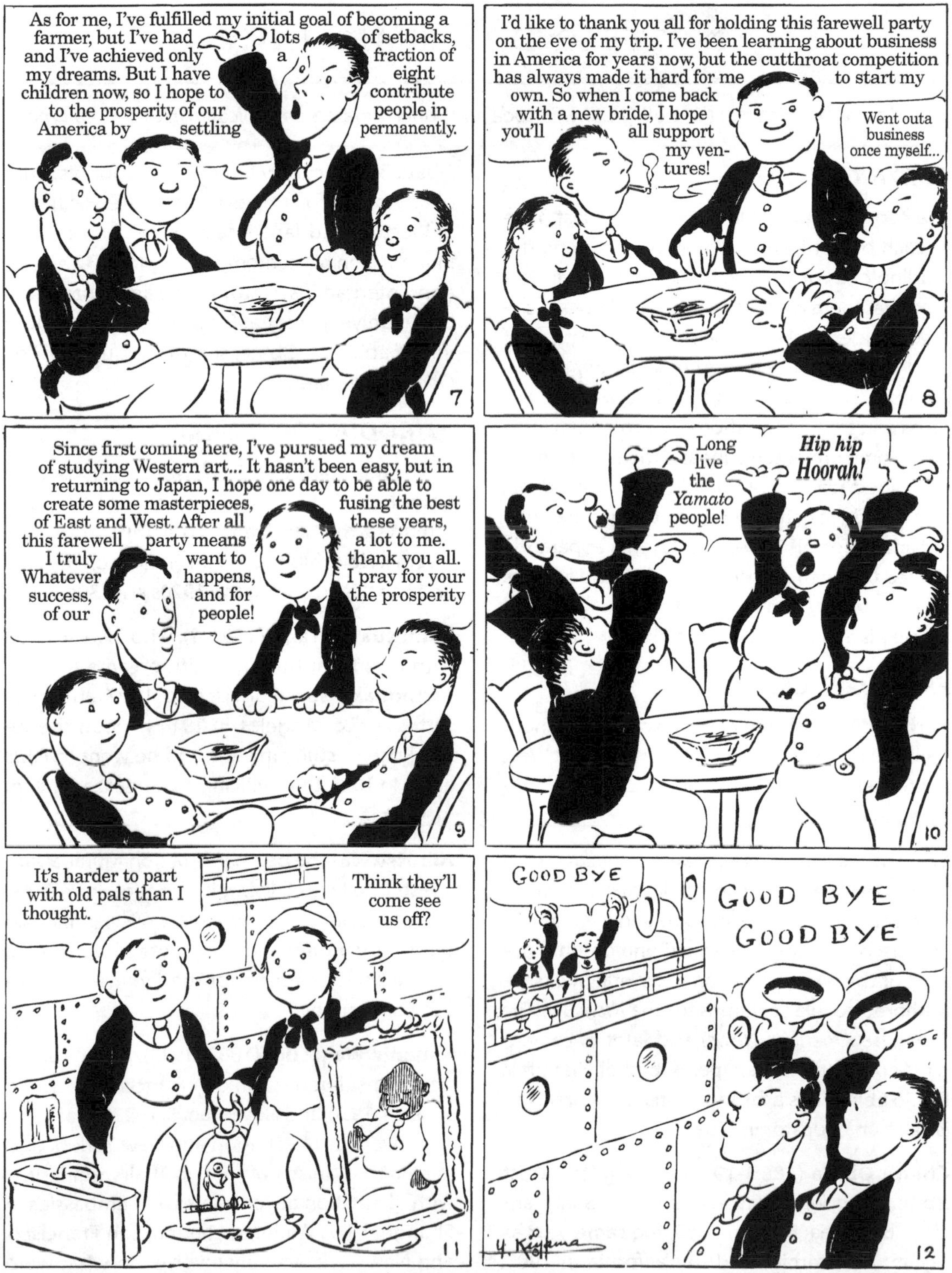

As for me, I've fulfilled my initial goal of becoming a farmer, but I've had lots of setbacks, and I've achieved only a fraction of my dreams. But I have eight children now, so I hope to contribute to the prosperity of our people in America by settling permanently.
I'd like to thank you all for holding this farewell party on the eve of my trip. I've been learning about business in America for years now, but the cutthroat competition has always made it hard for me to start my own. So when I come back with a new bride, I hope you'll all support my ventures!
Went outa business once myself...
Since first coming here, I've pursued my dream of studying Western art... It hasn't been easy, but in returning to Japan, I hope one day to be able to create some masterpieces, fusing the best of East and West. After all these years, this farewell party means a lot to me. I truly want to thank you all. Whatever happens, I pray for your success, and for the prosperity of our people!
Long live the *Yamato* people!
Hip hip Hoorah!
It's harder to part with old pals than I thought.
Think they'll come see us off?
GOOD BYE
GOOD BYE GOOD BYE
Y. Kiyama

NOTES AND COMMENTARY

Works cited are listed in the Bibliography. Episode and panel numbers are indicated in the left column.

COPYRIGHT PAGE

The copyright notice is pasted on the last page of each book Kiyama printed. When having the binding of a copy of the book repaired, I discovered that there is another notice underneath the first. It is identical in format, but lists the place of publication as "The Inpaku Association, 174 8th Avenue, Oakand, California." This was the address of a local association of people from Kiyama's home prefecture. "Inpaku" derives from the combined reading of two old regions of Japan, Inaba and Hōki, and refers to the general area of today's Tottori Prefecture. Kiyama apparently started to use the association's Oakland address as a temporary contact point and then decided to use his San Francisco address.

FRONTISPIECE

Perham W. Nahl (1869–1935) was a prominent California artist and a member of the East West Art Society, which promoted an East-West synthesis in art.

Shunshūrō was the pen name of Kazuo Ebina (1886–1956), a Japanese intellectual and writer who came to America in 1910 and lived in San Francisco for several years off and on until the start of the war. In addition to several books, he authored regular columns for the *Nichi Bei* (*The Japanese American News*) and later became a chief editor and newspaper publisher. His father, Danjō Ebina, was a famous Christian, a nationalist, and an educator in Japan.

Chiura Obata (1885–1975) was a gifted artist from Japan who was active in the San Francisco Bay Area. Born in 1885, the same year as Kiyama, he immigrated to California in 1903.

Obata is particularly famous today for his stunningly beautiful scenes of Yosemite. His fusion of Western and Japanese art styles had a major influence on his contemporaries. In 1932 he was appointed an instructor in the art department of the University of California, Berkeley. For more information on Obata, see the exquisite book *Obata's Yosemite*.

INTRODUCTORY REMARKS

Kazuo Matsubara (1894–?) was an artist born in Hawaii who settled in San Francisco in 1912 and attended the San Francisco Art Institute with Kiyama. He exhibited in San Francisco, Oakland, and San Diego during the 1920s and '30s.

Kamesuke Hiraga (1890–?), who also studied with Kiyama at the Art Institute, came to post-earthquake San Francisco in 1907 and later settled in Los Angeles. In 1914 he won the Julian Prize to study in Paris, and he went to Paris again in 1925, thus fulfilling an unrealized dream of Kiyama.

Hibutsu was the pen name of Koh Murai, a Japanese intellectual living in America from 1900 on. He was involved in a variety of scientific and business ventures and later wrote a book on the naturalization process for the Japanese American community.

Kaname Wakasugi (1883–1943) was the Japanese consul general in San Francisco between June 24, 1930, and November 8, 1933. He attended universities in Oregon and New York before joining the Ministry of Foreign Affairs and served with distinction at consulates and embassies in Shanghai, Los Angeles, London, San Francisco, and New York. Actively involved in what were ultimately futile Japan-U.S. negotiations to head off World War II, he tragically passed away of illness when returning to Japan on a civilian exchange ship in 1943.

THE FOUR IMMIGRANTS

1 Arrival in San Francisco

1.2 The **island** referred to here is presumably Angel Island in San Francisco Bay. This is the notorious island through which thousands of Asians were processed and often detained for long periods when they tried to immigrate to the United States. The vast majority were Chinese, but many Japanese were also held here temporarily. The immigration station was not opened until 1910, so in 1904, when Kiyama actually came to America, inspectors would have boarded ships in port and detained suspect immigrants in sheds at dockside in San Francisco. This episode is therefore probably a composite of later Japanese experiences, but it is conceivable that Kiyama's friends were sent to the quarantine station on the island, which was run by the U.S. Marine Hospital Service and had been in operation since 1892. For both Japanese and Chinese, "bad eyes" caused by infectious eye diseases could result in detention and being shipped back. On Angel Island today, Chinese graffiti and poems can still be seen on the walls of some of the old holding cells, which are preserved as a museum. To read many of the poignant poems, see *Island: Poetry and History of Chinese Immigrants on Angel Island, 1910–1940*, by Him Mark Lai et al. A few Chinese were held up to two years on the island. During World War II, the island was sometimes used to hold Japanese POWs.

1.4 **Zōni** is a special dish of rice cakes boiled with vegetables and eaten at New Year's.

1.8 **Mr. Ushijima, the "Potato King"** refers to one of the most successful and famous Japanese immigrants of the period, Kinji Ushijima, known to Americans as "George Shima." Ushijima (1864–1926) succeeded in growing potatoes in the Sacramento Delta area, partly by reclaiming swampy land and using the latest techniques in irrigation and draining. He owned vast tracts of land and died a millionaire, but in his later life he increasingly had to battle discrimination against Japanese. He served as the first chairman of the Japanese Association when it was formed in February 1908. There is a memorial and gravesite to him in the Japanese cemetery in Colma, south of San Francisco. The Shima Tract, in the Delta area, is also named after him.

Yamato is the ancient name for Japan. In *Planted in Good Soil*, author Masakazu Iwata writes that the early immigrants, whether poor or well off, had a "deep sense of racial and national pride" and an assurance that "each was a member of the *Yamato minzoku*, or Yamato Race, ruled, according to traditional Japanese history, by a line of emperors 'unbroken from ages eternal.'"

1.11 Early immigrants often boarded at local Christian churches or Buddhist temples and were assisted in a variety of ways, including finding work. Here they are met by a Buddhist elder or priest, and the welcoming meal appears to be held in Chinatown.

2–10 "Schoolboys"

2.8 In most Japanese-English dictionaries, the word **ketō** is listed (if listed at all) as simply meaning "whites" or "Westerners," but it is a derogatory term for which there is no perfect translation. "Hairy, ugly whites" might best convey the nuance. Ironically, *ketō* is written with the characters for "hairy" and "Tang" (as in Tang-dynasty China), and has a secondary, now-in-disuse meaning of "Chinese."

3.7 **Hokinoichi Hanawa** (1746–1821) was a scholar in feudal Japan, blind from the age of seven. Despite his handicap, he was renowned as a scholar of the classics and as an archivist-editor.

3.9 If Frank finds American houses too "hard," it is because at this time almost all houses in Japan were single-story wood buildings with inner sliding walls of paper-based *fusuma* and *shōji*, both of which are relatively very soft to crash into! San Francisco houses are mostly wood, too, but they have brick and concrete foundations. In some of the wealthier, earthquake-resistant areas of the city, the houses are of masonry construction.

4.1 **Kōdōkan** is the name of the organization formed by Jigorō Kanō in 1882 to promote and teach judo. It is also the name of this judo school's *dōjō* (training halls) and of the most popular type of *jūjitsu*.

5.2 **Madam Tamaki** refers to Tamaki Miura (1884–1946), the first world-famous Japanese soprano prima donna, best known for her role as Madame Butterfly. Although she was widely known around the globe, she did not actually perform in America until 1920.

5.6 According to Hideko Kiyama, Henry's family ran an inn in Neu, Japan. It might have been customary for the servant-maids to scrub the backs of their employers, but males would normally not have done this.

8.2 The **Call Building** survived the 1906 earthquake. It can still be seen today at 703 Market Street, at the intersection with Third, but it has been extensively remodeled and renamed the "Central Tower." Built in 1898, at 315 feet, it was for years the tallest building in San Francisco (the tallest west of the Mississippi, for that matter). It was the home of *The Morning Call* newspaper.

8.3 This is presumably Union Square, which today is still a popular spot for what are now called "homeless" people. **I.W.W.** stands for Industrial Workers of the World. At the time the I.W.W. was thought of as a rather militant labor union, but apparently Charlie did not share this view! In *The Issei*, Yuji Ichioka notes that some Japanese student-workers were attracted to the I.W.W. exactly because it did not subscribe to the racism common to other unions.

Built in 1904, the **St. Francis Hotel** on Powell Street facing Union Square today remains one of San Francisco's premier hotels. It is often used by visiting presidents and in 1998 was part of the Westin chain of hotels.

8.4 Judging by the sign in the background, Charlie and Frank have walked over to Chinatown and are standing in front of a Chinese-owned store. Although both Japanese and Chinese immigrants were discriminated against and faced many similar problems, they were not always on the best of terms, as this interchange indicates. Things weren't helped by the fact that Japan had generally sided with the imperialist powers in Asia against China, had been embroiled in its own war with China in 1894–95, and by the time of this story had already turned Taiwan (not to mention Korea) into a colony.

8.6 There were many bordellos throughout San Francisco when Henry Kiyama and his friends lived there, but they were especially common in the Barbary Coast area and in Chinatown. Women of a variety of races often inhabited tiny "cribs." Ichioka's *The Issei* includes an account from the turn of the century in which not Chinese but Japanese prostitutes in Chinatown are described as being exhibited in a "kind of cage," dressed in gaudy red garments with painted cheeks and wearing "a peculiar wreath-like ornament upon the head, which instead of being a crown of a pure and noble womanhood was the emblem of shame."

9.5 **Dr. Kurosawa** is certainly modeled after Kakusaburō Kurosawa, an actual doctor who served the Japanese community for many years. A prominent figure in the local community, Kurosawa served as vice chairman when the first Japanese Association was formed in 1908 and later headed the organization.

9.9 The correct spelling of **Haward St.** is "Howard St."

10.1 Henry Kiyama studied art in San Francisco at what is today known as the San Francisco Art Institute. The institute was formed in 1871, but around the time Henry Kiyama first arrived in the city it was known as the **Mark Hopkins Institute of Art**, and it was located in the former Nob Hill mansion of financier Mark Hopkins, at the corner of California and Mason streets. During the 1906 earthquake the mansion was destroyed by fire, and when the school was rebuilt it operated as the San Francisco Institute of Art, California School of Design. In 1926 the school assumed its present location at 800 Chestnut Street in the North Beach area. It remains one of the top art schools in America.

12–14 Working on a Farm

In episodes 12 through 14 the class differences in the Japanese immigrant community are highlighted, as Frank and Charlie are definitely not cut out for farm work and are very different from the other Japanese they meet. It was common for city-based student-laborers like them to work part time in the San Joaquin Valley and in the Sacramento River delta area, where farmer-entrepreneurs such as George Shima were busy developing the land and where much human labor was needed.

12.2 **Stockton** is a town around 80 miles east of San Francisco, in the fertile San Joaquin Valley.

12.3 **"Blanket-boy"** and *buranke-katsugi* ("blanket-toters") are terms Japanese used to refer to their countrymen who were rural migrant workers.

12.5 See 2.8.

12.12 In the original Japanese, the "boss" character declares them to be on a "floating island" built on *gama gusa*, which is a type of cattail or bulrush. The delta is famous for its tule reeds, so that may be what is meant here. It is doubtful that the island was actually "floating," but it was probably on highly unstable, reclaimed land formerly covered with water and reeds. Much of the rich delta farmland today is reclaimed and irrigated.

14.1 **Sacramento**, the capital of California, is around ninety miles northeast of San Francisco. The Sacramento Capitol building dates back to 1869 and was rebuilt after the 1906 earthquake. It is 210 feet high at the top, which made it a very imposing structure around the time of Charlie and Frank's visit. Because ordinary citizens could then freely enter the building, the young men are very impressed with the openness of American government. Today liability and safety issues have constrained this openness, and the public is no longer allowed access to the cupola near the top of the structure.

15   Death of a Parent

15.8   In the original Japanese text Henry offers Charlie *tekkan biiru* (literally, "iron pipe beer"), which was an amusing way of saying "tap water."

15.10   With space at a premium, in 1901 San Francisco prohibited further burials within its city limits. Most cemeteries already in San Francisco were thereafter moved to the neighboring city of Colma in San Mateo County. Before 1901, Japanese gravesites were scattered in various cemeteries in San Francisco, but after a Japanese prostitute died of disease in 1879 and was refused burial in the local Gibson Chinese Church cemetery, the Japanese community began developing its own cemetery. The current Colma cemetery has been operated by the Japanese Benevolent Society of California since June 1901, when, according to its brochure, the Society was established with donations from Japanese individuals and companies. In 1906 the Society also received a grant from Japan's Emperor Meiji "to (1) assist sick, disabled, or destitute Japanese in California, and (2) to create and operate a common cemetery for Japanese in California."

16–18   Decadence

At the beginning of the century, San Francisco's Chinatown offered young men many forms of entertainment—ranging from gambling to opium dens to sex—that could easily lead to their ruin. In the early years of the Japanese community, when the population was overwhelmingly male, gambling by single young men was often a serious problem.

16.2   *Baahk gap piu* was a popular Chinese game similar to modern keno. According to Ichioka in *The Issei*, it meant "white pigeon card" in Cantonese, because in old China pigeons were used to announce the results of lotteries in rural areas. The Japanese, bastardizing the Chinese pronunciation, called it **bakappei** or *bakapyō* and wrote it with the characters for "horse" and "deer," which gave it the double meaning of "fool's card." **Fantan**, one of the oldest Chinese games of chance, was also popular among Japanese immigrants, and it was played with coins and a brass cup on a table. Fast and simple to understand, it was called *shiigo* or *shiikoi*, from the Cantonese word *sei gok*, which means "four corners," for the four "gates" marked on the table.

17.2   Here Charlie is having what is known as his *hatsuyume*, or the first dream of the New Year. In Japan this is supposed to indicate one's luck for the year, and Charlie has been lucky, because he's seen the lucky symbols of Mt. Fuji, a hawk, and an eggplant!

18.2   This is presumably where the Japanese men get work referrals, and it is probably affiliated with a Buddhist or Christian church. The men appear to be playing the popular Japanese board game of *go* to pass the time. The sign on the wall reflects the menial types of work available to them.

19   The Shoe Salesman

The **Russo-Japanese War** (1904–5) forms the backdrop for this episode. In the space of around fifty years, Japan had modernized and joined the European imperialist nations in jockeying for power on the Asian continent. The conflict with

Russia grew out of a dispute over Manchuria and Korea and resulted in a resounding defeat for Russian forces. The defeat of a major European and "white" empire's forces by an Asian island nation of "little brown men" shocked people in the West and quickly established Japan as a world power. In the United States, Japan was at first viewed as the underdog in the conflict with giant Russia and was overwhelmingly supported; later, the same victory was used to portray Japan as a military threat and to agitate against Japanese immigrants in California. Peace negotiations between Japan and Russia were presided over by U.S. President Theodore Roosevelt. The war was enormously popular in Japan, and crowds rioted in Tokyo when it was ended, furious that they had unjustly been deprived of further victories and the chance to obtain a huge indemnity from Russia.

19.1 Admiral Heihachirō **Tōgō** (1846–1934) was Japan's most famous hero of the Russo-Japanese War, roundly defeating Russian fleets at Port Arthur in 1904 and in the battle of Tsushima in 1905. Given the story line of Kiyama's comic book, this episode likely refers to the Battle of Tsushima, which occurred on May 27, 1905, and resulted in destruction of Imperial Russia's Baltic Squadron.

19.7 At first glance, the model for the building in the background here appears to be the California Palace of the Legion of Honor, an art museum that did not open until the end of 1924 and thus does not fit with the story's time line. Careful examination, however, shows it to actually be the Spreckels Temple of Music, a bandshell built in Golden Gate Park in 1900, right next to the popular Japanese Tea Gardens.

19.8 When Frank mentions a lack of women in California, at this stage in history he is referring to a lack of women for Japanese men. Given discrimination, socializing freely with respectable white women was extremely difficult (marrying them was against the law), and in the early years of the immigrant community there were very few Japanese women. In *The Politics of Prejudice*, historian Roger Daniels notes that around this time there were almost eight males for every female in the population over fifteen years old.

19.9 **Cliff House**, which overlooks the Pacific Ocean, has been a favorite spot to eat and drink in San Francisco since 1863. It has been rebuilt several times.

19.10 One of the famous views from Cliff House is Seal Rock, which is still inhabited by a colony of seals.

20–23 The Great San Francisco Quake

The earthquake struck early on the morning of April 18, 1906. It registered an awesome 8.25 on the Richter scale and is now believed to have killed over 3,000 people (original estimates were far lower, as officials apparently tried to minimize the destruction). It left much of the population homeless. The worst damage was done not by the quake but by the fires that ensued.

20.6 **Namu Amida Butsu** means "I sincerely believe in the Amida Buddha" and is often said when facing death or when praying for the souls of others.

20.12 After the earthquake, fires broke out all over the city, but water mains had also burst, so there was little the fire department could do. When a fire storm resulted, the Army general in the Presidio took over firefighting operations and instituted martial law. He ordered buildings on the periphery of the fires to be dynamited to create fire breaks, but in most cases this was ineffective.

21.4 The **checkpoints** Charlie refers to are the *sekisho* of feudal Japan, which were used to prevent or control the movement of people throughout the country. They were not abolished until 1868, when Japan began modernizing.

22.4 Today the epicenter is believed to have been around Point Reyes, just north of San Francisco.

22.12 The original gag here is based on the expression *yoraba taiju no kage,* or "If you're going to lean against a tree, it's better to lean against a big one."

23.1 Many Japanese immigrants seem to have hit on the idea of going into the restaurant business at this time, serving American-style food. According to Daniels in *The Politics of Prejudice,* by the end of June the Asiatic Exclusion League tried to get whites to stop patronizing such restaurants. In October a boycott was begun, windows were smashed, and some owners were beaten.

23.2 There certainly would have been advantages in obtaining a **"non-immigrant" visa**, as it would have higher status and privileges.

23.6 **Fusakichi Ōmori** (1868–1923) was a pioneering seismology professor from the Imperial University in Tokyo who came to San Francisco in 1906 shortly after the earthquake to investigate the damage. Along with a Professor T. Nakamura of the same university, he was stoned and attacked by angry whites. One of those responsible for the attacks was portrayed as a hero by the local press. Making the attacks doubly disturbing was the fact that the Japanese government and the Japanese Red Cross had donated more money to help the stricken city than all other foreign nations combined. Ōmori

is sometimes referred to as the "father of seismology" in Japan.

25 Working in a Store

25.2 Why does Charlie speak of his dad as being alive, when in an earlier episode he led us to believe he is dead? This is one of the main puzzles of Kiyama's story line, and it may never be solved.

25.9 In feudal times, Japanese society was organized into four classes—samurai, farmers, craftsmen, and merchants—with the merchants theoretically on the bottom of the social ladder. Samurai, as the elite, sometimes beheaded people from lower classes who insulted them.

26 A Crisis over Japanese School Children

Organized groups like the Asiatic Exclusion League, backed by labor unions and otherwise "progressive forces," advocated the segregation of all Asian children in San Francisco schools. With newspapers conducting inflammatory anti-Japanese campaigns, after the 1906 earthquake there were boycotts waged against Japanese-owned restaurants and frequent attacks on Japanese individuals in the city. On October 11, 1906, the San Francisco Board of Education ordered all Japanese and Korean school children to join the Chinese, who were already segregated. This action caused an uproar in Japan and led to the unprecedented involvement of a U.S. president—Theodore Roosevelt—in local San Francisco politics. Roosevelt considered the anti-Asian California legislators and politicians "idiots" and was genuinely concerned that San Francisco's inept handling of its Japanese school children might bring Japan (which had just defeated the Russians) and the U.S. to the brink of war. The problem was eventually resolved by a compromise known today as the 1907–8 "Gentlemen's Agreement" with Japan. Japanese children were allowed to attend San Francisco schools (unless, according to one frequent complaint, they were overage, or had limited English ability); in February, Congress passed an immigration act that Roosevelt signed, ending further Japanese immigration via Hawaii, Mexico, or Canada; and Japan agreed to stop issuing visas to Japanese laborers going to the United States. For a good description of this, see *Theodore Roosevelt and Japan* by Raymond A. Esthus.

26.5   Although the kanji characters Kiyama wrote here look as though they should be pronounced "Katada," and he did have a classmate named Setsurō Katada, they certainly represent Otosaburō Noda, a staff member of the Japanese American Industrial Corporation. In one other place, Kiyama uses the same kanji character with the pronunciation. According to Yuji Ichioka's *The Issei*, an Otosaburō **Noda** was dispatched by the Japanese American community in San Francisco to Washington, D.C., in April 1907 to consult with the Japanese ambassador. Whether he actually met Roosevelt is doubtful.

26.6   One of the sources of anti-Japanese sentiment in California was the influx of poor, unskilled laborers. Often they first immigrated to Hawaii (not annexed by the U.S. until 1898), where they worked on plantations and then later moved to California under part of a sophisticated labor contract system. The "Gentleman's Agreement" put a stop to this Japanese immigration via Hawaii.

26.7   Although first-generation Japanese immigrants could not become naturalized, their children, having been born in the United States, were automatically citizens.

27–28   *Japanese Immigrants Arriving via Hawaii*

27.2   The building in the background is the Ferry Building, completed in 1898. Until the Bay

Bridge and the Golden Gate Bridge were built, ferries were the main mode of transportation across San Francisco Bay, and the Ferry Building was one of the busiest spots in the city. Although the big clock on the tower stopped in both the 1906 and 1989 earthquakes, the building survived, and—prominently located at the end of Market Street— still serves as a proud symbol of San Francisco.

27.8   See 2.8.

27.9   As an educated student-laborer, Charlie clearly regarded his fellow countrymen who arrived as poor laborers as a bit of an embarrassment. Although much of the anti-Japanese sentiment in San Francisco can be attributed to ignorance and racism, many members of the established Japanese community were themselves concerned about the quality and behavior of laborers arriving from Japan and about the impression it might give Americans of Japanese in general. Also, since Japan had long been isolated and had only recently modernized and cast off its feudal system of government, there was a burning desire on the part of most people for their country to be recognized as a **"first-rate"** nation on a par with the industrialized West.

28.2   Physical attacks against Japanese had become quite frequent at this time. Some are described in Daniels's *The Politics of Prejudice*. One issei man interviewed by President Theodore Roosevelt's investigator stated that "the miscreants are generally young men, 17 or 18 years old. Whenever the newspapers attack the Japanese the roughs renew their misdeeds with redoubled energy."

28.3   See 27.2

28.5   Until Japan's feudal system was overturned in the mid-19th century, most Japanese never ate meat, mainly for religious reasons. After 1853, it soon became fashionable among urbanites to eat meat, but it was still very expensive.

28.7 In Kiyama's time, there were **Japantown**s, or Japanese communities, scattered in several locations around the city, including South Park, the intersection of Grant and Dupont streets by Chinatown, and the Western Addition. Today, what is known as Japantown in San Francisco is centered around the intersection of Post and Buchanan streets on the edge of the Western Addition. Because of the incarceration, displacement, and dispersion of Japanese Americans in World War II and their subsequent assimilation into mainstream society, San Francisco's Japan Town no longer plays the same role it did in Japanese American life. Increasingly, it is the home to Japan-based corporations and a growing Korean-American community.

28.12 Theodore Roosevelt issued executive order No. 589 on March 14, 1907, after being authorized to do so by Congress on February 18. It barred Japanese immigration (mainly of laborers) to the U.S. via Hawaii, Mexico, and Canada and took effect on July 1, 1907. In the original version of *The Four Immigrants*, Kiyama uses the character for "end", implying this was the *last* day of the ban; since it does not make sense historically, this presumably is a lettering mistake.

29   *Enjoying an "Illumination" Show*

Around 1907, tensions between Japan and America escalated to a war scare. Japan, having emerged victorious from its war with Russia, had greatly increased its armaments budget, which made many Americans very nervous. When combined with the anti-Japanese agitation in

California, this resulted in predictions of war, with preposterous rumors of Japanese spies and of invasions by Japanese troops from Mexico. In Japan a similar reaction took place. Theodore Roosevelt's response was to send the Atlantic Fleet around the world, and to show the flag in Japan. The fleet was popular in Japan and very well received, but there was a hidden message. As Roosevelt wrote in a letter in 1916, "the voyage of the battle fleet … was really an answer to the very ugly war talk that had begun to spring up in Japan; and it was the best example I know of, 'of speaking softly and carrying a big stick.'" For an account of this see Esthus's book, *Theodore Roosevelt and Japan*.

29.1 The **Atlantic Fleet**, also known as the "Great White Fleet," visited San Francisco between May 7 and July 7, 1908.

29.6 **Goemon Ishikawa** was a famous Japanese robber said to have lived in the late 16th century. Much of his life is shrouded in mystery (or legend), but he was reportedly executed by being boiled alive in a huge pot on August 24, 1594. In later Kabuki plays, he was often romantically portrayed as a type of Robin Hood. His name today survives in the expression *goemon buro*, which refers to taking a crude, fire-heated bath, usually outdoors.

29.7 **Danjūrō** Ichikawa is the lineage name of over eleven generations of Kabuki actors, starting in the 17th century. The founder was especially renowned for his dramatic flourishes and exciting portrayals of warriors.

30   *A Visit by the President*

30.1 **President** William Howard Taft (1857–1930) visited San Francisco on October 13, 1911. He probably had a better knowledge of Japan than any previous president. As Secretary of War in the Roosevelt administration, he had visited Japan in 1905, and the Taft-Katsura Memorandum that resulted in effect gave Japan a free hand in Korea in exchange for recognition of America's rule over the Philippines. In 1907 Taft had again visited Japan to reassure Japanese about anti-Japanese sentiment on the West Coast and to discuss immigration issues, as well as fears of war.

30.3 **Market Street** was the busy main street of San Francisco in 1911, and it remains so today.

30.5 **Kanshin** (Han Xin, ?–196 B.C.) was a famous general in the Han Dynasty in China. Of an impoverished background, as a youth he was forced to crawl between the legs of a tormentor, but he endured this humiliation and went on to become a legendary figure for his service to the emperor. From this incident comes the expression (now rarely heard) of "going between the legs like Kanshin," used to indicate enduring humiliation.

30.10 At 5'10" and over 300 pounds, Taft was probably the heaviest, and horizontally largest, president ever.

31 When the Golden Gate Bank Failed

On March 29, 1909, the San Francisco branch of the **Golden Gate Bank** (Kinmon Ginkō), shuttered its doors with a note saying, "closed for three days for arrangements," but never re-opened. That year seven Japanese-immigrant-owned banks failed.

31.9 **Monterey** is a beautiful seaside town around 110 miles south of San Francisco. Best known for tourism today, during Kiyama's time it had a thriving sardine industry with many canneries. It was the setting for John Steinbeck's famous novel *Cannery Row*.

31.12 The original Japanese joke here revolves around the expression *nawa wo kakeru* (literally, "to tie up"), which also means "to arrest."

32–35 The Panama-Pacific International Exposition

The **Panama-Pacific International Exposition** was held in San Francisco from February 20 to December 4, 1915. Ostensibly, it was to celebrate the opening of the Panama Canal, but even more than that it was a celebration of the recovery of San Francisco from the 1906 earthquake. By all accounts, it was one of the most successful and beautiful fairs ever. It covered 635 acres of what is today known as the Marina District of San Francisco, and it was designed and built with top talent. By the time it closed, over 18 million people had attended. Over twenty-four nations participated. The government of Japan contributed over half a million dollars, making it one of the largest foreign donors. In addition to a Japanese tea house, there were Japanese gardens and displays of Japanese manufactures and handicrafts, and demonstrations of *sumo* wrestling with the normally semi-naked wrestlers wearing full underpants. The gardens were very popular and according to the fair's guidebook replicated the grounds of a famous Japanese temple, "trees, sods, and even the stones having been brought over and rearranged in exact semblance of the original." Marjorie M. Dobkin (writing in Burton Benedict's *The Anthropology of World's Fairs*) notes that the Exposition Board led the opposition to some of the more virulent anti-Japanese forces in California at the time, in particular the move to exclude Japanese immigrants from the right to own land in California.

32.5 **The End of the Trail** was the name of an enormously popular twenty-five-foot statue by James Earle Fraser. It depicted an exhausted Indian and his horse, symbolizing the end of resistance to civilization. The statue was later moved to the Cowboy Hall of Fame in Oklahoma City, Oklahoma.

33.5　The **Zone**, also known sometimes as the "joy zone," was the name of the sixty-five-acre amusement area of the Exposition near the Fillmore Street entrance. There were exciting rides and exhibits and shows, some of which were quite adult in nature.

33.8　The building in the background is the Palace of Fine Arts, the only original structure from the fair that still stands today. Of a universally acclaimed design by Bernard Maybeck, in 1998 it housed a theater and a hands-on science museum called the Exploratorium. Because of its otherworldly beauty and harmony with the landscaping and ponds around it, the site is a prized backdrop for wedding photos.

33.12　**Kuroto** is slang for a black person. It is not a nice term, but literally just means "black person"; it does not have the same associations with slavery and racism that many English colloquialisms have. There is an associated double entendre, as *kuroto* also means "professional." As with his depictions of Chinese, here Kiyama has employed a style used by European American cartoonists at the time to caricature African Americans.

34.7　This is from a famous poem by Fujiwara-no-tomoyasu-no-musume (936–95), a court noble. The poem expresses her feelings after her husband leaves her for another woman.

34.9　The **Telescope** refers to a ride in the Zone part of the fairgrounds, known as the Aeroscope. It was built by famed engineer Joseph Strauss, who later oversaw construction of the Golden Gate Bridge. In reality, the Aeroscope could only take passengers up to 285 feet, but in those days even such a height was an unprecedented, dizzying experience.

35.2　During construction of the fair, accidents in the city increased. In this particular interchange, however, Frank is certainly referring to the famous stunt pilot, Lincoln Beachey, who performed acrobatic stunts in his airplane regularly at the fairgrounds. On March 14, while flying a monoplane doing loop-the-loops over San Francisco Bay, Beachey crashed and was killed.

36–39　*The Rice of Colusa*

Colusa is a county located in the central part of the Sacramento Valley of northern California, 90 miles northeast of San Francisco. It is intersected today by Interstate 5, running north-south, and State Highway 20, running east-west. The Sacramento River runs along its eastern border, and the rich, fertile soil in the area, when irrigated, has been a prime area for a variety of crops. It is one of the first places in California that rice was grown. According to Akiji Yoshimura, who wrote "A Brief History of the Japanese in Colusa County" for the local county historical society, rice was introduced into the county in 1911, and by 1915 over 12,000 acres were under cultivation. This attracted hundreds of Japanese investors and laborers to the area. The most successful lived "high on the hog," "taking in the bright lights of San Francisco and tossing their money around with reckless abandon so uncharacteristic of the usually frugal Japanese. But those were fabulous times, when fortunes were made and lost."

36.7　**Masamune,** a famous brand of *sake*, is another way of saying "Japanese *sake*."

37.3　The **Specie Bank** was the Yokohama Specie Bank. Many immigrants kept their money at its branches on the West Coast.

39.10　**Overland** was the name of a popular car early in the 20th century. Later known as the Willys-Overland, it was eventually manufactured in not only the U.S., but Canada and the U.K. In 1914, the Overland Model 79 cost $950, which was a fortune for a janitor.

39.12 The original gag in this episode revolved around the word *kome*, which normally means "rice." In the last frame, the husband says, *Ore wo kome ni mite iru kara da* ("It's because you always look down on me") with the same-sounding *kome* used in a different meaning.

40–43   Picture Brides

Picture brides were women who came from Japan to marry men in the United States, usually knowing them only through photographs. It was an extension of the traditional arranged marriage system in Japan, and it often involved close consultation on the part of the respective families. For poor, single men in the United States who could not afford to return to Japan and search for a wife or find mates locally (where there were few Japanese women and marrying a white was often illegal), it also was one of the only practical ways for them to ever get married. Most of the marriages turned out to be successful. But as can be imagined, many of them did not, and Japanese-language papers of the time in America frequently ran stories of runaway brides. For a clever cartoonist, the "picture bride" system provided lots of amusing material. For the pro-exclusionist forces in California, it also provided ammunition for them to depict Japanese women as being downtrodden and the victims of a new type of slavery. In 1920 the Japanese government stopped issuing passports to "picture brides." In episode 43, even the relatively well-educated Fred has mixed feelings about the system, but he goes ahead with it anyway, and it seems to work out—in a fashion!

40.8 **Ono-no-komachi** was a woman poet of legendary beauty and talent in the early Heian period (early 9th century), who has been revered down through the ages.

41.4 When Fred mentions the **sake vows** back home, he is referring to *san-san-kudō*, the nuptial cups of *sake* exchanged at Shinto weddings.

44–45   The Great War in Europe

World War I began in Europe in 1914 and lasted until 1918. America entered the war on April 6, 1917. Japan entered the war on the Allied side much earlier, when it declared war on Germany on August 23, 1914, but its activities were mainly limited to Asia. In the United States, many issei immigrants enlisted in the U.S. military, even though as noncitizens they were exempt from the draft. Patriotism was certainly one motive, but many also hoped that by fighting for the United States they would be able to gain citizenship. For most this did not come true, at least until 1952 when the immigration laws were finally changed.

45.8 **Kiyomasa Katō** (1562–1611) was a samurai general who served the famous warlord Hideyoshi. He distinguished himself in a series of battles in Japan and fought overseas in Hideyoshi's second invasion of Korea in 1597. His nickname was "Tiger."

45.9 For Japanese American readers around the time this book was published, Charlie's comment would probably have elicited an ironic, slightly bitter laugh, because most of the elements of his plan—to buy land, marry a white woman, and obtain citizenship—were illegal at this time.

45.12 The building in the background is San Francisco's present City Hall. Construction of it was completed in 1916.

46 *Influenza*

In 1918 an **influenza** epidemic killed over 20 million people around the world and over 548,000 in the United States. In San Francisco, between September and January 1918, over 3,500 people died, most between the ages of twenty and forty. As in other cities, authorities tried to prevent the spread of the disease by making people wear masks, not realizing that the virus easily permeated gauze. On November 1 a "mask ordinance" went into effect, requiring all citizens to wear one in public. Fines ranged from $5 to thirty days in jail, but in the end most San Franciscans became tired of the masks and started ignoring the regulations (it was hard to smoke wearing them, for one thing!).

46.3 Charlie and Frank are standing in front of a store called **Goshadō**, although only the first two characters of the word are visible. First established in 1906, when Kiyama created *The Four Immigrants* it was located at 1698 Post Street and sold a variety of goods, including books. At the end of 1998, it was only a block away, on the corner of Buchanan and Sutter, and still run by the original family.

46.10 In English the epidemic was also known as the "Spanish Influenza"; it is now generally believed to have started in Kansas.

46.12 The original joke here revolved around a pun on the word for "king" (*ōsama*) and a word for death (*ōjō*).

47 *Prohibition*

47.1 The 18th Amendment to the Constitution was submitted for ratification to the states by Congress on December 18, 1918, and went into effect at the beginning of 1919, ushering in the era known as Prohibition. From then until 1933, when it was finally repealed, the sale of alcoholic beverages was illegal.

47.11 Making home-brew *sake*, or traditional rice wine, was a common practice among many issei.

48 *The Turlock Incident*

Turlock is a town about 110 miles southeast of San Francisco, near Modesto on Highway 99. During the night on July 20, 1921, Japanese laborers in Turlock were awakened by an armed band of white men who loaded them onto trucks, drove them out of town, and warned them never to return again. Similar incidents occurred in several other towns in California. Six whites were later tried, but it was hard to find Japanese willing to testify, and only one was able to make a positive identification. An all-white jury acquitted the defendants in ten minutes. Even the Japanese Exclusion League condemned the incident, fearing it would discredit their cause. For more information, see *Japanese American History*, edited by Brian Niiya, and Ichioka's *The Issei*.

48.12 The original Japanese gag here revolves around a pun on the expression *naki ne-iri*, literally, "go to sleep crying." It is used to describe situations when there is no choice but to endure or "grin and bear it."

49 *The Alien Land Act*

49.1 Early Japanese immigrant families were sometimes accused by those in favor of exclusion of having too many children, but as Roger Daniels points out in his book, *The Politics of Prejudice*, their average birthrate statistics were skewed by the fact that most of the women came during their prime childbearing years.

49.4 Although Kiyama has left the dates blank here, he is presumably referring to the Alien Land Act passed by the California legislature in November 1920, which was in turn an attempt to strengthen a similar act of 1913. It forbade "aliens ineligible to citizenship" from owning land and banned their leases, and by default this largely meant the issei and other Asian immigrants who were not allowed to become citizens. This law was emulated in other states and tested in the U.S. Supreme Court in 1923, which voted against the issei. One way to get around the law was to register land in the name of children born in the United States, who were citizens by birth.

49.7 **Margaret Sanger** (1883–1966) was an early advocate of birth control as a means of improving the life of women. Starting in 1912, she initiated pro-birth-control movements and formed several organizations. From 1922 on, she also visited Japan several times.

50 Meant for Each Other

50.6 **Dodoitsu** is a Japanese popular love song in a 7-7-7-5 syllable pattern. Charlie starts to sing, but since there isn't enough room to write the whole song, Kiyama just has him say, *dodoitsu*.

Waka is a favorite type of thirty-one-syllable poem.

50.12 In Japanese the gag in this episode revolves around an untranslatable double meaning phrase-pun. The episode is titled "Nita Mono Fūfu," which means "A Couple Who Resemble Each Other." When written without ideograms, however, it could also be read to mean "Blowing on Something Cooked." In this final panel, therefore, little John says "I'm blowing on this cooked food before I eat it."

51 Mutual Downfall

51.6 *Benkyō*, which normally means "to study," has a secondary meaning of "working hard" or "discounting," and when prefaced with *dai*, or the character for "big," it means "big bargains." The signs in front of the competitor's store use this secondary meaning. Although no one seems to remember a grocer by the name of Daibenkyō, in 1998 there was a confectionery shop named Benkyodō on the corner of Buchanan and Sutter streets, dating back to 1906.

51.12 In the background, the Chinese man yells an obscenity at the two men in Cantonese.

52 Good Bye

52.3 Frank refers to the banning of all immigrants from July 1, 1924, on. Kiyama is referring here to the Immigration Act of 1924, which was signed into law on May 24, 1924, by President Calvin Coolidge. This bill was a response to a general belief that all immigration should be limited, but while limiting European immigration, it rejected even a token quota for Japanese immigrants, effectively excluding them from the United States. The American ambassador to Japan resigned in protest, and in Japan the law was perceived as deeply insulting. Along with other discriminatory legislation and measures passed against the Japanese in the United States at national, state, and local levels, the Act contributed greatly to the rising tension between Japan and America that eventually led to World War II. It also meant the effective end of immigration from Japan to the United States.

Afterword

What happened to Henry Kiyama after he went back to Japan?

It is not entirely clear at what date the story ends, although we know that it is before 1924, when the very restrictive Immigration Act was passed. From the Kiyama family history and from newspaper articles provided by his daughter and son-in-law, it is clear that Kiyama returned to Japan in 1922, and that he took a painting titled "Negro" with him, which was exhibited in Japan at an exposition in Tokyo in March of the same year. Presumably this is the painting he shows himself carrying in the last episode before getting on board the ship to return to Japan.

In 1923, at the age of thirty-nine, Kiyama married, and within a year had a daughter, Hideko. This marriage soon dissolved, and in 1924 he returned to San Francisco alone. There he established his own art studio, and, as we have seen, by 1927 he had not only exhibited his paintings and drawings in a variety of places but also created the comic story that would become *The Four Immigrants*.

In March 1927, one month after exhibiting the art for his comic, Kiyama returned to Japan again for a stay of several years. In 1931 he drew the illustrations for a Japanese collection of Native American children's stories, and on March 3 he also had his own comic book printed in Tokyo at Kumaya Printing. That same year he returned again to San Francisco with the books for sale. He continued living in San Francisco for several years, presumably at 1901 Sutter Street, which is the address given on the copyright page of his book.

In 1937, Kiyama returned to Japan for another visit. Although he planned to return again to San Francisco, and apparently hoped to eventually make his way to Paris, he was forced to abandon this idea because of worsening international conditions. Relations between Japan and the United States had soured, and Japan was already embroiled in war in China.

In his fifties by this time, Kiyama lived in Neu, the town of his birth, taught art at a local girl's high school, and continued painting and occasionally exhibiting. He also drew several social satire cartoons, and later during the war took in refugee children from Japan's bombed-out cities. His daughter describes him as someone who might have been thought of as rather eccentric, who loved to paint, and who kept animals, but she notes that they came through the war in relatively good shape because they lived in a rural

The mature Kiyama. Courtesy Kiyama Family.

area that was never bombed and where food was relatively plentiful.

Immediately after the war, Kiyama apparently hoped to publish a sequel of sorts to his San Francisco comic documentary. Although only the pencil drawings survive, he did create a very funny story about two Japanese Americans named Ben and George visiting Japan and experiencing severe culture shock (when they do such things as use mixed public baths for the first time). Alas, Kiyama apparently never inked this story, and it was never printed or published. On April 24, 1951, at the age of sixty-six, he passed away of kidney disease.

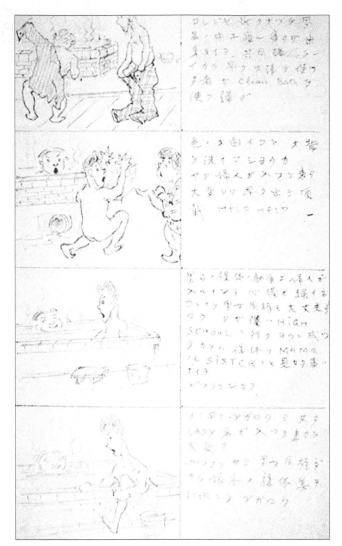

Panels from Kiyama's unpublished sequel. Courtesy Kiyama Family.

Many of Kiyama's original paintings and drawings are in the vault of the Yonago City Art Museum, as is the original artwork for *The Four Immigrants*, which Kiyama carried back to Japan. The comic artwork is mounted on large panels, of which, oddly, there are 156, despite the fact that the book itself is only 112 pages including the front matter. This mystery was finally solved when I realized the artwork pages and the printed pages are divided differently. Each episode consists of twelve panels, but Kiyama drew only four panels per page of artwork; in the printed book each page has six panels. The total number of episodes and panels in the book pages and the artwork panels correspond exactly.

Perhaps because of the long boat ride back to Japan, and the intensity of the humidity and heat, there is a slight spotting and discoloration of the original artwork. As a result, this English-language reproduction has been created by scanning the pages of a printed copy of Kiyama's book—rather than his original artwork—into a computer, erasing the Japanese, and then inputting English in its stead. Any errors of translation and interpretation are all mine. For the historical record, several panels in Kiyama's work were flipped for readability. By order of episode and panel numbers, they are: 6.10; 8.8; 9.9–10; 10.1, 4; 11.2–3, 7–8,10–12; 21.1–2, 7; 22.6; 24.4; 25.6; 32.3, 7–10; 33.1–5; 38.5–6; 40.1–12; 41.1–12; 43.1; 46.5–7.

Many people have encouraged me and helped me in this quixotic project, and I would like to thank them all. The following deserve special mention: the Kiyama family of Hideko, Teruaki, and daughter Akiko; and Takako Aoto, the assistant curator of the Yonago City Art Museum. For reading over the translation and notes and making comments, thanks go to Ben Kobashigawa, Leonard Rifas, and Eddie and Margie Schodt. For exceptional help in deciphering problematic passages and general historical advice: Seizo Oka and the Japanese American History Archives; also, Yuki and Aiko Ishimatsu and Yuko Kitaura. For archival assistance, thanks to librarian Jeff Gunderson of the San Francisco Art Institute. For advice on fonts and lettering, thanks to Tom Orzechowski and Lois Buhalis, and to Toren Smith. Finally, general but effusive thanks and promises of good karma go to Amy Barach, Don Best, Cullen Curtiss, publisher/friend Peter Goodman, Allison Hunt, Milton Katz, Yurika Kimijima, Raymond Larrett, Mikio Okada, Shogo Oketani and Leza Lowitz, Karl Matsushita of the Japanese American National Library, Taye Sasaki, Keiko Tokioka, and Shigekuni Yamada.

Frederik L. Schodt
San Francisco, 1998
http://www.jai2.com

BIBLIOGRAPHY

Becker, Jules. *The Course of Exclusion, 1882–1924: San Francisco Newspaper Coverage of the Chinese and Japanese in the United States*. San Francisco: Mellen Research University Press, 1991.

Benedict, Burton. *The Anthropology of World's Fairs*. Berkeley: Scolar Press, 1983.

Blackbeard, Bill, and Martin Williams, eds. *The Smithsonian Collection of Newspaper Comics*. Washington, D.C.: Smithsonian Institution Press and Harry N. Abrams, 1979.

Choy, Philip P.; Lorraine Dong; and Marlon K Hom. *The Coming Man: 19th Century American Perceptions of the Chinese*. Seattle: University of Washington Press, 1995.

Clauss, Francis J. *Angel Island: Jewel of San Francisco Bay*. San Francisco, Briarcliff Press, 1982.

Crosby, Alfred W., Jr. *Epidemic and Peace, 1918*. Westport, Conn: Greenwood Press, 1976.

Daniels, Roger. *The Politics of Prejudice: The Anti-Japanese Movement in California and the Struggle for Japanese Exclusion*. Berkeley: University of California Press, 1977.

Esthus, Raymond A. *Theodore Roosevelt and Japan*. Seattle: University of Washington Press, 1966.

Ewald, Donna. *San Franciso Invites the World: The Panama-Pacific International Exposition of 1915*. San Francisco: Chronicle Books, 1991.

Gordon, Ian. *Comic Strips and Consumer Culture, 1890–1945*. Washington, D.C.: Smithsonian Institution Press, 1998.

Hansen, Gladys. *San Francisco Almanac: Everything You Want to Know about Everyone's Favorite City*. San Francisco, Chronicle Books, 1995.

Hata, Donald Teruo, Jr. *"Undesirables": Early Immigrants and the Anti-Japanese Movement in San Francisco, 1892–1893, Prelude to Exclusion*. New York: Arno Press, 1978.

Herman, Masako. *The Japanese in America, 1843–1973: A Chronology and Fact Book*. Ferry, N.Y.: Oceana Publications, 1974.

Horn, Maurice, ed. *The World Encyclopedia of Comics*. New York: Avon Books, 1977.

_____. *The World Encyclopedia of Cartoons*. New York: Chelsea House Publishers, 1980.

Hughes, Edan Milton. *Artists in California, 1786–1940*. San Francisco: Hughes Publishing, 1989.

Ichihashi, Yamato. *Japanese Immigration: Its Status in California*. San Francisco: R and E Research Associates, 1970.

Ichioka, Yuji. *The Issei: The World of the First Generation Japanese Immigrants, 1885–1924*. New York: Free Press, 1988.

Iwata, Masakazu. *Planted in Good Soil: The History of the Issei in United States Agriculture*. Vols. 1–2. American University Studies, series 9, History, vol. 57. New York: P. Lang, 1990.

Kawakami, K. K. *The Real Japanese Question*. New York: MacMillan, 1921.

Knopf Guide San Francisco. New York: Alfred A. Knopf, 1993.

Lai, H. Mark; Genny Lim; and Judy Yung. *Island:*

Poetry and History of Chinese Immigrants on Angel Island, 1910–1940. Seattle: University of Washington Press, 1991.

Maki, Itsuma. *Tekisasu mushuku/Tani Jōji cho* (Vagabond in Texas, by Jōji Tani). Tokyo: Shakai Shisōsha, 1975.

Niiya, Brian, ed. *Japanese American History: An A-to-Z Reference from 1868 to the Present.* New York: Facts on File, 1993.

Obata, Chiura. *Obata's Yosemite: The Art and Letters of Chiura Obata from His Trip to the High Sierra in 1927, with Essays by Janice T. Driesbach and Susan Landauer.* Yosemite National Park: Yosemite Association, 1993.

Oka, Seizo. "Biography of Kyutaro Abiko." Series in *Hokubei Mainichi,* September 3–November 1, 1980.

Okazaki, Suzie. *Nihonmachi: A Story of San Francisco's Japantown.* San Francisco: SKO Studios, 1985.

Penrose, Eldon R. *California Nativism: Organized Opposition to the Japanese, 1890–1913.* San Francisco, R and E Research Associates, 1973.

Richards, Rand. *Historic San Francisco: A Concise History and Guide.* San Francisco: Heritage House Publishers, 1997.

Sandmeyer, Elmer Clarence. *The Anti-Chinese Movement in California.* Urbana: University of Illinois Press, 1991.

Schodt, Frederik L. *Manga! Manga! The World of Japanese Comics.* Tokyo: Kodansha International, 1983.

_____. *America and the Four Japans: Friend, Foe, Model, Mirror.* Berkeley: Stone Bridge Press, 1993.

_____. *Dreamland Japan: Writings on Modern Manga.* Berkeley: Stone Bridge Press, 1996

Sekai daihyakka jiten (Great World Encyclopedia). Tokyo: Heibonsha, 1972.

Yoshimura, Akiji. "A Brief History of the Japanese in Colusa County." *Wagon Wheels, 1969.* Colusa County Historical Society, September 1969, pp. 4–12.

--*-*-*

The following San Francisco newspapers, published during Kiyama's years in the city, were used as primary source references. Those marked with an asterisk contain either articles on or references to Kiyama.

* Nichi Bei (The Japanese American News)
* The San Francisco Bulletin
  The San Francisco Chronicle
* The San Francisco Examiner
* Shin Sekai (The New World)
* Sōkō Shūhō (The San Francisco Weekly)

Printed in the USA
CPSIA information can be obtained
at www.ICGtesting.com
JSHW052028110124
55254JS00006B/37